D1320238

PIRANDELLO
AND THE CRISIS
OF MODERN
CONSCIOUSNESS

ANTHONY CAPUTI

PIRANDELLO
AND THE CRISIS
OF MODERN
CONSCIOUSNESS

UNIVERSITY OF ILLINOIS PRESS

URBANA AND CHICAGO

Library of Congress Cataloging-in-Publication Data

Caputi, Anthony Francis, 1924–
Pirandello and the crisis of modern consciousness.
Bibliography: p.
Includes index.
1. Pirandello, Luigi, 1867–1936—Criticism and
interpretation. 2. Consciousness in literature.
I. Title.
PQ4835.I7Z54125   1988   852'.912   87-10801
ISBN 0-252-01468-5 (alk. paper)

○○○○○○○○○○○○○○○○○

*Publication of this book was supported
in part by a grant from the Hull Memorial
Publication Fund, Cornell University.*

○○○○○○○○○○○○○○○○○

Per le tre carissime

CAROL   MARY   PAULINE

CONTENTS

ACKNOWLEDGMENTS

AMONG the generous and tough-minded friends and colleagues who have helped me with this book I would like to single out the following for special thanks: Giuseppe Mazzotta and Richard Gilman of Yale University, Gian-Paolo Biasin of the University of California at Berkeley, Pietro Pucci, Anita Grossvogel, Walter Slatoff, and David Grossvogel of Cornell University, Wylie Sypher, professor emeritus of Simmons College, and Adrienne McNair. For much-appreciated financial support I wish to acknowledge with gratitude the American Philosophical Society and the Cornell Humanities Faculty Research Committee.

INTRODUCTION

OUTSIDE ITALY Luigi Pirandello is usually seen as a master ironist who wrote largely about the mind and its quirky paradoxes. Unfortunately, that view of him is sufficiently true to be dangerously misleading. In what follows I shall wish to take issue with it, not to prove it wrong so much as to demonstrate its inadequacy. In doing so my assumption is that Pirandello was a key figure in that shift of sensibility by which the consciousness with its many-layered life replaced the inherited structures of tradition in the West as a matrix of value. Pirandello was of course not the only writer interested in that shift: it was in the air, in Proust, in Svevo, in Joyce, in all the writers drawn to contemplate and explore the crisis of interior life. But Pirandello has a special importance because he developed a vision of modern man in which consciousness as he understood it became the central issue in a new philosophy of behavior. In his work he provided a commentary on consciousness and its intricate workings of dazzling subtlety and completeness. He was neither wildly excited nor cheered by what he saw; yet neither was he paralyzed by cynicism and gloom. He was melancholy, sometimes outraged and bitter because he saw difficulty everywhere, and often irritated and exasperated by the human need to create oneself continuously, to define and redefine oneself, one's situation, and the value of what one did. He was bedeviled by the irony that one frequently knew that one's creation was a deceit. At the same time he was often amused by the spectacle, and occasionally filled with wonder by it.

Pirandello began where Matthew Arnold began, with the conviction that the world was in disarray, that the system of beliefs that had provided coherence and continuity for centuries had broken down, and that the new sciences could yield little more than organized barbarism. Arnold's remedy, of course, lay in the direction of the highest culture, a culture characterized by sweetness and light and achieved through education in the humanities and, especially, literature. Like Pirandello he saw the problem and its solution in subjective terms: culture was for him a condition consisting in "becoming something rather than in having something, in an inward condition of mind and spirit, not in an outward set of circumstances."[1] But Arnold saw the achievement of this inward condition in terms of a largely coherent, integrated mind. For him the mind was governed by dependable faculties: as individuals internalized the best that has been thought and said, they transmuted it into a capacity for criticism that became the sign of culture. For Pirandello the mind was far from coherent and integrated: it consisted of many faculties and strata, some of them subconscious. As individuals internalized the world around them, they processed their contacts with it by way of a consciousness that they were continuously structuring and restructuring, even as, at the same time, another part of the mind was monitoring this process. Culture for Pirandello was the experience, dense and authoritative, created within the consciousness.

Consciousness, then, is the key issue, and especially consciousness in Pirandello's understanding of it. But before I can turn to Pirandello and before I can hope to discuss anything so mouth-filling as the crisis of modern consciousness, I must try to clarify the sense of that term as I shall use it. That in itself is not easy not only because the term comprehends so much, but because what it comprehends is itself often elusive. Moreover, consciousness has a maddening way of slipping into self-consciousness, and so rapid and complex are the interpenetrations of the one with the other that—let me admit it now—it is virtually impossible to keep them entirely separate. And yet they can be kept separate, much as form and shadow can be, and they must be if I am to do justice to Pirandello's analysis.

In keeping with that analysis, I shall take consciousness as the broader term and understand by it that part of our mental apparatus that functions in wakefulness. Of course my problems begin at once, for we all know that at different times we function in highly different states of wakefulness, ranging all the way from intense efforts at consecutive reasoning to those barely wakeful moments when our eyes begin to glaze over. To oversimplify that variety somewhat, I will understand by consciousness three basic activities. First, I will understand by it being wakeful to something, such as a change in light or the approach of a person; in other words, experiencing something in the environment, as in the statement "I was conscious of her standing behind me." Secondly, I will understand by it having present in the mind a sense of a subject some part of which may not be in evidence or in the environment, as, for example, having present in the mind an extended sense of a person. This second meaning brings with it a dimension of knowledge in time and a further dimension in associated systems of experience. Thirdly, I will understand by the term all that activity that might be described as purposeful, diligent reasoning.[2]

Pirandello frequently compared consciousness to a piazza and to a net, figures that suggest containers, largely passive in character. But we should note that what piazzas or nets normally contain is itself highly active and that they themselves are continuously filling and emptying. Taken in toto, in fact, consciousness, as Pirandello understood it, and as I shall understand it, is distinctly active because it comprehends all those busy faculties that process the data of experience, frame impressions, formulate arguments, draw conclusions, and distill judgments. Hence it is both matrix and machine, distinct from the rest of the mind chiefly because it operates in a state of wakefulness.

Now by self-consciousness I shall understand the reflex function of consciousness that enables it to watch itself as its various faculties operate. Self-consciousness, too, occurs in linear time, but it additionally creates a kind of disjunctive time as it causes the consciousness to focus on itself again and again, revisiting, so to speak, what it has itself created. This reflexive dimension actuates still further arguments, conclusions, and judgments, greatly complicating the consciousness. As we shall see, Pirandello's sensitivity to this layering and dynamic interplay was extraordinarily acute.

Of course both consciousness and self-consciousness are mysteriously connected with that body of life in each of us that is not conscious, which lies below the threshold of twilight, pulling us this way and that, conditioning, directing, bending impressions and arguments and judgments. No one underestimates the influence of this darker zone on conscious life; clearly it contributes continuously to our interior landscapes and their changing character. But it is also different from the consciousness: it is not responsive to the will, and it is scarcely responsive to the efforts of memory and reason. Altogether, it plays so mysterious a role in determining judgments and framing arguments and identifying values that it is usually left by philosophers and moralists for the psychoanalysts to worry about. In any event, it figures hardly at all in Pirandello's attempts to make sense of the consciousness and its crises.

Let me try to illustrate all this in the simple example of a man going to a baseball game. He is a man with everyone's idiosyncratic burden of prior life: parents, a particular childhood of mixed joys and sorrow, thirty years, let's assume, of all the experiences that have made him what he is on this sunny afternoon as he starts up the ramp of the baseball stadium. Some small part of this past is fugitively conscious. He remembers the first time he came to this stadium, with his father many years before. He recalls, too, the last time he was there, when his home team had lost in extra innings.

He recalls, furthermore, that his team is now one-half game out of first place and today is playing the team in first place. These thoughts and memories, as well as many others both relevant and irrelevant, flash through his mind, become conscious, even as he notices the heat of the sun, the hardness of the seat, the shadows cast by the stadium roof along the third-base line, the smell of beer in the passing vendor's box. These fragments and strains constitute some part of his consciousness as the teams take the field and he begins following the game, noting individual performances and events, making numerous judgments about them as superior, inferior, exceptional, even beautiful, developing arguments about strategy, lamenting or rejoicing at different stages of the contest. Throughout the afternoon he sees the game by way of the peculiar dynamism of his consciousness, and he watches himself seeing it, perceiving himself in different ways at different moments, pausing in the welter of onrushing thoughts and sensations to muse that now he is thirty years old, so different and yet so like the boy of ten who had come to this ballpark. How nice it would be if his father were with him! As he leaves the stadium he may evaluate the game as a whole—good, exciting, dull—or even the day as a whole—agreeable, exhilarating, upsetting. In all this, of course, he has been subject to more than the data provided by the events on the playing field and around him in the grandstand and welling up from his past; as a person he has been more—perhaps much more—than what I am identifying as his conscious life. By his consciousness I mean those events that have been present to his mind, those that he has wakefully received and processed, and those that have made up his pleasure or pain, *his* idea and judgment of what he saw and experienced. By his consciousness I refer to his continuous and at the same time discontinuous efforts to bring order, meaning, and value to that afternoon in the baseball stadium.

Consciousness, then, consists of not merely all that is present to the mind, but also the mind's efforts to shape it. In attempting to describe it, of course, I have discovered nothing new: consciousness and self-consciousness have been with us and we have known them for much of human history. And yet as we think of their efforts to shape, to process and construe, we recognize that these efforts differed considerably at different times in human history, even as their biological apparatus remained largely constant. We can easily imagine, for example, that men and women in the Egypt of the tenth century B.C. processed the data of their experience in ways quite different from those of the Christians of fourteenth-century France. And the great commonplace about the Renaissance is that it initiated the gradual substitution of private value systems for the structures that had organized experience for more than a millennium. The story of that slow dismemberment through the seventeenth and eighteenth centuries and beyond is too complex to rehearse here, but it is possible to say that it led to a time when finally the mind itself came under critical scrutiny and the consciousness and its shadow self-consciousness were plunged into a series of crises.

By what I call the crisis of modern consciousness I mean the most recent of the major upheavals to which consciousness has been subject since the Renaissance. If the Renaissance saw the earliest breakup of the medieval orthodoxy, the modern period, beginning with the romantics and culminating in this century, marks that stage in which not just traditional ways of deriving coherence and value were lost but the capacity for deriving alternative coherences by way of the reason has been undermined as the reason itself has been subverted as an authority. As the idea gained ground that every mind is a relative instrument, subject not to the grand program for coherence provided by Christianity or, for that matter, by any other traditional orthodoxy, but subject to its own conditions, a new variability and a new insecurity were born. Not only did men and women not look to external sources for guides to value, they no longer looked to reason. Instead, they looked to consciousness and in it found not so much a tool as a multiform life that could give shape to itself and monitor itself in the process.

But what is so modern about that? you ask. Certainly there is nothing especially new in "watching oneself live," in Pirandello's phrase. Lyric poets have watched the play of their emotions as they have loved, suffered exile, and lamented the passing of loved ones since the Greeks at least. Hamlet is a textbook case of a figure who is mesmerized by the play of his mind on itself. The romantics exalted self-study into a creative act, called it genius, and made a way of life of it. Do we in fact see consciousness so differently from John Donne or the gallants cultivating a filigree detachment in Restoration comedies?

A simple answer to this question is that we see consciousness with sufficient differences to make a great difference. To begin with, we are much more preoccupied with it than any previous age has been: ours is a time, after all, when we talk explicitly and rather solemnly about consciousness-raising. In our century, beginning a couple of decades before its onset and then most distinctly after the First World War, consciousness became the principal source of value for those for whom traditional values had been lost. For the first time wakeful life and the exercise of watching that life in ourselves have become the focal field in a new attempt to rationalize civilized life. To be civilized, to be human in the light of this new vision, came to mean to stock the mind and memory with information, skills, and experiences that would enrich the operation of consciousness. Indeed, this is what is meant by a liberal education! Experiencing the self, highlighting the present in the context of the past, keeping a cool hand on the reins of event while savoring it consciously—in Pirandello's phrase, creating oneself from moment to moment and day to day (even as you are conscious that other agents contribute to that creation): all this became the core of life for those who had abandoned earlier guides to value. We no longer visit twelfth-century churches to practice the devotion for which they were designed, but, guidebooks in hand, to dovetail what we can recover of the meaning of the place into our carefully cultivated consciousness of human history. We no longer fill our minds and train our hands to serve others, but to serve our idea of ourselves as we serve others.

Now the story of consciousness in this century is largely the story of those conceptions or versions of it that have been highly influential in shaping the experience of twentieth-century men and women. Pirandello defined and commented extensively on one such conception, in his case an extraordinarily influential one because it provided the basis for many others. Other, notably current, versions of it might include a Marxist-revolutionary model, a feminist model, and various minority models, to name a few. To illuminate this general subject further before homing in on that part of it marked out by Pirandello, I should like to look briefly at another influential and distinctive conception of consciousness, that defined in the work of, among others, George Bernard Shaw. Unlike the post-structuralists, I am not interested in structures of consciousness as structures of discourse, though I see the value of that kind of analysis; I am primarily interested in describing models of consciousness as replacement structures for traditional orthodoxies lost. I shall begin, that is to say, by acknowledging that there is an unexamined structure and/or system in the mode of discourse adopted by any writer, including Shaw and Pirandello, but I shall give most attention to the model constructed and its uses in rationalizing experience and deriving values from it.

That I choose Shaw as an important commentator on consciousness may surprise some readers. We are inclined to associate this interest with inordinately self-conscious individuals, retiring and introspective creatures stymied by their own thought, J. Alfred Prufrocks and Leopold Blooms. In any event, we scarcely think of Shaw, who seemed to be talking perpetually, who had an answer for everything, the image of self-confidence and aggressive argumentation. And yet the intellectual structure on which the vast array of Shaw's work rests gives a major place to consciousness and self-consciousness.

He began where all those who make consciousness the central source of value begin, by dismissing the structures of tradition: Christianity, the gentlemanly code, traditional ideas of country, community, and family. Indeed, he did more than dismiss them: he spent the greater part of his long life and career trying vigorously to root them out, to free the mind of obsolete ideas and values so that the mind might look at itself and its condition fairly and build a world responsive to its real needs. For him this process of liberation entailed nothing more or less than the destruction of society. His fervent belief was that once society had been destroyed (through education and persuasion, of course, not revolution), once the mind had been freed, the mind would then construct a world on roughly the plan provided by Fabian socialism. Of course he was doomed to disappointment. But he never despaired. Through all the many years of his untiring efforts to assist in this process, through all the many plays and essays and speeches, Shaw was sustained by the conviction that the world would ultimately succeed because it was governed by the principles of a creative evolution. To be more precise, through all his decades of effort to change the ways men and women saw themselves and thought about themselves — when Fabian gradualism seemed to be working not at all — he took refuge in the belief that nature, life, has a purpose and is in fact slowly working that purpose out.

His argument goes something like this. Through all the aeons of its existence life has been driven by an inner will, or call it a force. This force has worked slowly and often wastefully, it has made many starts that have ended in failure, but it has labored long enough that by now its purpose is clear. That purpose is to create an organ by which to attain self-understanding and self-mastery. An inner compulsion to know, to understand: this was for Shaw and the creative evolutionists the propelling force driving life, the mystery of life revealed. Not natural selection or the survival of the fittest but a will to understand and to control through that understanding. The Holy Ghost was for Shaw a scientific fact, or at any rate a metaphor for the fact of mind and the ambitions of mind operating in all things. To quote Don Juan, one of his principal spokesmen:

Life is a force which has made innumerable experiments in organizing itself; . . . the mammoth and the man, the mouse and the megatharium, the flies and the fleas and the Fathers of the Church are all more or less the successful attempts to build up that raw force into higher and higher individuals. . . . Life has not measured the success of its attempts at godhead by the beauty or bodily perfection of the result. . . . Life has been driving at brains—at its darling object: an organ by which it can attain not only self-consciousness, but self-understanding. . . . [Hence] I sing not arms and the hero, but the philosophic man: he who seeks in contemplation to discover the inner will of the world, in invention to discover the means of fulfilling that will, and in action to do that will by the so-discovered means. . . . That is the law of my life. That is the waking within me of Life's incessant aspiration to higher organization, wider, deeper, intenser self-consciousness, and clearer understanding.[3]

To put all this more briefly, the life force by way of its evolutionary method is driving at intelligence, intelligence that will make possible ever richer, denser, and more intense states of consciousness and self-consciousness, states of consciousness that will yield greater understanding and control. Hence the great value of consciousness and self-consciousness for Shaw; hence Don Juan's choice to go to heaven, where these faculties are cultivated.

Don Juan's decision to leave hell is of course a decision to quit all that men and women have invented to give their lives quality but that has no reality. "Hell [again Don Juan explains] is the home of the unreal and the seekers of happiness. [It is like earth, where] men and women play at being heroes and heroines, saints and sinners. . . . Here you call your appearance beauty, your emotions love, your sentiments heroism, your aspirations virtue, just as you did on earth, but here there are no hard facts to contradict you, . . . nothing but a perpetual romance, a universal melodrama."[4] Hell, accordingly, is a rarefied version of a world made up of illusory structures, some derived from tradition and believed to be real, but actually false, some known to be unreal but accepted in the absence of anything else to fill the vacuum. In other words, hell too provides a model of consciousness, and for those who approach life with the Devil's assumptions, accepting it is a necessity. Don Juan (and of course Shaw) will object that because he knows this model and its constituent structures to be inauthentic and knows the life they make possible to be an exercise in make-believe or theater, he can finally only be bored by them. Don Juan leaves the romance of hell, the "Palace of lies" and its boredom, to go to heaven, despite its austerities and lack of glamour. There he can "contemplate that which interests [him] above all things, namely Life: the force that ever strives to attain greater power of contemplating itself."[5] There he can bring to his conscious life not merely richness but also authority.

Now Shaw was more precise, though always speculative, about the states of consciousness and self-consciousness most highly valued by his philosophy. He makes heroic, if sometimes rather grotesque, attempts to define these states in the Ancients, those characters in *Back to Methuselah* who live 700 and more years and whose consciousness is so intense that "one moment of the ecstasy of Life as they live it would strike the rest of us dead."[6] In the never-to-be-reached future when all individuals will have disappeared, Shaw associates this intense conscious life with a vortex of energy, "a whirlpool of pure intelligence" comparable to the whirlpool of force with which life began. But here we move away from anything that has meaning for most of us. Shaw is useful in the story of modern consciousness because he clarified a model of consciousness that continues to have wide currency in our time, despite the qualifications that must be made in the outline just provided.

Consciousness as Shaw understood it is, in fact, rarely met in imaginative literature; indeed, it is rarely met anywhere in precisely the detail provided by Shaw. And yet it is at the center, I believe, of that widely held, if often unacknowledged, attitude of our time that assumes that the human condition is getting better. For the majority of those who believe in progress, whether they hold this belief overtly or secretly, consciousness is the prime agent in enlarging our knowledge and control. It is, as Shaw everywhere implies, an emphatically problem-solving faculty, critical, analytic, experimental rather than poetic, and it operates squarely on the assumption that the mind can possess itself of authentic knowledge, can, that is, push beyond the illusory projections of the moment. We see a fair example of a person coming to this kind of consciousness in the Maiden in *As Far as Thought Can Reach,* the last of the plays making up *Back to Methuselah.* She is maturing, and she knows it, as she says, "Now the world is opening out for me. More than the world: the universe. Even little things are turning out to be great things, and becoming intensely interesting."[7] She begins to deplore the trivialities of ordinary life, and most of all to deplore sleep, because through it we lose "half our life in a state of unconsciousness." Her destiny is to move gradually closer to the contemplativeness of Don Juan and then beyond that toward the conscious ecstasies of the Shavian Ancients.

For many this model of consciousness is a central source of value in an age otherwise poor in them. It postulates an optimistic, constructive view of the mind. It positions the individual in a universe that is coherent, and progressively more coherent as the consciousness makes fresh conquests of it. We might say with Shaw that those drawn to this model do in fact believe that nature is making toward self-understanding, self-control, and self-realization. Unless I'm very mistaken, this is the version of consciousness often—not always—to be met in those whose views of life are primarily influenced by science or the social sciences.

At any rate, this is what Shaw has to tell us: for those for whom received civilization is a bust, the work of the world consists in confronting one's own consciousness freshly and fairly. It consists in a mode of being that is essentially a mode of thinking, a continuing process of probing, analyzing, examining. Its great advantages are that it occasionally yields real knowledge; its great solace is that it saves one from frivolity.

But if Shaw was repelled by the frivolity of living with fictions, others were persuaded of the desperate need to live with them. If Shaw was convinced that life has purpose and coherence, others anguished that it was largely a mystery. If Shaw saw the mind as the darling object of creation, others saw it as a frail, uncertain faculty capable of little more than self-deception. This second group includes most of the artists and writers of the century, and very notably Luigi Pirandello. The widely influential model of consciousness to be met in his work will require careful and detailed definition.

1

●●●●●●●●●●●●●●●●●●●●●●●

A WORLD OF WORDS

All life is crushed by the weight of words!
The weight of the dead!
—Pirandello, *Henry IV,* act 2

IN A WELL-KNOWN passage from one of his brief efforts at autobiography Pirandello says of his birth that on a June night in time of plague he had fallen like a firefly on an arid Sicilian headland known locally as Chaos.[1] Whatever the poetic excesses of this account, the circumstances of his Sicilian origins explain much about his later interests. Born of patriots and superpatriots in the most conservative region of the island, Pirandello grew up in an atmosphere combining rigid social formality, Garibaldian liberalism, and primitive superstition. His maternal grandfather had died in exile after the defeat of the separatists in 1848; his father and uncles had fought with Garibaldi. Throughout his youth his family lived in modest wealth in Agrigento (then called Girgenti) and Palermo, where, in addition to an adoring mother, he enjoyed nurses, servants, a tutor, and the other amenities afforded by his father's thriving sulphur mines. Only during the summer of 1886, when, newly engaged to his cousin Linuccia, he initiated a brief life of business with his father in Porto Empedocle, did he come into close contact with the squalor and brutality of Sicilian life. For the rest he was a darling son and student, first in Palermo, then in Rome—until expelled for offending a Latin professor—and finally in Bonn, where he took a doctorate in romance philology.

After his father had extricated him from the ill-advised liaison with Linuccia, he set up as a young man of letters in Rome. The Roman literary scene of the early 1890s was a heady mixture of Gabriele D'Annunzio and the verists led by Luigi Capuana, and initially Pirandello allied himself with the verists, then to withdraw to his own position with the independence that would characterize most of his literary life. He met writers, editors, and critics, and developed deep and lasting friendships with men like Ugo Ojetti and Ugo Fleres. He wrote a great deal. Even before officially taking up his literary life he had published a volume of poems and a few essays; now on the first tide of the literary vitality that would sustain him throughout his career he published poems, stories, and essays and wrote two novels and an indeterminate number of plays. In 1894 he agreed to an arranged marriage with Antonietta Portulano, the daughter of his father's business partner, and brought her to Rome, where they had three children in the next five years. By the end of the decade he had begun to win a modest reputation among literary peers.

If there appears little in all this of the time of plague or the headland called Chaos, and equally little of the young litterateur grappling with anything so monumental as the crisis of modern consciousness, the fact is that Pirandello was always a man of elusive contradictions. Middle-class husband and father, furnishing apartments, cashing the monthly checks from his father, walking with his family in the Villa Borghese, he was at the same time, like Shaw, deeply suspicious of traditional values and violently hostile to traditional structures. In his earliest letters to his sister Rosalina, where his somewhat posturing despair suggests youth and too large a dose of Giacomo Leopardi, the edge of his pessimism nonetheless cuts with unmistakable authority. The fact is that even before his family had lost its money and his wife had had the first of the attacks that were to lead to her mental collapse, he was already setting the main features of the vision he was to refine through the rest of his life. He was nineteen when he wrote the following to Rosalina from Palermo:

I trust you with everything: you understand me sufficiently. And yet don't think that my unhappiness is unfounded and that I'm taking some easy way.... Don't believe it: you'll be badly misjudging me. Meditation is a black abyss, peopled by obscure phantoms, guarded by despairing dejection. No ray of light ever penetrates there, and the desire to have light plunges you ever more deeply into the dense darkness.... It's an unquenchable thirst, a relentless madness; the darkness floods you, and the silent immensity freezes you. We're like poor spiders that in order to live have to weave themselves a delicate web in some corner; we're like poor snails that to live carry their fragile shells around on their backs; or like poor molluscs that have their shells at the bottom of the sea. We are spiders, snails, and molluscs of a nobler race, admittedly; we wouldn't want a web or a shell. But a little world, yes, both to live in and to live from. An ideal, a feeling, habits, a line of work—that's the little world or shell of this large snail called

man. Without them life is impossible. When you succeed in living
without an ideal because life, when considered closely, seems an
enormous puppet show without connection or rationale, when
you've learned to do without feeling because you no longer respect
or care for men or things and you, therefore, lack habits, which
don't develop, and an occupation, which becomes contemptible—
when, in a word, you live without life, think without thoughts, feel
without a heart, then you don't know which way to turn: you'll be a
homeless wayfarer, a bird without a nest. I am like that.[2]

Setting aside the oratorical rotundity of some of this, we must note that
Pirandello is already talking about created worlds and the invented structures
that make life possible. Life is a puppet show: in the letter of 10 December
1887 to Rosalina and her husband one needs a carefully contrived artifice
(*inganno*) to live it; and in the letter of 9 March 1888 the principal culprit
in this life of elaborate pretense is one's compulsion to penetrate illusions.
And all this before he had gone to Bonn!

We have no idea what prompted this gloom. Perhaps his self-betrayal in
the affair with Linuccia, whom he at first desperately loved and then
suddenly, unaccountably, no longer wanted, shook him more deeply than
anyone has guessed. The fact is that the temperament and many of the
issues that were to govern his long preoccupation with consciousness were
already evident. In the letter of 10 December 1887 he said:

I am not sad; I laugh, laugh so that it is a joy to all. I am he who has
seen the earth on which all of us gather, little men and big, from a
point of vantage a bit too high, and it appeared to me—dissuade me
who can—a lemon. At this height one laughs, like mad folk. Am I
speaking seriously? Oh what foolishness everything is! and what
foolishness to say that everything is foolishness! We know nothing,
we learn nothing, but words; for a word we live or die, suffer or
experience pleasure. . . . Everything one does are things that one
says. . . . How can you resist laughing when you hear sentences like
these? I want to but I cannot. I can but I must not. Wish, can, must:
words, words, words. It is unfortunate to come to this conclusion
and to think like this, but unhappily one does think! Blessed is he
who can stop halfway and before old age comes on can marry
illusion and preserve it lovingly.[3]

The irony, the bitter laughter, the exasperation of the later Pirandello
were already in evidence. The emphasis on "words, words, words" as the

nonstuff from which lives are fabricated was prophetic of the intense attention he was to give to rhetoric in his earliest assaults on the inauthenticity that he saw on all sides.

Until more is known about Pirandello's life during these years, perhaps from the letters that the family has still not released, the fullest evidence of what he thought and felt remains his published writings. His first book of poems, *Troubled Joy* (*Mal Giocondo,* 1887), is unified by the figure of the young poet trying to balance joy and the loss of his ideals. In "Romances" of that collection he is the young cavalier in the manner of Ludovico Ariosto's heroes, lost in a magic wood, beset on all sides by mystery, enticed by nymphs, dreaming of a night of love with the dangerous Alcina. In "Mirthful Poem III," in which he alludes to the Emperor Domitian's practice of hunting flies and pretending they were his enemies, we hear of his hope, despite his persistent sluggishness and the deadly tedium of action, of threading his life, like a wingless fly, on the stiletto of his writing as Domitian had done his enemies on a needle. Occasionally flashes of irony, irreverence, and bitter wit surface; and when they do, the tone later so important can be heard. But for the most part the world is lost in an endless night, and, as the winds howl outside, in his breast the poet hears the roar of inner discord (*dissidio interno*). As Gösta Andersson has shown, inner discord is the shaping principle of Pirandello's earliest work,[4] discord intensified by doubt, the "severe giant" that undermines everything.[5] He achieves something like a resolution in the last poems in the collection, but it is Stein's answer from *Lord Jim* of submerging oneself in the destructive element. Having lost all direction and purpose, Pirandello wants to "sink in the voracious / sea . . . of human affection. / Only in this way . . . , / by losing himself in others and that feverish / . . . hurly-burly, / can he stop thinking meanly of human meanness."[6] This gesture is part of the broader dedication to literature that closes the collection.

The gesture was far from empty. The industry to be met at all stages of Pirandello's career was already evident in the 1890s in the long list of stories, novels, essays, collections of poems, and unproduced plays written by then. He complained that he was having difficulty publishing;[7] and it is true that much of this work was not printed immediately, and some of it—most of the plays—not at all. But in what was published, and especially in the essays and reviews, the young man of letters assembling the theory that with little change would serve as the basis for not only his work, but his life, is clear. And the aim of much of this early work was not simply a representation of inner discord, but an analysis of the crisis of values at its roots.

"Art and Consciousness Today" ("Arte e Coscienza d'Oggi"), a long essay published in 1893, offers a textbook account of what Joseph Wood Krutch would later call the modern temper. Modern science and philosophy have deprived us of our central position in the universe and most traditional sources of coherence and value. The old norms have crumbled! All certainty is gone!

> In minds and consciousnesses an extraordinary confusion reigns. In their interior mirror the most disparate figures, all in disordered attitudes, as if weighed down with insupportable burdens, are reflected, and each gives a different counsel. To whom should we listen? To whom should we cling? The insistence of one counsel overrides for a moment the voices of all the others, and we give ourselves to him for a time with the unhealthy impulsiveness of someone who wants an escape and doesn't know where it is. Meanwhile, we almost all show off our contempt for traditional opinions. . . . We simulate a discreet indifference toward all that we don't know and would actually like to know; we feel bewildered, lost in an immense, blind labyrinth surrounded on all sides by impenetrable mystery. There are many paths, but which is the true one? Go that way and there are people in a hurry, each giving airs of understanding something; and they seem so certain that now and then one of us, assailed by doubt, will stop and ask: "Am I the only one doesn't understand anything?" . . . No one dares to see his path through to the end; we stop halfway and turn around to look at the others, doubt on our lips. . . .
>
> The old norms have crumbled, and the new ones haven't arisen and become well established. It's understandable that the idea of the relativity of all things has spread so much within us to deprive us almost altogether of the faculty for judgment.[8]

In our desperation, he goes on, many of us turn to God, others to the aridities of sciences, still others to an aesthetic dilettantism. But none of these alternatives serves to generate intense desire or strong need in us, and lacking all conviction we fall back on an openness and tolerance that acknowledge our confusion.

The great importance of "Art and Consciousness Today," as well as of such pieces as the review of Antonio Fogazzaro's *Little World of Yesterday* (*Piccolo Mondo Antico,* 1895) and "Renunciation" ("Rinunzia," 1896), in which the same arguments, even the same sentences and phrases, recur, is that they focus the crisis of values as substantially a crisis of consciousness.

Modern consciousness, Pirandello concludes in "Art and Consciousness Today," suggests the image of an anxious dream, a continuous cacophony of discordant voices. In the review of *Little World of Yesterday* he plays this inner discord off against the old-fashioned world of the novel.[9] In "Renunciation," taking his cue from the recent discoveries of Marconi, he reviews the effects of scientific discoveries on consciousness, concluding that science has not only destroyed most traditional structures of coherence, but in converting life into an abstraction for the purposes of anatomizing it, it has destroyed life itself.

> And now in our blindness, we let ourselves be dragged along and live by nature itself, governed by context, by inherited customs and who knows how many prejudices derived from inveterate habit and imitating others, by forces never taken into account by consciousness, never pondered, by chains whose links have not been counted nor weight measured — we live committing acts and speaking words without considering their value or understanding their necessity. We are herded together and driven by time, like cattle, toward some final destruction, without making the supreme effort of forming an idea of ourselves or developing a criterion for our actions, without any perception of the causes that determine our way, and accepting, without thinking, life as it little by little reveals itself in effects daily sadder and sadder.[10]

Without God, without guides, enveloped in mystery and ignorant even of its own nature, consciousness is an inferno of activity producing chaos. The causes are in the world and its past, but the effects, which themselves then become causes, center in the consciousness.

But let me pause to consider a linguistic complication that has a crucial bearing on the large argument I am trying to make. In Italian the word *coscienza* means both consciousness and conscience, depending on the context; the same is true of the French *conscience*. We even see something of this ambiguity in English in Protestant discussions of conscience, where the "light" of conscience occasionally suggests the wakeful state of consciousness but where conscience is usually the faculty in control of one's actions. Now the fact that there is only the one word in Italian prompts Italians to see consciousness and conscience as closely related. Of course Pirandello used the word in both senses and, what is trickier, in both senses at the same time. This explains how he could collapse, as he did in "Art and Consciousness Today," questions of moral conscience into a broader discussion of what I have described as consciousness. "What will be the norm of conduct?" he asks; "Which actions will be judged good, which bad, which just or unjust?" In addressing these questions, he turns not to ethical premises but to various models of consciousness as proposed by philosophers and explores their suitability for deriving ethical systems. He comes to rest on Herbert Spencer's argument that an adequate ethic requires a rational structure of thought unifying clear ideas of being, knowing, and acting; in other words, a consciousness ordered by a super-imposed rational structure. In this way ethical coherence derives from cognitive coherence, and conscience and consciousness are one.[11]

In fact, Pirandello set up Spencer's and other philosophical foundations chiefly to knock them down, to argue that, like the conception of life provided by modern science, these models of consciousness reduce what is exceedingly intricate and mysterious to abstract system. By accepting such formulaic reductions we "renounce" (see his "Renunciation") the full dimensions of both life and consciousness. Yet even as he rejects this view of conscience's calibrated dependence on a coherently structured consciousness, he retains the assumption that a dependence exists: conscience operates within consciousness, or, to put that another way, consciousness has at all times a moral dimension. Consciousness for Pirandello was, as we shall see, a matrix for other faculties, highly inclusive; for some thinkers, surely, too inclusive. But far from reflecting a rational idea of the world, as Herbert Spencer would have it, it suggested its own indeterminacy in its always shifting, changing version of the world.

The affliction of modern consciousness, as Pirandello understood it in the 1890s, was that it had lost the focus that inherited cultural structures had made possible for many centuries: it lacked the means to order, define, and regulate the data of experience; the familiar categories, the time-honored distinctions, the unexamined standards and loyalties that had given shape and meaning to experience had been lost. The crisis of modern consciousness consisted in its need to discover a new idea of itself and of the world, a way to structure itself that would enable it once again to derive values coherently. In Pirandello's view this crisis worsened in the course of his life, and World War I was a catastrophic proof of the mounting chaos. One of Berecche's friends in the story "Berecche and the War" ("Berecche e la Guerra," 1914) comments, "We have lived forty, fifty, sixty years, feeling that things as they were could not continue, that the tension of spirit that bit by bit became more violent had to fly to pieces, that finally the explosion would come. And it has. Tremendous. . . . the anxieties, the distresses, the anguish, the torment of such a long wait will find an outlet and an end."[12] In 1930 the unnamed protagonist of *As You*

Desire Me (*Come Tu Mi Vuoi*) raves hysterically about this life of the mad, lawless, and desperate, all driven by an obscene fury to amuse themselves. Even as late as 1932 in the story "Lucilla," Pirandello constructed an elaborate image of lostness in the figure of the young woman raised in a convent, treated like a plaything by the nuns, now wandering, unprepared, through a dark, brutal, mysterious world. Pirandello never championed a pat solution to this condition, though at different times he considered various. In "Art and Consciousness Today" he saw art not as a solution but as the way to keep closest to life and ultimately to produce the "unique secular book" that would point the way out of the tumult and devastation. "We are certainly at the vigil of a great event,"[13] he wrote in an optimistic moment, though at twenty-six he could do little more than hope for the hero who would write the book.

Yet even at twenty-six Pirandello was already deeply engaged in the problem of structuring the consciousness against this backdrop of chaos. He apparently read deeply in the philosophers. At Bonn one of his three final examinations had been in philosophy and doubtless included extensive work in the German idealists. As Mathias Adank has shown, the influence on him of Kant, Hegel, Schopenhauer, et al., was profound: the assumption that the world exists only as idea, that we create it, ourselves, and our lives, permeates his thought, if, as we shall see, in idiosyncratic form.[14] By the first decade of the new century he was also deeply read in Henri Bergson and in the new psychologists. But as Antonio Gramsci pointed out many years ago, the method of his thought traced unmistakably to the French positivists and Cartesians.[15] We must never forget that Pirandello was trained in the German philological tradition and always saw himself, to some extent, as a romance philologist. The positivist method of this discipline gave a crucial early focus to his thought that lasted throughout his life.

Given his pride in his philological training, it is not surprising that among Pirandello's earliest responses to the crisis of consciousness were several essays on language and the symptoms of that crisis in language. More remarkable, perhaps, is that instead of drawing him off into narrow, specialized studies, romance philology led him to a deeper reading of the general crisis. In one of his earliest pieces, "Dishonesty of Feeling in Art" ("La Menzogna del Sentimento nell'Arte," 1890), he dealt with the tendency of social convention to distort emotion, a tendency that he traced all the way back to the decline of Greek civilization. In the romance tradition of the Middle Ages, for example, he found a serious disjunction between form and feeling. Quite simply, he could not accept the emotional content of chivalric literature, in which emotion was dictated by convention, hence fixed by the mind and inauthentic to the point of dishonesty. The life of the Provençal aristocracy, in his view, was "often false and superficial, a life that could not help giving us an art often false and superficial."[16] Unfortunately, its tradition of fitting experience to convention and of prescribing the forms of love and grief persisted beyond the chivalric age in the work of Petrarch and his followers.

In "Modern Prose: After Reading Verga's *Mastro Don Gesualdo*" ("Prosa Moderna: Dopo la Lettura del *Mastro Don Gesualdo* del Verga," 1890) Pirandello traced the factitiousness of modern Italian prose to the Italians' insecurity about their language. Italian readers prefer bad translations of French and English works to Italian works, he argued, because the translations have more life and vigor; even the Italian classics, by which he meant some, are unbearably heavy because oppressed by a spurious concern with form. This sad condition results, he explained, from the fact that Italian is no single language but many, each modified by the writer's dialect. To compensate for this variability, Italian writers often borrow from other languages and literatures and imitate in them what they believe to be literary quality. By this process they write an artificial, lifeless prose, one in which the writing itself and the experience it is intended to treat are rarely close. The big job—he saw it almost as a mission—must be to "stop this tidal wave of form . . . and promote the unity of language,"[17] by which he meant the integrity of experience and writing. To put it simply, Italian writers must shake off the practice of writing about words and return to writing about experience.

By 1895 Pirandello had moved to a still more definitive argument. In "How We Speak in Italy" ("Come si Parla in Italia") he confronted the distinction between spoken and literary Italian, explaining again that because there was no single spoken language, but many, the confusion had prompted Italian writers to practice an ersatz literary language deficient in distinctive character and genuine color. An impediment to the free and natural development of Italian, this literary language suffocates creativity; in fiction, he explained in "How We Write Today in Italy" ("Come si Scrive Oggi in Italia," 1895), it is a confection derived largely from foreign models, typically more French than Italian. The tendency to imitate, always a fault in Italian writing, and lately worse than ever before, amounts to a "deliberate and conscious negation of sincerity [a term to become fundamental to his aesthetic vocabulary], a falsification for the sake of falsification."[18]

Finally, the argument underlying all this discussion crystallized in

"Excesses" ("Eccessi," 1896) in the crucial distinction between words and things. Here for the first time Pirandello's version of the words-things formula common to antiromantic theory emerged clearly as he took issue with the contention that the study of Italian literature in the schools should consist of a study of its facts, or, as some would call them to emphasize their substantiality, its things. He objected that this plan was wrongheaded and misguided because scholars were looking for things in a literature that had nothing to do with things, in a literature, more precisely, of words. In this kind of writing, whether old or new, charlatanry is the key principle, and the excesses of studying charlatanry are as little helpful as the excesses of practicing it.

This distinction between words and things is fundamental to Pirandello's conception of the creative process as it operates both in the production of literary works and in the shaping and structuring of experience. More broadly still, it is central to what he saw as the deeper issue of inauthenticity at all levels of experience. "The evil is this," he said in his introduction to Alberto Cantoni's *L'Illustrissimo* (1905): "although we wish to believe the contrary, we are still dominated by rhetoric and we still follow . . . its laws and precepts, not only in literature, but in all the expressions of our lives. Rhetoric and imitation are at bottom one."[19]

The debate over words and things had begun in the eighteenth century in the work of such Enlightenment figures as Ludovico Muratori, Francesco Algarotti, Giuseppe Baretti (Dr. Johnson's friend), and Melchiore Cesarotti.[20] To begin with it consisted of attacks on the older rhetoric, especially that of the sixteenth-century Arcadians and the Accademia della Crusca, the Florentine society empowered to monitor Italian vocabulary. In the nineteenth century Francesco De Sanctis used the words-things distinction in his discussion of what he called the new literature[21] and probably furnished much of the intellectual base for Pirandello's view of it. De Sanctis, too, chafed at the rhetoric and falsity of much of Italian tradition; but he saw hope in the new literature launched by Carlo Goldoni, who had restored the word by shifting emphasis from the word as sign to the life signified by it. In describing Italian writing's lack of interior authority, De Sanctis even used the term *sincerità* and spoke of creating a new consciousness to replace the operatic consciousness that had kept Italian life superficial.

In many respects Pirandello seemed virtually a disciple of these views, and he may well have been for as far as they went. But however much he may have owed to De Sanctis, he did not share his optimism that the new literature was already with us, or the corollaries that a new consciousness was already in the process of being made and that the direction toward a superior reality had already been established. Nor did he believe, as De Sanctis and his predecessors had, that a purified order of words could in fact describe the order of things. Things, in Pirandello's conception of them, were forged à la Hegel et al. in the consciousness, which itself was made, unmade, and made all over again, day by day and hour by hour.

Writing about things rather than words, accordingly, did not consist simply in the "nude exposition of facts" in the manner of the verists.[22] For all their many virtues, according to Pirandello, the verists were wrong in thinking that they could see experience objectively, without imposing on it properties of their own vision, or that in focusing on its exterior they were seeing it whole. Although the imitation of nature should be simple and "nude," he agreed, it should also be complete: the facts or things presented, he went on, paraphrasing Niccolò Tommaseo, should "embrace or outline the causes of things, and even in part the effects."[23] Things, in other words, are not merely exterior facts, but things with a will (*volontà*) or, to use the technical term, an intentionality of their own; moreover, they are things with an intentionality as we perceive it. Hence things are more like events than hard-surfaced facts, events with a complex interior-exterior existence. As Pirandello never tired of pointing out, "Life is a continuous and indistinct flux and has no form beyond that which we from time to time give it, infinitely variable and continuously changing."[24]

It was against this conception of things that Pirandello defended Giacomo Leopardi against the charge that he had slighted colors and the details of landscapes in his poetry, a serious fault for critics of romantic bias. Actually, Pirandello explained, Leopardi was more interested in "human things" (*cose umane*) than in the things of exterior nature; he was interested in things, that is, in this special sense, as keys to the peculiar amalgams of exterior and interior reality that make up our experience, things in the sense suggested by the Father's speech in *Six Characters in Search of an Author* (*Sei Personaggi in Cerca d'Autore*, 1921), when he says, "We all have within us a world of things, each a world of things of his own."[25]

Things thus understood, "human things," are traced in "Subjectivism and Objectivism in Narrative Art" ("Soggettivismo e Oggettivismo nell'Arte Narrativa," 1908) to a deep, neglected level of consciousness where the artist frees them and joins them to the materials capable of giving them expression. As Gösta Andersson has shown, Pirandello's account of how the apparatus of mind, spirit, and emotion selects and organizes these materials was largely derived from Gabriel Séailles, from whose *Essai sur le Génie dans l'Art* (1883) Pirandello appropriated not merely ideas, but long, crucial passages. Séailles, too, had profound affinities with Bergson.

For him the process of artistic creation was organic and intuitive, every faculty functioning with every other in a "free, vital movement of spirit," a phrase that Pirandello used again and again. But where Séailles saw harmony as the end of the process, Pirandello could conceive of a work characterized by bitterness and distress, and where Séailles understood instinct to dominate, Pirandello insisted, as we shall see, on a "free, vital movement of spirit" that comprehended reflection and intellect.

Pirandello's commentary on the words-things opposition, then, was at one and the same time an attack on the world of words, both in literature and in experience, and an exploration of alternatives to their inauthenticity in structured consciousness. For all his reputed sweetness and generosity with family and friends, he could be downright nasty in matters of literary and cultural bankruptcy, and he was probably never shriller than when discussing the high priest of the tradition of words in his time, Gabriele D'Annunzio. D'Annunzio runs through Pirandello's essays like Doctor Moriarty through the novels of Conan Doyle. There is a story that one day Pirandello had run out of cigarettes and had turned to some D'Annunzio had sent him—D'Annunzio was always making small gifts to people. In trying one and finding it scented with roses, he threw it down and in a rage exclaimed, "Always the same!" The dilettante par excellence, master of a splendiferous style in his writing and his life, D'Annunzio summed up everything Pirandello detested; he was rhetoric incarnate, that "distinguished swindler." In an interview given in 1926 and published first in *Observer* and then in *Living Age* Pirandello said flatly, "He is, I believe, in everything just the opposite of what I am. He is all pose and pathos—and very excellently, almost classically, acted repose. For myself, I feel that I am of the modern, throbbing life."[26]

Perhaps most pernicious of all D'Annunzio's unsavory traits was his imitation of foreign models (occasionally he even wrote in French!); for Pirandello imitation was the surest way to literary corruption. It had surfaced as a persistent problem as early as "How We Write Today in Italy" and in the following year had become the central issue in "Neo-Idealism," ("Neo-Idealismo," 1896). By 1905, in his essay prefatory to Cantoni's *L'Illustrissimo*, he examined at length the fashion of seeing life through the "spectacles of Paris," formerly supplied by Stendhal and Company, now by the Brunetière Corporation, and explained their relation to the deeper problem of inauthenticity in Italian life and writing. Imitation went hand in hand with the ideal of *scriver bello*, writing beautifully, both in the work of D'Annunzio and throughout the tradition of words. Like Goldoni, Pirandello wanted to write well, *scriver bene*, not beautifully, even if that should be construed as writing badly by the cultists of beauty. As late as "The New Theater and the Old" ("Teatro Nuovo e Teatro Vecchio"), a paper first given in 1922 but then given again with a few changes in 1934, Pirandello came back to the paradox that writing badly often went with having original vision; the great like Dante and Ariosto wrote badly because they did not look at the world with the spectacles of others. They looked not at words, but things.

In later essays he would dilate on the cultural implications of the words-things distinction. In the first lecture on Giovanni Verga, given in Catania in 1920, his opposition of Verga and D'Annunzio leads to an extended contrast between the style of things and the style of words, the first a style that constructs from within, beginning with the sensuous content of experience, the second a style that constructs from outside, from words, the signs of things. These rival styles dominate Italian litera-ture in two almost parallel lines of development, two continuous groups of writers. Dante as against Petrarch. Machiavelli as against Francesco Guicciardini. Ariosto as against Torquato Tasso. Alessandro Manzoni as against Vincenzo Monti. Verga as against D'Annunzio. While the tradi-tion of things subsists in the spoken language—the dialects rich in idiom and vibrant with the tension of people living—the tradition of words promotes the literary language.[27]

In the second lecture, given before the Royal Academy of Italy in 1931, Pirandello went straight to the rival traditions and to their cultural and political implications:

> [There are] two human types that perhaps every people compre-hends within its stock: those who construct and those who readapt, the necessary spirits and the creatures of luxury, the first endowed with a style of things, the second with a style of words. [These] two great families or categories of men living in the bosom of every nation are in Italy, perhaps more than elsewhere, easily distinguished. But only to one who is very familiar with our life and knows how to look within.[28]

Italy, in Pirandello's view, is especially given to the tradition of words: it honors the heroes of that tradition and exiles or ignores all others; it thrives on the sentimental image of an easy, happy, sun-drenched people, a nation of singers, lovers, and dreamers so often met in that tradition. Flamboyance, panache, romance: these constitute the cultural rhetoric of a spiritually bankrupt people!

Thus Pirandello's examination of the alternatives to inauthenticity began with his commentary on things in the special sense of "human things" and then led to his long, discontinuous discussion of structuring consciousness. Selecting and organizing the human things that underlie genuine art and authentic experience are tantamount to capturing life in its fullness and mystery. Pirandello was never as precise as we might wish about this process, but he was clear that the exterior things selected were always merely the exposed facets of a larger reality mostly hidden from view. This reality is like a polyhedron, he explained repeatedly: we cannot by its nature see all sides of it at once, and we cannot turn all sides of our being, also like a polyhedron, on it at once. The best we can hope for is that two facets of these subjective and objective polyhedra touch. By giving expression to that contact, simply and honestly, we comprehend the whole. He put it like this: "In each of our acts all being is; the act that shows is connected simply with another contiguous to it, yet at the same time it refers to the totality of being. It's like that facet of a polyhedron that touches the respective facet of another, and yet does not nullify the facets facing in still other directions."[29] The process of artistic creation consists in catching the thingness of this contact through the "free, vital movement of spirit," of uniting in consciousness the physical presence of the subject with our experience of it past and present, our sense of its way of being—and all this accompanied by our awareness of our effort to effect this unity. Human things, the deep reality (realtà profonda), the thingness of the touching facets of two polyhedra: these fill out the extended sense of Pirandello's use of the term "things" in the famous distinction.

Things in this sense are the alternative to the inauthenticity of a world of words. Things in this sense clarify how Pirandello could on the one hand say that the world is only what we make of it and on the other claim that "the world is not limited to the idea that we have of it" and that "in our representation [of it] . . . we must commit ourselves to realizing it as much as we can."[30] These statements are consistent as long as we understand that "making an idea of the world" means approaching our experience of the world with a respect for mystery, both in the world and in us, with a lively awareness of those facets of the polyhedra not overtly evident in the moment of contact. This tolerance for mystery predicates a readiness to hold many elements in the consciousness at once, in suspension, to make of creation a moment of fusion rather than resolution. This readiness, as we shall see, was fundamental to Pirandello's conception of creative consciousness.

The figure of the polyhedron, or rather of the polyhedra in contact, provides our first access to the complex issue of Pirandellian consciousness. The figure suggests how little human agents can know of what they are meeting in the world and how little they know of themselves as they do. But it also leaves a good deal of the process in darkness. It suggests virtually nothing about how the consciousness will process any given human thing, and nothing at all about the character of consciousness.

Pirandello's early commentaries on consciousness, though they fall short of a full account, add important details to the rough outline provided by the polyhedra figure. One of the earliest of these is that given by the character Gregorio Alvignani in *The Outcast* (*L'Esclusa,* 1901), when, in a chapter omitted from the definitive version of the book, he attempts to define consciousness as he defends his behavior toward Marta Ajala, the novel's protagonist.[31] Alvignani is a brilliant amalgam of weakness, self-deceit, and intelligence. A local lawyer soon to go off to the Chamber of Deputies in Rome, he is mistakenly thought by everyone to be Marta's seducer and is at least partly responsible for her ostracism by her husband and the community. Yet he concludes, deriving his arguments from his scholarly work on the transformation of morals, that he need take no responsibility for what others think or for the consequences of what they think: his conscience is his own. Later, when during a second encounter in Palermo Marta in fact succumbs to his advances and becomes pregnant, he ultimately ends the affair by arguing that she does not love him; Marta, shocked by the charge and at the same time overwhelmed by the ambiguity of her feeling, cannot deny his claim. What Alvignani, good man though he fundamentally is, never sees is that he is using Marta in the same way he uses his work in ethical relativity, as a diversion, and that he is manipulating her reconciliation with her husband in a bad faith that he does not remotely suspect in himself. Alvignani is a man of words, a master of rhetoric and self-flattering argument. He makes choices and finds arguments to support them, but they somehow add up to a person vastly different from the one he intends. Like Pirandello, he is the author of a paper entitled "Art and Consciousness Today," the paper he comes to Palermo toward the end of the book to give.

In his discussion of consciousness with Luca Blandino, however, Alvignani makes a number of telling points. It is not, he begins, the structure of norms derived from Christianity; nor is it the promptings of intuition; nor a structure determined by the so-called laws of thought; nor the product of pragmatism or any of the other "isms" current in the world. It is absolute unto itself, though it cannot exist in isolation. It is extremely difficult to develop a precise idea of it because it is so much a part of us: in fact it is ourselves, that with which, inevitably, we strive to form an idea of it.

Yet some of its traits are reasonably clear. Alvignani admits that despite the autonomy of individual consciousness it does not exist in isolation because he finds it impossible to conceive of himself in isolation. His idea of himself is always in part his perception of the ideas that others have of him. By consciousness, then, he means his idea of a community of consciousnesses, all consistent with one's own, not simply an idea of one's own waking mind, but of one's waking mind in a community of like-structured minds. This idea is self-generated and always highly tentative because in any contact with the world (the polyhedra in contact) one has so little under direct control. Both the exterior and interior worlds are continuously changing, seeking form, but in flux. Yet this consciousness is all I have, Alvignani concludes, and it is sufficient. "It is," Pirandello would say repeatedly, "our artifice for living."[32]

This general picture of consciousness as a self-generated, always tentative structure provides a necessary focus for Pirandello's more detailed analysis of it. Unfortunately, he scattered the steps of this analysis in his many explanations of the creative process. In his view artistic creation occurred spontaneously yet consisted of activities that could be distinguished from each other. In a figure analogous to that of the polyhedra in contact, the work of art was a living organism that sprang from what he most frequently called a germ that had become lodged within the author. In "Subjectivism and Objectivism in Narrative Art," after fulminating against the critics' concern with exterior form, he spoke of the work's interior principles and of the germ from which the work develops, "naturally and spontaneously flowers, according to the germ's own vital, interior laws," its will or intentionality.[33] The plant metaphor was, as it had been for Séailles, his favorite means of describing the process. The work as germ grew and could grow only as the laws of the germ predicated: an acorn into an oak, a grain of barley into barley.[34] Sometimes, instead of "germ," he spoke of "images" as "the perennial source of art": "My works are born from live images . . . [that] pass through a veil of concepts which have taken hold of me. My work . . . is never a concept trying to express itself through images. . . . It is on the contrary images, often very vivid images of life."[35]

But whether germ, images, or yet another term, larva, the stimulus, so to speak, takes root in the artist and grows according to its "vital laws." There is a useful passage summing up the initial phase of the process in Pirandello's review of A. Lauria's *Le Garibaldine* (1905), where he speaks of "the germ from which the work of art will develop like an organic, living being. It's necessary that there be in him [the artist] . . . the terrain suitable to fructify this germ. The work of art is born not from the crude fact, but from the fecund emotion of the artist, who gathers this fact to himself and lets it mature within himself."[36] And again in the notes heavily indebted to Séailles published as "The Secret Notebook" ("Il Taccuino Segreto"): "The image is already something living: it relates to the spirit almost as the cell does to the body."[37] Then in his appendix to *Art and Science* (*Arte e Scienza,* 1908), in a splendid passage describing the final phase of the process by which the germ-image-larva of a dog is transformed into a creation, he says, "When will it become creation? When I stop contemplating it as an object in myself, when it begins to will in me what I for its sake want for it, when it ceases to be mere theoretical contemplation and becomes action, when its simple theoretical form becomes form in fact, technique, that is, a free spontaneous movement toward form, no longer an objectification, but subjectified."[38] Perhaps all this is most tersely summed up in his body-spirit-body formula: the body, sometimes called material, moves through the spirit of the artist to become a new body, the created work. In "Sicilian Theater?" ("Teatro Siciliano?" 1909) art consists fundamentally in "subjectifying the objectification."[39]

These various metaphors for the creative process represent what in nonmetaphorical terms might be described as the process by which experience is given definition and made conscious. This process consists in bringing one's knowledge, past experience, and present sense of a subject into a fresh focus as one contemplates it, and it includes one's self-observations as the attempt is made to achieve this focus. Each germ or image or larva has its own will or laws in the sense that it has a particular way of being in our experience, a particular life. The "free, vital movement of spirit" present in all phases of the process of achieving this focus is the free and congenial congress of the separate activities of consciousness.

Throughout his long career Pirandello stated and restated this theory with virtually no change, defining as he did a small group of terms that make up the framework of his aesthetic. Among the most frequent of these is *spontaneità* ("spontaneity"), which can perhaps best be defined as that sudden rush in the free, vital movement of spirit to select and organize the expressive material. In "The Comedy of the Devils and the Tragedy of Dante" ("La Commedia dei Diavoli e la Tragedia di Dante," 1916) he described Dante's creation of Farinata as a moment of arrival, "*new* as regards the treatment of material that is moving and still warm and that stirs within him in an *intensely active instant* [*momentaneità attiva* (his italics)]."[40] In his review of G. L. Ferri's *La Camminante* (1906) he emphasized the sudden, impulsive character of the process: "The image wills itself and provokes, consequently, immediately, that harmonious, spontaneous, and natural movement that effectuates in sensuous form outside what the image was within the artist who conceived it and brought it to maturity."[41] Pirandello found no contradiction in the assertions that on the one hand he saw creation as a largely involuntary event, as spontaneous as characters suddenly appearing in his rooms and making their demands, while on the other he saw himself as a thoughtful writer who contemplated and reflected. As we shall see presently, the intellect, reflection, or critical faculties were, for him, readily assimilated to "that harmonious, spontaneous, and natural movement" that creates. All his life he hostilely resisted the view that he was a cerebral writer. For him the mind, like the emotions, worked in darting rushes.

The sister term to *spontaneità* was *sincerità,* that quality that should be dominant in the artist during the creative process. Most simply, *sincerità* was rigorous honesty, an unfailing fidelity to things as far as one could accurately know them. In "Sincerity and Art" ("Sincerità e Arte," 1897) he found the idealist view of what could be known of subjects too modest in its claims. Where his friend Ugo Ojetti had argued that since the world is only one's idea of it, one must not range beyond the self, Pirandello countered, "For me the world is not only an ideality, that is, it is not limited to the idea that I make of it for myself: outside of me the world exists for itself and with me, and in my representation I must determine *to realize it* [his italics] as much as I can, creating for myself something like a consciousness of it in which it lives, in me as it does in itself, seeing it as it sees itself, feeling it as it feels itself. Then there will be no need for symbol or appearance: everything will be real and living."[42] The distinction is important because it sets him against the subjectivism that in the work of D'Annunzio and his followers became a monumental narcissism. For Pirandello the world could be known in small part, however great the difficulty; and by enabling the germs of subjects to fructify within him, the artist could grasp some measure of their intentionality. *Sincerità* required taking that limited knowledge into account, while at the same time retaining the fullest respect for mystery.

The artist governed by *sincerità,* then, would draw on both inner and outer worlds, simply and directly, without preestablished formulas or systems, without, above all, resort to rhetoric or imitation. As the free, vital movement of spirit ripened the germ of the work, spontaneously, *sincerità* permitted the work virtually to compose itself. "All the masters say 'Work simply,'" he insisted in "The Secret Notebook," and "that means have a strong feeling that dominates your vision and your hand as it does your spirit: be almost ingenuous, sincere."[43] At bottom *sincerità* is very like the candor that Massimo Bontempelli argues to have been the primary quality in both Pirandello's work and his life, candor in the sense of natural simplicity, a determination to penetrate to essentials, and a profound sense of and humility before the large areas of mystery in life. These qualities made building with authority possible and predicated an unremitting opposition to the world of words.

Yet *sincerità* as Pirandello understood it must be sharply distinguished from the sincerity of a Rousseau or Wordsworth. At all points Pirandello admits that being honest consists in recognizing that most of the time one is inevitably dishonest: one is true to a self that is continually showing another face. Pirandello had tremendous compassion for those who did not make this admission, the self-deceivers, and his compassion extended not only to those who deceive themselves for what might be seen as a noble end, but also to those who deceive themselves for ignoble, even squalid ends. By contrast, the highest creation and the richest experience consist in holding in suspension everything that consciousness governed by *sincerità* forces one to acknowledge.

The other terms in Pirandello's aesthetic identify still other facets of the creative process. "Technique" is the process itself of composing or creating, that by which the free, vital, spontaneous movement of spirit shapes the work. "Form" is the final shape of the work; inseparable from technique, it is not imposed from outside, as in the work of imitators, but evolved within the artist. "Style," on the other hand, is the peculiar disposition of the artist to compose or create one way rather than another; like technique, it comes into play as the germ matures within the artist, generating the free and natural movement of spirit that ultimately produces the work.

Small wonder, then, that Pirandello opposed the imitation of models and rhetoric with such hostility. For him originality could be achieved only through the free and natural congress of germ with the artist's sensibility: the uniqueness of this congress produced the original work. In the same way, modernity was in no way a special quality restricted to the avant-garde. According to Pirandello, Giovanni Papini, avant-garde poet and theorist, succeeded usually in being only extravagant despite all his violent efforts to appear original and modern.[44] A truly original work by a contemporary artist could not fail to be modern as well.

Altogether, Pirandello's understanding of the creative process makes it clear that treating or giving expression to things, in his extended sense of that term, was far more than merely producing sensuous images. It involved first reacting with *sincerità* to a stimulus to create, that is, reacting with the highest responsibility to what is and is not known. Next it involved assisting at the maturation of that stimulus within the spirit to produce a work of optimal fullness and density. The difference between this process and those of rhetoric or imitation was the difference between the traditions of things and words, the difference between authenticity and inauthenticity in art.

What cannot be emphasized too often is that what Pirandello had to say about authenticity in art he also believed to be true of experience. With the single marginal difference that art is disinterested while life is not, the process by which one shapes or gives form to one's experience is identical with that by which one creates works of art. In *Umorismo* (1908), in a passage he was to use again in "Irony" ("Ironia," 1920), he declared, "We all have, more or less, a will that prompts in us the motions by which we create our lives. This creation . . . requires in greater or lesser degree, as art does, all the functions and activities of the spirit, of intellect and imagination, as well as will. And whoever has these and succeeds in bringing them into play in greater degree will succeed in creating for himself a higher, broader, and stronger life."[45]

Whether in making works of art or in the shaping of experience, then, Pirandello's response to the world of words consisted essentially of giving expression to human things. That aim comprehended, moreover, not merely a particular way of seeing the world, literary tradition, and the processes by which art and experience are forged, but a particular conception of the consciousness as the prime faculty for all experience and the source of all value. In a world that had seen the recent collapse of the structures that had for millennia supplied coherence and order to human life, this shift to consciousness was an event of the profoundest cultural importance. Although the world was dying within an empty superstructure of fossilized words, Pirandello could still speak of creating a rich life for oneself. The key to this life lay in using the consciousness well, in first recognizing the world of words for what it was and then living, as, according to Pirandello, Giovanni Cena had, one's own poetry.[46]

2

●●●●●●●●●●●●●●●●●●●●●●●

IN SEARCH OF
AUTHENTICITY: *UMORISMO*

B Y 1908 Pirandello's life had settled into a pattern that was to last through World War I. The straitened circumstances following his family's loss of its money had forced him to continue in the provisional teaching position he had taken at the Magistero, the women's teaching college in Rome. To secure a permanent post there, he published a collection of essays entitled *Art and Science* and gave what he described as a year of misery to writing a long monograph on humor, also published in that year. Meanwhile, he continued to write poems and fiction and gave increasingly more time to looking after the children and Antonietta, whose mental health continued to deteriorate. By this time their marriage had become a round of quarrels, separations, and long, bitter truces punctuated by the briefest of ecstatic reconciliations.

Umorismo, the most ambitious of his theoretical productions, offers a detailed examination of that special power fundamental to both authentic experience and to what Pirandello would call humoristic writing. The monograph consists of a careful study of the term itself, of the history of commentary on it, of the history of humoristic writing and of its major figures, and of the extended implications of *umorismo*'s special outlook as Pirandello understood it. Pirandello was scholarly with a vengeance, many times more thorough than he had been in his earlier treatment of the subject in the essays on Cecco Angiolieri, far more lavish in examples and variants than his basic purpose of setting out a clear understanding of *umorismo* seemed to require. But his method served him well: through all the detail he gradually illuminated both the conception and a sense of its qualitative implications for experience.

Essentially, the monograph deals with the way things, in Pirandello's conception of that term, are shaped and organized within the consciousness and at the same time mediated by a humoristic way of seeing. This mode of perception, or power of reflection, as he frequently called it, involves a kind of x-ray vision that provides both positive and negative images simultaneously. We see the old lady made ridiculous by her excessive makeup, and we laugh because she is trying so hard to appear a young lady. But at the same time we see that she suffers with this mask because she wears it to hold the love of her much younger husband. *Umorismo* is this way of treating the image of the woman. More a way by which many faculties collaborate than a single faculty, it was for Pirandello the dominant modality for modern consciousness.

Pirandello was never ideally precise about it. At different places in his work he called it a "creative power," a "sense of contradiction," a "special psychic physiognomy," and a "more or less diffuse state of spirit."[1] But most frequently he referred to it as a special kind of reflection both caused by a sense of contradiction (*sentimento del contrario*) and the cause of that sense.[2] It can be both cause and effect, paradoxically, because it functions in concert with that strong feeling that fosters growth in the germinating seed, both stimulating and becoming part of that growth. "Reflection," he explained, " . . . is a kind of projection of the very activity of imaginative creation: it is born of the image, like a shadow from a body. . . . It is in the creative germ itself."[3] Thus, although the power is most frequently called a special kind of reflection, it is not at odds with the spontaneity of artistic creation. It is present at the birth and throughout the growth of the work; it is itself "almost a form of feeling."[4]

As the early chapters of the monograph make clear, the term *umorismo* had wide currency at the time and a general meaning consonant with Pirandello's, if less precise and less elaborately articulated than his. It was defined and explained by theorists and studied in most major periods of art and literature,[5] and many writers, like Ugo Fleres, used it without explanation. As early as 1890 Pirandello had written to his former teacher Ernesto Monaci that he was going to do a study of three humorist poets of the Middle Ages,[6] and his essays on Angiolieri provide his first highly scholarly examination of other theorists (a striking instance of the young Pirandello taking on the "professors") and a penetrating commentary on how this "profound and subtle philosophical sense" is produced. Even Benedetto Croce had written on *umorismo,* only to dismiss it as an indefinable subjective state, provoking a quarrel that continued throughout Pirandello's life and beyond.[7]

Pirandello's quarrel with Croce went deeper than the dispute over *umorismo* and aesthetic theory, though these matters always remained to the fore; it provides a useful perspective on Pirandellian *umorismo*. Ironically, Croce and Pirandello had a great deal in common: both were southern; both opposed rhetoric and mannerism in literature and advocated a quality like Pirandello's *sincerità;* both derived a great deal from De Sanctis. But with the first salvos from Pirandello in 1908 in *Art and Science* and *Umorismo,* it was clear that their differences were profound and irremediable. Croce replied with a review of *Umorismo* in his periodical *La Critica* in 1909; Pirandello responded in his revised edition of the monograph in 1920, then renewed his assault in a review in 1921 of Croce's essay on Dante. Croce lashed out again at the time of Pirandello's Nobel Prize in 1934, Pirandello again in 1935, Croce yet again in 1938, two years after Pirandello's death, and even so late as 1948 in a review of Arminio Janner's book on Pirandello.

Despite this saga of give-and-take, the quarrel at all points turned essentially on a disagreement about the nature of the creative process, including the place of *umorismo* within that process. In his first attack of 1908 Pirandello went to the heart of the matter by accusing Croce of having distorted the creative act in limiting it to a single faculty, the intuition. The famous Crocean formula "intuition equals expression" represented for Pirandello a process that converted a content into a form, with intuition serving as the transforming agent. He objected that that was too simple, a "mechanical objectification," too much like the way science imposes abstractions on nature. By that process only the qualities already present in the content would be carried over into the finished work; nothing would be added by the perceiver or artist. It left no place for feeling, will, or mind, and denied to the process what Pirandello saw as basic, a spontaneous collaboration of many faculties, an effort of the whole spirit to evolve a form from the creative germ lodged within. In stressing intuition Croce had "separated with clean cuts of the knife the several activities and functions of the spirit otherwise bound inseparably together and in continuous, reciprocal action"[8] and had produced a rigid intellectualization of the creative process, "an intellectual aesthetic without intellect."[9]

Croce in his turn struck at Pirandello for his imprecise terms, his lack of logical rigor, his want of clarity and system; in short, for his failure to behave like a philosopher. Most important, he would yield no ground to Pirandello's assault on his conception of the creative process. In his view thought played no role in artistic creation, and Pirandello's attempts to smuggle it into a process that at the same time he called spontaneous Croce found laughable. At this distance, and with all due respect for Croce's greatness, it seems clear that he misread Pirandello. He stubbornly insisted on literal meanings for terms for which Pirandello intended extended meanings; he persistently translated what he saw as Pirandello's technical weaknesses and want of theoretical rigor into a general shallowness of vision.

The nub of their differences was the role of the intelligence or the critical faculty in creativity. For Croce the act of creation was a noncritical process, while for Pirandello it engaged the whole spirit, including the intelligence, or, as was usually the case in his own work, humoristic reflection. For Pirandello, accordingly, artistic creation was a largely conscious process, while for Croce it was not. It would surely be a mistake to say that it was unconscious for Croce, but he deemphasized calculation, artistic choice, self-conscious management, or anything resembling the contradictory, critical sense characteristic of *umorismo*.

But their differences went deeper than this. Croce's insistence on system and Pirandello's ostensible lack of it in his insistence on the dynamic interplay of all parts of the spirit trace to markedly different convictions about the mind itself. Croce was a man of reason who operated from the assumption that logic and its categories embraced all life and provided the framework for reasonings about it. The formula "intuition equals expression" defined one such category in a larger aesthetic, itself part of an all-embracing philosophy. Pirandello, on the other hand, nourished a deep distrust of the mind: he was convinced that it could never apprehend more than a small part of life at one time—one facet of the polyhedron—and could develop only imperfect reasonings about that because the rest was unknown. He described logic as "an infernal little machine," a kind of pump and filter that puts the heart in contact with the mind, extracting from the fullness of experience a pathetic distillate called ideas. With these we reason and construct philosophies. But all in vain: as a guide the mind is capable only of flashes and short sprints; the rest, and most notably its so-called system, is illusion.[10]

To take a crucial issue, Croce believed in history: he believed that the past could be known and reasoned about in the present; he believed further that our knowledge of the past might be used to direct the present. For Pirandello history was a smear of fragmentary myths and fables, an embalmed, denatured reduction of events never grasped in their entirety in their own time and largely created anew in the present.[11] And philosophy was little better. In his letter of 23 December 1916 to his son Stefano, then a prisoner of war, Pirandello cautioned him against wearing himself out with books of philosophy. "I've read them all for you, and on your return I'll tell you what they say. Very little, very little, my son."[12] The fact is that Pirandello often saw reason the problem solver as a tyranny akin to madness. Some of his most playful and amusing stories turn on what might be called the reason of unreason. In "Set Fire to the Dross" ("Fuoco alla Paglia," 1905) the peasant-zealot Nazzaro is rigorously logical about helping Simone Lampo expiate his sins by "setting fire to his dross." He not only disposes of dross by freeing Don Simone's birds, but he also literally burns his "dross" (*paglia*) by setting fire to his pitiable portion of grain (*paglia*).

Yet even as Pirandello continually undercut the claims of reason, he insisted on the presence of intellect in the creative process. In doing so, however, he appears to have meant something quite unlike reason the problem solver and builder of structures, and something more like *umorismo*, that special reflection consisting in a sense of contradiction, that power of intellect to probe and break up. This way of receiving and managing the data of experience produced not reasoned resolutions, but states of irresolution and tension. "In the conception of a humoristic work, the reflection does not retire and remain invisible, that is, subordinate to the feeling, almost a mirror in which the feeling reflects itself; on the contrary, it asserts itself in the role of judge; it analyzes the feeling, detaching itself from it; it decomposes the image."[13] What results is a state of critical presence inimical to Croce's system, a state of suspension congenial to the humorist's open, always partial, always changing way of seeing. In Pirandello this reflection was an indispensable part of creative consciousness.

To some extent Pirandello's objections to Croce trace to his greater concern with the surface that the work of art finally is. For him Croce was simply too abstract about artistic creation. Pirandello preferred to think of a literary work as a living thing, the fruit of a seed, grown and living, a human thing transformed into a created surface. Indeed, Pirandello's pervasive emphasis on the created surface reveals a good deal about him. Despite all the claims that can be made today that he was a kind of predeconstructionist, that he was continuously deconstructing roles and personalities, he differed markedly and crucially from the current analysts of discourse in that he persisted in seeing the elements he had deconstructed as parts of a seething, intact surface. He loved these surfaces, it is clear; not simply the elements and principles that explained them, but the surfaces themselves redolent with the sweat of deception and self-deception. His critics have frequently characterized him as intellectual and cerebral, and compared with the majority of his artistic contemporaries, he probably was. But his drama and fiction were never, or very rarely, cerebral to the extent of breaking his surfaces up, dissolving them into their abstract components in the style of postmodernist theater.[14] He was never drawn to dramatize the process of discourse[15] or the deconstructed process of playing at being someone; not, I think, because he would have disdained these subjects, but simply, I suspect, because it never occurred to him to relinquish surface for its underlying structure. Even in his most difficult and most famous play, *Six Characters,* he breaches natural probability but sustains throughout a surface that, operating within its own probabilities, is wholly coherent. Indeed, the majority of his revisions for the definitive version of 1925 were calculated to solidify that surface.

This fondness for surfaces is perhaps a response to the darkness that Pirandello found surrounding them. Much that he said and did can best be understood by recalling his conviction that the world, the world of limited surfaces, was enveloped in mystery, a place where cringing creatures create and perpetuate illusions to hold off the terror. In such a world *umorismo* is not simply a phenomenon to be met in art and literature, but a way of dealing with the world and, most important, a way of winning authenticity for experience. Instead of a world presided over by the Eternal Father, we live, as Pirandello put it in a letter to Antonietta in 1893, in an "immense labyrinth."[16] He used the labyrinth metaphor frequently, a labyrinth always plunged in thick darkness, with human figures trying to find their way with the help of their little lanterns, the flickering light of their uncertain minds, illuminating only the immediate ambience, terrifying themselves with the shadows that the light of their minds creates. It is the night of one of his best stories, "Ciaula Discovers the Moon" ("Ciaula Scopre la Luna," 1912), in which Ciaula's terror of the dark, on a night when he had to work late at the mine and, his lamp gone out, had lost his way in the tunnels, yields to tears of joy upon his emerging from the mine and discovering the moon. Although Pirandello would later emphasize less the labyrinth, night, and darkness and emphasize more the world as theater, these earlier images and metaphors continued to be prominent in his thought to the end of his life.

But the mystery and confusion of this background exist within the individual as well. There consciousness sets out tentative limits and makes possible some measure of control and coherence, even though beyond its barriers lie vast reaches of the unknown that are forever slipping back under and through the fencing. Hence the closeness of normality to madness and the desperate need to develop what Pirandello called, with due acknowledgment to Giovanni Marchesini,[17] artifices for living, the fictions, roles, self-serving conceptions that enable us to construct little worlds with which to stand off the mystery. These creative fictions—Pirandello had recognized their importance as early as the letter in 1886 to his sister Rosalina with its passage on the spider, snail, and mollusc—constitute the central material of any given state of consciousness, the organizing principle for the moment, so to speak, in that they give temporary focus and a fugitive coherence to the individual. More than anything else, they are the matter that humoristic perception works on, analyzes, decomposes, disintegrates into unresolved contradictions, and then holds in suspension. With the help of *umorismo,* we are able, in our great need, to use these creative fictions even as we perceive them for what they are.

And yet this is not all. In addition to helping us to live with outer and inner darkness and confusion, this power of reflection enables us to watch ourselves as we struggle to live. *Umorismo* not only dominates the consciousness, it also makes it reflexive, imposing on it an important dimension of self-consciousness. Pirandello's phrase for it, *vedersi vivere,* to see or watch oneself living, comprehends in the word "living" watching ourselves not only as we seize as much of the thingness of any moment as possible, perceiving as we do that even this interior-exterior thingness is largely illusory, a system of constructs and masks, but also as we devise and shift these constructs and masks, and even as we recognize that we are devising, shifting, and living them. The state of tension and irresolution produced not only contains contradictions, accordingly, it also frames and focuses these contradictions, clarifying, as it does, an intricate field of differentiable qualities and meanings, hence values. The preeminent value, of course, is that of making inauthentic structures the basis for a new kind of authenticity. By admitting their arbitrariness and at the same time recognizing their crucial importance we bring a distinctive authenticity to the act of creation.

Umorismo, then, is the genius of Pirandellian consciousness. It is not so much a single faculty, like reason, memory, and fantasy, among others, as it is a coordinating power that monitors the data of experience for *sincerità.* It functions as part of the free, spontaneous movement of spirit, adjusting, correcting, qualifying, shaping the materials moving toward form yet still in suspension.

Like the distinction between words and things, Pirandello's conception of *umorismo* persisted virtually unchanged through his long career. He came back to it repeatedly in his essays and reviews, explaining it, defending it, tracing its ramifications beyond the realms of art. Still more important, it was at all stages crucial to his fiction and drama.

Indeed, if the theoretical pieces yield the clearest exposition of *umorismo,* it can be met in all its fullness only in the fiction and drama because only in represented actions can we gauge the intricacy and density intended by a phrase like "sense of contradiction." For Pirandello this fullness followed from living with things rather than words, from engaging in the world with *sincerità,* which is to say with an honesty that forces a persistent awareness that experience is as much created as evolved, from an unremitting sensitivity to the partialness, factitiousness, transience of what is made conscious, and from a mirror image of all that as we watch these processes. But for examples of this fullness we must turn to the work, and for the first, impressive examples, to the fiction.

"Sunlight and Shadow" ("Sole e Ombra," 1896) has very few of the qualities with which Pirandello's name later became associated, yet it is extremely rich in the humoristic vision that underlay them. The title, like those of many of his early works, stresses opposing elements in suspension, while the story shimmers darkly with a sense of planes of energy moving in different directions, of a life at once painful and delicious, squalid and full of wonder. Essentially, it is the story of Ciunna's last day, of his determination to drown himself rather than face the humiliation of prison for his theft of 2,700 lire, of his journey to the port to do it, of his change of heart after a day with his friend Tino Imbrò, and of his final recognition that he must go through with it after all because by now his suicide note has been discovered and everyone thinks him dead.

The grotesque, difficult, tragicomic condition rendered in these events is, as in so many of Pirandello's best stories, present in the first paragraphs.

> Amid the branches of the trees that formed a kind of airy, green portico for the long avenue around the old city's walls, the moon appeared suddenly, by surprise, and seemed to say to an extremely tall man who had ventured forth alone in the perilous darkness, at so unusual an hour
>
> —Yes, but I see you.
> And, as if he felt himself discovered, the man stopped and, pressing his large hands to his chest, said with intense exasperation
> —It's me. Yes, me. Ciunna!
> Gradually, above his head, all the leaves, rustling in endless waves, seemed to confide the name to each other:
> —Ciunna. Ciunna. As if, having known him for many years, they understood why he walked alone like this, at this hour, along

the fearsome avenue. And they whispered about him and about what he had done. Ssss. Ciunna! Ciunna![18]

In these few lines the vastness of the night and the smallness of even this large man interpenetrate. The moon chides, as a friendly schoolteacher might do, "Yes, but I see you," and that cosmic familiarity plays against the finite intensity radiating out through the leaves, "rustling in endless waves," in the name "Ciunna."

This technique of texturing Ciunna's day by orchestrating qualities not merely contradictory but from different orders of experience is fundamental to the story. It is clear a few lines later in Ciunna's imagined dialogue with the Inspector, in the Inspector's homely formality as the explosive discovery of Ciunna's theft is made. It is everywhere in ironic details. On what he intends to be his last day Ciunna awakens to realize with a start that he has slept soundly, had put his shoes out to be polished, and has now put on his ordinary suit to save the better one. He goes to the port to drown himself, having rejected the poison he has in his pocket, and there meets his friend Tino Imbrò, who, himself exultant because his wife has returned to her mother, insists on a celebration, innocently promising to cure Ciunna of any and all of his ills. At first Ciunna, stupefied by the irony, resists the proposal that they go for a swim, but he finally agrees, privately seeing it as a preparation; he even tries unsuccessfully to hold himself under. Then he eats spaghetti alle vongole and drinks Tino's special wine as the holiday meal becomes for all in the trattoria a banquet. Reminded at last by the unsuspecting Tino of the *affaruccio* ("dear little piece of business") that he had come to the port to transact, he goes down to the water and decides that 2,700 lire is after all not reason enough to die. Instead of death by water, he chooses to buy a kilo of mullet to take home to his grandchildren. Only on the difficult climb back up the hill in a carriage does he remember the suicide note and conclude that he must go through with it.

In the course of his last day Ciunna experiences two awakenings: the first in the morning, after which, still hazy with sleep, he sets out for the port; the second in the carriage on the ride home after he had been saved by his day with Tino. He passes from the first through a period of stupor at the ordinariness of everything on this day of days, to the bliss of the ride down to the port, intensely sensitive and delighted by the most commonplace events, "as if . . . he felt compensated for everything," then to the camaraderie and joy of the dinner. In the carriage, after he has decided to live, he feels himself coming out of a dream; he imagines himself wandering through the moon-drenched field and a dog barking at him somewhere in the distance. At last, having remembered the note and taken the poison, he awaits death, puzzled at first that it does not come, and then writhes in his final agony as the unsuspecting carriage driver begins to sing.

In addition to defining the grotesque, seriocomic quality of Ciunna's day, this surface of incongruities serves, through Ciunna's responses, to fill out our perception of him. He is himself a humorist with a humorist's appreciation of life. Indeed, the power of the story derives in large part from our awareness of his great love of life. Far from being a cynical suicide, he has a notable capacity to enjoy—the donkeys decorated in the style of the region, the beggars on the road, the spaghetti alle vongole—a capacity commensurate with his physical size. He would steal to feed his son's children, but die rather than degrade his life by going to prison. When the warm and generous Tino acknowledges him his master, he calls him "immense Ciunna."

Yet the humoristic sensibility that controls all this belongs not to Ciunna but to the authorial voice. The point of view of that voice is very close to Ciunna's, close enough so that we feel acutely Ciunna's anguish at the whiteness of the moon in his last moments; at the same time it is sufficiently detached so that the fullness of Ciunna's outline is clear against this background of sunlight and shadow, this world elusively out of control much as his daughter-in-law's too-frequent pregnancies are out of control.

Much the same structure by contrasts is evident in "The First Night" ("Prima Notte," 1900), though there the vision is tempered less by comic values than by intense poignancy. The title refers to the wedding night of Marastella and Don Lisi Chirico, and the story opens with a detail that encapsulates all the homely effort and anguish of Mamm'Anto's dream to see her daughter happily married: Mamm'Anto' setting out and counting the items of the trousseau that she has lovingly assembled.

> Four nightshirts.
> Four sheets.
> Four skirts.
> Four, that is, of everything. She never tired of showing her daughter's trousseau, put together one piece today, another tomorrow, with the patience of a spider.
> —The goods of poor folk, but clean.[19]

And clean, white, chaste in its purity everything is, like the hope of Marastella's marriage. But Mamm'Anto' weeps almost too much, and the narrator is careful to point out that the chest from which she takes the articles is "like a coffin."

The wedding day unfolds quickly and simply to reveal that the inordinate weeping, Marastella's and her friends' as well as Mamm'Anto's, is explained by a disaster of a year before, when Marastella's father and Tino Sparti, the young man she should be marrying, were drowned. By now the dream of a golden lad has been swallowed by the difficult circumstances in which her father's death has left her. Don Lisi Chirico, an older man, a widower, means security to her; but he is also the custodian of the local cemetery, and he will take her there to live. The wedding procession, indeed, is like a funeral cortege.

Within this rather sentimental framework Pirandello treats the wedding day and first night so that the narrative progressively intensifies the poignancy of this couple mismatched in everything but heartbreak and goodwill. Marastella is predictable enough: beautiful, frightened, submissive not merely to her mother but to a destiny that seems to mock and torment. But Don Lisi Chirico, shaved for the occasion and looking like an old, if docile, goat, upsets the expected pattern: instead of being a vulgar, unpleasant man, he is sweet and thoughtful, heartbroken himself for the loss of his wife a year before, acutely sensitive to his bride's anguish. Unfortunately, if he can save Marastella from fear, he does embody as well the death of her dream. When he rings the "Angelus" on the cemetery bell, he signals both the visitors' departure and the beginning of Marastella's residence in the house of the dead. In the concluding image Marastella weeps at her dead fiancé's grave while he cries out at his wife's, and "the moon looked down on the little cemetery on the plateau. It alone saw those two black shadows on the graveled path near two tombs, in that sweet April night."[20] Again the situation is defined by commonplace events and details that suddenly reveal sides and dimensions unlooked for: a funeral in a wedding. And again there is no resolution but a recognition and acquiescence, both rich with a sense of the ambiguous density of the condition set forth.

Pirandello's mastery of the short story form was quick and sure. In his first decade of writing he perfected a repertory of narrative styles and techniques, each in its way adaptable to humoristic purposes, though each differing somewhat in the kinds of values stressed. In any fiction, of course, the perception of the experience rendered depends utterly on the point of view from which it is seen. For Pirandello, acutely sensitive to the relativity of all perception, point of view was accordingly a technical issue of the first importance and probably the one most pertinent to his expression of *umorismo*.

An important part of Pirandello's response to the world of words was, as we have seen, to fix on human things, the always distinctive meetings of an individual with the world; he looked for authenticity in the thingness of these experiences. Yet he vigorously denied that this thingness was exclusively subjective. In the exchange with Ugo Ojetti in "Sincerity and Art," an exchange concerning what can be known and written about honestly, he made his position quite clear. Arguing that art can deal only with subjective, hence individual, experience, Ojetti had said: "The world is my representation; the world is an ideality. The world is my representation, and for man thinking the world (that is, everything external to the 'I') exists only according to the idea one has of it. I don't see what is, but what I see is."[21] Pirandello objected by arguing that external to the "I" many things (in our usual sense of that term) exist, and the individual has some consciousness of them. Although these things can be brought to consciousness (realized) only partially, as they are made "human things," the individual must commit himself to making conscious as much of them as possible. That is, the individual must bring things to consciousness while acquiescing in their will (*volontà*) and while accepting them with as much of their contiguous mystery as possible. By assuming this responsibility he could argue that the world is largely what each human being makes of it, but that it is possible to fashion ideas of it, realizations of it, of great authority.[22]

Pirandello's conclusion for the writer, therefore, is not surprising: one must give to the things perceived their aspect and color, their own life and not one's own manner, but one must also speak in one's own person and in one's own way. To put this slightly differently: in constructing a story as perceived by a narrator, the writer creates a surface that is defined by the narrator's voice and then grounds the story in it. In so doing the writer acknowledges that the account being rendered is relative to the perception of the narrator and declares that the fiction is not only this story but this relative account of it. The events of the narrative, the characters in the narrative, everything making up the narrative take up a place on the plane of the speaker's experience of them, speaking for themselves as far as possible. That plane becomes the story.

Thus Pirandello looked for the human things of his fiction less in the external world than in someone's experience of that world, less in what we usually call facts than in his or his characters' perception of facts. He discovered early that the narrator's voice was the best of all vehicles for humoristic vision. A voice like that in "Sunlight and Shadow," comic, tender, melancholy, bitter, could sustain an extraordinary gamut of qualities while mixing tones ranging from defeated to ecstatic.

A masterpiece in this vein is the early novel *A Place in Line* (*Il Turno*, 1902), in which the narrator is perfectly attuned to the grotesque comedy of Pepè Aletto's wait for the hand of Stellina through two marriages. In the first she marries Don Diego, a well-to-do old man who marries for the fifth time because he loves the company of the young, but who stubbornly refuses to die; in the second she marries Pepè's former brother-in-law, the tyrant lawyer Cirò Coppa. Romantic expectations are everywhere undercut. Although Pepè is young and handsome, a golden lad to Stellina's golden lass, he is weak and a bit dull. To begin with, he has to be aroused to think himself in love with Stellina, as she does with him; then having endured humiliation after humiliation he emerges with Stellina at the end, after Coppa has literally consumed himself in his own jealous rage—able to go on, but far more mutilated than wise. Yet the story of Pepè and Stellina is at all points something more than the structure of episodes leading to their far from romantic union at the end: it is that system of events and details as they are mediated by the sensibility of the narrator, as they are colored, shaped, and adjusted to a vision emphatically humoristic. Consider the account of the scene in which Pepe, Stellina, and Marcantonio Ravì, Stellina's father, watch at the sickbed of the apparently dying Don Diego, Stellina's husband of convenience:

And for the whole course of the sickness, they stinted on no attention to Don Diego, clinging to a thread of life as if to a twig at the edge of a precipice. They vied, intent and solicitous, to sit with him. As if their consciences truly found relief and joy in lavishing these attentions, each tried to free the others and take upon himself the whole burden. Thus among themselves they were all ceremony and prayers, urging each other to eat something and get a little sleep.

Pepè spared himself least of all. But the force with which he thus bravely resisted sleep and food did not proceed from his will: he could really neither sleep nor take food because his thoughts and feelings were so much on his own imminent happiness. He was there already: he was at the eve of his great fortune, sustained by the looks and words of Stellina in the full certainty, after these days of close intimacy, that she loved him and that she too felt herself on the threshold of a new, happy life.

Don Marcantonio, however, kept them under surveillance. "They're taking fire," he said to himself, twisting his mouth. Then one evening, as he passed along the corridor, he was surprised by the sound of a kiss in the darkened sitting room and he began to cough.[23]

An ambiguous surface fretted by details suggesting a mysterious serio-comic world and focused by a mentality conscious of its depths and texture: these are the main structural components in this passage and in the stories with humoristic narrators. Once Pirandello had mastered this structural conception, it was inevitable that he should take a further step by having a humorist narrator tell a story about himself; that he should discover, in other words, the expressiveness for humoristic purposes of the first-person narrator. In Pirandello's many stories with a first-person narrator the narrative voice with its peculiar emotional trajectory becomes the essential material of the story. Instead of calling attention to and registering understanding of the contradictions in the narrative, in Marastella's first night, for example, it embodies the human things and the causes of things; it is not only spokesman but also vehicle for the humoristic vision.

One of the earliest stories, perhaps the earliest, to use this point of view was "Who Was It?" ("Chi Fu?" 1896), a distressing tale of a young man's discovery that the young woman he loves has turned prostitute. Certain features of the narrative anticipate *The Late Mattia Pascal* (*Il Fu Mattia Pascal,* 1904), chiefly Jacopo Sturzi, the old man thought to be dead who has taken refuge in Rome from his wife and their daughter, the Tuda whom the narrator had lost when she had broken their engagement six months before. But the central figure is Luzzi, the young man who tells of his desolation, his descent to drink and vice, and his ghostly meeting on a stormy night with Sturzi, his former father-in-law-to-be. By using Luzzi as a first-person narrator Pirandello focuses in a single unity the numerous planes of reality intersecting within him on the crucial night. His suffering and disorientation, his self-disgust, his astonishment at meeting and talking with one he had thought to be dead, his mounting confusion and loss of control as he drinks and listens to Sturzi in the murky *osteria* and then follows him through the black storm: all these qualities amid the rising uncertainty and terror, culminating in the murder of Sturzi's wife, Tuda's mother and bawd. These fearful interior events dominate the story's foreground, chancy, even arbitrary, we are aware, but unquestionably the things of Luzzi's experience. Their coherence, here without the benefit of commentary even from Luzzi, constitutes the story's expressive core, the main source of the authority for its nightmarish vision.

In the abundant body of fiction produced by Pirandello his first-person narrators comprehend a vast range of voices and points of view. They are cranky, bemused, outraged, defeated, submissive, exalted: each embodies a specific experience of his world, and each has sufficient volatility to convey a sense of the world on the wing, as it is perceived through the lens of his individuality. By 1904, the year of *The Late Mattia Pascal,* Pirandello apparently felt that most effective for the expression of *umorismo* was a narrator at once sensitive, intelligent, witty, and high-spirited and at the same time rooted in a situation rich in grotesquely painful and funny possibilities, that is, angled to stress humoristic values.

Mattia Pascal is one of Pirandello's most memorable humorist-protagonists. The cross-eyed son of a widow rapidly losing her money to the manager of her estate, he is clever, rebellious to the point of domestic anarchism, affectionate and kind to those he loves, deeply skeptical, unprepared to take up a conventional work in the world, witty, and ironic. You can hear some of these qualities in the exasperated recognition of the first lines of the book:

> One of the few things, indeed perhaps the only thing that I knew for sure was this: that my name was Mattia Pascal. And I took advantage of that. Every time some one of my friends or acquaintances would demonstrate that he'd lost his senses to the point of asking me for advice or suggestions, I'd shrug my shoulders, narrow my eyes, and respond:
> —My name is Mattia Pascal.
> —Thanks, old man. I know that.
> —And that seems to you negligible?[24]

Or consider the amused annoyance with which he settles into his job as librarian after the comedy of errors that has led to his marrying Romilda:

> In a short time I became another from the one I had been. With Romitelli [the old librarian] dead, I was alone, devoured by boredom, in this out-of-the-way church, amid all those books, tremendously alone and yet without any desire for company. I could have spent very few hours there each day, but I was ashamed to be seen on the streets, impoverished as I was. I fled from the house as from a prison; better to be here, I told myself over and over again. But what to do? Hunt rats, yes; but is that enough?
> The first time I caught myself with a book in my hand, taken from one of the shelves without thinking, I felt a tremor of horror. Had I become like Romitelli and begun to feel the need to read, I as librarian for all those who didn't come to the library? I knocked the

book to the floor. But then I took it up again, and—you guessed it—I began to read, even I, with one eye only because the other one didn't want to take any part in it.[25]

As narrator, Mattia not only reflects a highly probable perception of bizarre contradictions, he is also the glass through which we see the events of the novel and all the other characters. His sainted mother; his good-looking brother; his explosive Aunt Scolastica; his timid and clumsy friend Pomino; Romilda, whom he woos for Pomino, saves from a worse fate, and then marries himself because he gets her pregnant; the Widow Pescatore, his termagant mother-in-law; not to mention all the others in Nice, Milan, and especially Rome: all these come to us as Mattia sees them, with that one eye that is a law unto itself. The novel is Mattia's experience of these figures and of the extraordinary series of events that leads him first to run away to Nice, then, after he has won a modest fortune in Monte Carlo and learned that he is thought to have drowned himself, to run away again and start a second life as Adriano Meis. His travels; his attempt to settle in Rome and his involvement there with Adriana Paleari, whom he comes to love and wishes to marry; his connections with her father, with her tyrannical brother-in-law, with Silvia Caporale, the middle-aged pianist-spiritualist medium, and with all the others; his second death in Adriano Meis' feigned suicide; and his return to Romilda, who, he finds, has remarried and borne a child to his old friend Pomino: these are the events, but always, unmistakably, Mattia's events.

Mattia Pascal is the best known of several Pirandellian protagonists who have the doubtful privilege of seeing themselves dead. At first he is dizzied by his new freedom: he luxuriates in the giddy delight of seeming to master his fate. But even in the first flush of exhilaration Fortune warns, as the good humorist knows something or someone must, that this sovereign detachment too will soon seem "curious," as curious as the young scholar in the railway carriage consuming himself with zeal to prove that Christ was the ugliest of men. And of course Mattia's subsequent experiences are more than simply curious: they trace a network of unexpected joys and blows, enticements and threats, all building steadily toward his recognition that it is not given to him, or anyone, to live a second life. His flight from the wreckage he leaves in the Paleari household and his return to his hometown and its anguish darken the picture toward the end of the book. But the world as we see it at the last is still the world as Mattia sees it: dark, painful, bitter, outrageous, yet also funny and beautiful and worthy of love. It is the world of Pomino's house on that ghostly night of

Mattia's return. He comes thundering in shouting that he is alive and berating Romilda, Pomino, and the Widow Pescatore for having wanted him dead; they quarrel about the best way to live with this irregularity; Romilda faints; the Widow Pescatore and Mattia rage; Pomino protests, aghast. Meanwhile, Mattia has picked up the crying infant, Pomino and Romilda's new baby, and tries to get her to fall asleep. Out of this a modus vivendi is wrenched.

Mattia Pascal, twice dead hence thrice born, is the principal medium for this humoristic vision. He is not the exclusive medium, as Moscarda would be later in *One, None, and a Hundred Thousand* (*Uno, Nessuno e Centomila*, 1925), because characters like Tito Lenzi and especially Anselmo Paleari with his lantern-philosophy (*lanterninosofia*) and his brilliant image of modern self-consciousness in the figure of the marionette Orestes provide a good deal of the book's commentary on the world. But Mattia assents to this commentary and his voice assimilates it as he tells his strange and wonderful story.

The Late Mattia Pascal is the closest of Pirandello's longer works to the central content of *Umorismo*. Piero Cudini has argued on the evidence of common elements that the novel was actually a source for the essay;[26] certainly Pirandello's dedication of the novel to Alberto Cantoni and of *Umorismo* to Mattia Pascal indicates that he abundantly appreciated the affinity. But even without this linkage the sense common to both is clear: experience is on the one hand atomistic, composed of elements continuously in flux, often in conflict, always fugitive; but on the other an end in itself because extraordinarily rich to those conscious of and honest about its complexity. In his review of Luigi Baccolo's book in 1938 Croce described Pirandello as a child angry and astonished at the difficulty of learning Latin.[27] Pirandello would agree that he was angry and astonished, and certainly that like Latin, life was difficult. He would object however that, like Latin, life can be learned. At best it can be studied, contemplated, held in the mind in as much of its fullness as possible and dominated there for a brief moment by the synthetic power he calls *umorismo*. Of course Croce was right: Pirandello never learned to master his anguish and to achieve the serenity that Croce thought the reward of art; what Croce never understood was that Pirandello deeply believed that serenity could not be achieved and that we must live with our anguish.

3

oooooooooooooooooooooo

A MEDITATION ON
CONSCIOUSNESS AND
SELF-CONSCIOUSNESS

A WORLD MIRED in the inauthenticity of words, art degraded by the
succubi of rhetoric, experience itself corrupted by false ideas of what it
is: these were the subjects that drew Pirandello's attention to consciousness,
the matrix within which experience, art, and the world were composed
and discomposed. How does consciousness work? What are its materials?
What faculties shape these materials? These are the questions he addressed
and to which throughout his life he provided a uniform configuration of
answers. Fashioning works of art and fashioning one's experience are
fundamentally the same; both art and experience build most securely on a
foundation of things. But permanence and fixity should not be looked for:
the world is in continuous flux, interior no less than exterior life. The data
of things, assisted by various faculties of mind, move toward form, drift
and coalesce, drift in suspension; and the consciousness that lights them
also watches them. To be alive and human is to be conscious of this
activity.

In all his discussions of words and things, of artistic creation, of *sincerità*
and *umorismo,* Pirandello was continuously talking about consciousness.
He tried to set its limits honestly, to mark it off from all those regions in
the individual that are inaccessible or in waking life obscured; he described
the processes that occur within it—the growth from germ, the movement
toward form, the persistent irresolution; he prescribed its legitimate uses in
the service of art and experience. Yet of all its functions and powers so far
discussed perhaps none is more important than its reflexive capacity, or
self-consciousness. This comprehends all the others, the constituent "human
things" as well as the fictions that organize them; it watches even as

umorismo discomposes and atomizes. It provides the mirror for consciousness, that which makes it aware of itself.

The most celebrated passage dealing with this dimension of consciousness occurs at the beginning of chapter 12 of *The Late Mattia Pascal.* Anselmo Paleari announces to Mattia that the tragedy of Orestes is to be performed by marionettes.

> Consider for a moment this curious idea. Suppose that at the climactic moment, just as the marionette playing Orestes is about to avenge the death of his father on Aegisthus and his mother, the paper sky of the little theater develops a tear. What would happen? What do you think?
>
> —I wouldn't know, I responded, shrugging my shoulders.
>
> —But it's very simple, Signor Meis! Orestes would be terrifically disconcerted by that hole in the sky.
>
> —And why?
>
> —Let me go on. Orestes would still feel the drive to revenge, would still be wildly passionate about carrying it out, but his eyes, at that instant, would go there, to that tear, through which, now, all sorts of cosmic wrongs would invade the scene, and he would feel his arms drop. Orestes, that is to say, would become Hamlet. The whole difference, Signor Meis, between ancient and modern tragedy consists in this, believe me: in a hole in the paper sky.[1]

The image catches beautifully the meaning of watching oneself live (*vedersi vivere*). Orestes disconcerted, full of his revenge but distracted by a detail that reminds him that he is only a marionette in a flimsy little theater, a creature invented by himself and others and set on a trolley-line of circumstance that leads to this moment: he is Orestes become Hamlet because he understands himself to be an actor on a stage where he knows any of a million other dramas could be playing.

Pirandello was acutely aware of this dimension of consciousness throughout his life and career, beginning at least with his letter to Antonietta of 5 January 1894, where he traced the relations between his great self and his little self.[2] The sad privilege of watching oneself live opens the way to many values presumably inaccessible to animals, but it is also fundamental to varieties of anguish known only to human beings. It highlights the malaise of being unhappy with the body one is trapped in. It points to guilts almost without form or cause, for which there are no courts, yet which gnaw. Most important, it is the only begetter of our sense of superfluity and the peculiar suffering that proceeds from it. For reasons unknown Pirandello's work during the war was full of a fascination with this superfluity. "The Train Whistle Has Sounded" ("Il Treno Ha Fischiato," 1914) provides a relatively simple case in Signor Belluca, who, living a life of drudgery to support three blind women, two daughters, and their seven children, hears in the train whistle a world lost to him. The narrator of "The Wheelbarrow" ("La Carriola," 1916) averts the temporary madness that overtakes Belluca by the grotesque exercise of holding his dog by her hind legs and walking her around his study like a wheelbarrow. He is a man completely estranged from the life he is living, who watches the self that is and is not himself and then finds a release for his anguish by momentarily destroying the dignified form in which he appears to live and at the same time avenging himself on the dog who in its simplicity knows how to live. In these figures self-consciousness inevitably complicates, making one aware both of what one could do and does not and could be and is not. This complication is the superfluity (*superfluo*) that Simone Pau examines at length in Pirandello's *The Notebooks of Serafino Gubbio, Cameraman* (*Quaderni di Serafino Gubbio Operatore,* 1915). It embraces both our awareness of possibilities unrealized and our sense of oppression under the excess baggage that these possibilities and their attendant fictions entail.[3] The world is better suited to animals than humans, Pau concludes, because they confront it simply and directly; humans, never.

In the years following the war, as Pirandello's artistic efforts centered increasingly in the theater, his attention focused more and more narrowly on self-consciousness, watching oneself live. "I have had the audacity," he said in an interview in 1925, "of placing a mirror at the centre of the stage. It is the mirror of intelligence. Man, while alive, lives, but does not see himself. Sentiment by itself is blind; I have therefore so managed that this blind man at a certain point should open his eyes and should see himself in that mirror and should stand as if frozen by the unthought-of image of his own life."[4] The drama of our meeting ourselves, seeing ourselves as fugitive fabrications or ghostly mirror images, this is the drama of consciousness and self-consciousness. The difficulty that this confrontation produces, Pirandello is quoted as saying by Adriano Tilgher, "that difficulty is my theater."[5] Of course in 1925 it was to be expected that he would place this interest at the heart of his theater. He was then writing largely for the theater, and, as we shall see, his detailed interest in self-consciousness was nourished and focused by his explorations of practical as well as theoretical theatricality. But a lively concern with self-consciousness is evident everywhere in his career, in the fiction as well as the plays, and in the plays that preceded those now best known for it. It is worth recalling that among the eight or so plays written before 1900, now lost, there were titles like *Rehearsing the Play* (*Provando la Commedia,* c. 1886) and *Facts That Are Now Words* (*Fatti che or Son Parole,* 1887).[6] One of the richest and most powerful studies of the drama of consciousness, in fact, is the long story "The Difficulty of Living Like This" ("Pena di Vivere Così"), a work he published in 1920 but was still revising at his death.

The story is an extraordinary evocation of Signora Lèuca's passage from a controlled self-consciousness in a life held within severe limitations to the blistering anguish of self-consciousness in a life thrown open to need. From the beginning her consciousness is reflected in her house: "A silence of mirrors, an odor of waxed tiles, the freshness of muslin at the windows: Signora Lèuca's house had been like that for eleven years. By now the rooms had been possessed by a strange deafness."[7] Since her husband had left her for another woman eleven years before, she had worked hard at her serenity: she had kept her surroundings immaculate; she had restricted herself to a narrow circle of women friends; to overcome her horror of the flesh, of all in life that soils, she had diligently engaged in acts of charity. But most of all she had cultivated a sovereign detachment, a capacity to stand off, observe, and under- stand the world around her. As the story opens and the parish priest and the lawyer try to persuade her to allow her husband to visit her, she is aware, as she has been for some time, that her house is not sweet, as the priest says, but merely silent, that her friends are innocents, good but limited women to whom she feels superior, that her acts of charity have always been more for herself than for others, and that the summit of detachment that she has reached is cold and austere. She has achieved the life of the mind watching, and she has left below the life of noise, movement, and confusion. She has no illusions about her husband: he had left her not because she had rejected him—she had not—but because he had wanted more than she could give; she has a sympathy for that, a "charity, as for all those unfortunates who, like him, feel life like a hunger that soils and is never satisfied."[8] But she is also utterly honest about herself, about the profound emptiness and vanity that over- takes her as she knits sweaters for the poor, about the hollowness of the admiration accorded her. She wants compassion for him and his bestiality, but also for herself as one who has denied herself in trying to be free from bestiality.

Enough, at last, of this insipid admiration! She is not made of marble; she has paid for this liberation.

And for the first time she felt bored—boredom, tedium, and aversion at all the order and neatness of her house.

. . . Hypocrisies![9]

Despite the story's length the other characters are distinctly subordinate to Signora Lèuca. Even Marco Lèuca, brutish, passionate, in part wracked by guilt, in part hypocritical: we see him in brilliant flashes in the important first interviews with Signora Lèuca, in the first when he goes down on his knees in shame, in the second when he confides to her the details of his turpitude and then silently accepts a hundred lire, and again when with his three daughters he moves into the house. But we have only glimpses of his earlier life with the other woman and only a report of his later elopement to Ecuador with Signorina Trecke's niece. The other characters are still more fragmentary: the three little girls, the neighbor women, the lawyer, and the parish priest. Structurally, virtually everything in the story contributes to the definition of Signora Lèuca's journey of spirit. Taking in the children and her husband on the death of the other woman serves to return her to a more vulgar and deeper life than she could know from the mountain top of detachment. She refurnishes her house, neglects herself after years of careful self-preservation, spends money and time so lavishly on the children that she has nothing left for her other charities. Yet she does all this still terrified that Marco will try to renew a physical rapport with her and at another level convinced that ultimately he will leave her again. At last he does leave her, abandoning the three girls, to go off with yet another woman. The lawyer and parish priest tell Signora Lèuca that she is well rid of him and has the best of it in having the children. But she knows that even that is not true. With Marco gone she takes no joy in raising children not her own. She will raise them, more acutely aware than ever that she will always live feeling that she has not lived; detached, alone, waiting. Her self-consciousness frees and enslaves: it lets her see and even understand her anguish; it even lets her see that she shares it with all humanity. But the price of this perspective is austerity of experience. The view from the heights opens the mind, but the chilling caution appropriate to heights tightens the heart.

Self-consciousness is the mirror of consciousness, that power within it that enables it to watch itself as structures are made and unmade, as decisions are taken, or not taken, as the fragments of experience coalesce briefly in coherent unities or do not. Consciousness frames all this activity. Although to be human is to live in one's consciousness more than in the exterior world, to do so is far from an unmitigated privilege. Serafino

Gubbio's philosophical friend, Simone Pau, sets the range most succinctly by contrasting the world of human creatures with the simple world of animals. At the one extreme is the abandoned horse in "The Good Luck of Being a Horse" ("Fortuna d'Esser Cavallo," 1935): he wanders through the town looking for something to eat, his good luck being that he does not think or worry. At the other is the voracious bookworm of "A World of Paper" ("Mondo di Carta," 1909), a man who lives entirely in the world of his reading. When he goes blind, he hires readers, but cannot bear their voices and discharges the last when she tells him that the book she is reading about the cathedral at Trondheim is in error; she knows because she has been there. To a large extent, Pirandello's studies of characters sickened, incapacitated, and tormented by consciousness are the predictable amplifications of his early concern with stressful tedium (*tedio angoscioso*) and interior confusion (*dissidio interno*). In stories like "Let's Dispose of This Worry" ("Leviamoci Questo Pensiero," 1910), in which Bernardo Sopo is destroyed because his ability to anticipate problems sets in motion pressures he cannot bear, consciousness is shifting, unreliable, deceptive, and painful. Helped to distance by study and discipline in a scholarly figure like the old Cosmo Laurentano of *The Old and the Young* (*I Vecchi e i Giovani,* 1913), it is often the basis for the blackest pessimism.

The processes of constructing a consciousness and of sustaining a life by means of it are of sufficient importance to justify our lingering briefly on images of other Pirandellian characters in moments of self-contemplation. No one of these characters exemplifies a model in all details, of course, since each is idiosyncratic; but taken together they clarify the conscious life still further. The example provided by the young Lando Laurentano in *The Old and the Young* as he ruminates on the condition of Italy and compares the noisy agitation of the sparrows in his garden with the life fixed in the books in his library comprehends the entire phenomenon:

> Even he, inevitably, with the concepts and opinions that he sought to form of men and things, with the fictions that he created, with the affections and desires that he felt, even he fixed this continuous flux of life in himself and all around him in determinate forms. Even he, in this body, was already a determined form, a moving form that could follow up to a certain point this flux of life until, already growing more rigid little by little, the movement that slowed down gradually would stop altogether! Indeed, on certain days he felt a strange antipathy toward his own body. . . . In the mirror [his features] seemed to belong to a stranger. Within his body, meanwhile, in what

he called the spirit, the flux continued indistinct, flowing under the banks and limits that he imposed in composing a consciousness for himself, in constructing a personality. But all these artificial forms were liable to crumble if assaulted by the flux in a moment of storm; and even that part of the flux that did not run unseen under the banks and beyond the limits, but that he made clear to himself and that he had with care channeled into his feelings, into the duties that he had imposed on himself, into the habits that he allowed himself, even these could in a time of flood uproot and overturn everything.

There, he gasped in one of these moments of floodtide! For these reasons he had immersed himself completely in the study of new social questions, in the criticism of those who, armed with powerful arguments, aimed at demolishing at its foundations a structure of things convenient for a few, unfair to the majority of men, and to awaken at the same time in this majority a will and desire that would give impetus to undermining, destroying, and scattering all the forms imposed in the course of centuries, centuries in which life had been heavily rigidified. Would this will and desire emerge in a majority strong enough to bring on a collapse quickly? The requisite consciousness and education were still lacking. To make them conscious, to educate them: here was an ideal! But when to actuate it? Even this was slow work, long and requiring patience.[10]

In this passage Lando reviews the whole process of composing a consciousness and a personality by arbitrarily setting limits on the inner and outer flux and imposing forms on what has been selected for the material of a life. He creates *his* forms for "men and things" according to *his* "concepts and opinions"; he even channels some part of the flux into his duties and feelings and habits, always aware that a "moment of storm" could sweep the whole structure away. The passage is quite remarkable for its emphasis on Lando's deliberation in all this. What he has constructed as his consciousness and personality explains why he has "immersed himself completely in the study of new social questions" and the "criticism of those who . . . aim at demolishing" the status quo. He even ponders the problem of the specific mission that his consciousness and personality predicate for him: providing the education to raise, as we would say, the consciousness of the people. He sees that this is a long, slow, and difficult task.

Other characters stress other parts of the process and see it in different terms. Leone Gala in *The Game of Parts* (*Il Giuoco delle Parti,* often translated *The Rules of the Game,* 1918) is a totally committed Pirandellian humorist and one of the most explicit of Pirandello's commentators. He has understood the game (*ho capito il giuoco*), he explains to Guido, his wife's lover, in the sense that he has seen through the fabric of arbitrary structures that life is; this knowledge has enabled him to empty himself of life's illusions, to want nothing, and to take his pleasure from watching others from a distance. Near the play's beginning he counsels Guido to do the same, to empty himself of life so that, disengaged, he too will want nothing and can thus withstand the attempts of others to fix or define him. The same intellect that struggles with Guido's muddled interior life and slyly fixes it in precise forms, he explains, is marvelously suited to play the game of watching others live. But to insure that once emptied he will not float away, he must also supply himself with ballast, the support (*pernio*) of a concept for living. "To restabilize equilibrium, so that you can always stay on your feet, like those comic toys that you can push as you wish and that always remain upright because of their lead balance. Believe me, we are no different. But it's necessary to know how to manage this emptiness and this fullness; otherwise you find yourself on the ground and in outlandish attitudes." His support, he goes on to explain, is cooking. It protects him, not so much from chance, or the tyranny of nature, or the eyes of others, as from himself and what chance can do to his delicate equilibrium. "You must protect yourself from yourself, from the feeling that chance suddenly provokes in you and with which it attacks you! You must parry it immediately, drain it off; you must extract your concept from it, and then you can even play with it." He then compares such threats to the unexpected arrival of a fresh egg. "If you're ready, you'll take it, you'll perforate it, and you'll suck it." And the empty shell is your concept, which you can play with further, or smash.[11] The whole passage is a justly famous example of the cerebral game-playing that is doubtless a dimension of creating and sustaining a consciousness. The chief value of this kind of play is a sovereign clarity.

The Game of Parts, written in the year following Pirandello's success with *Right You Are* (*If You Think So*) (*Così è* [*se vi Pare*], 1917) provides his most explicit analysis in drama to that point of the ways of consciousness. The movement of act 1 is gamelike as it sets the traditional triangle of husband, wife, and lover in a rationale with the symmetry and precision of a geometrical flower. Silia Gala has separated from Leone out of exasperation at his superiority. Because he has understood the game, he has urged her to embrace his freedom, to empty herself of life and live with detachment. But Silia is "full of unhappiness because she is full of life";[12] she cannot free herself of the messiness of living, and she sees Leone as her incubus because his example reproaches her for failing to do so. He accedes to her every request; he obeys her every command; he stands by and watches as she consumes herself with the fever of living. And she hates him for it. At the end of the act she stumbles into what looks like a suitable vengeance when she obliges him by the game of their society to challenge a man who has inadvertently insulted her. Guido Venanzi, by contrast, is more conventional: he is innocent of Leone's reasons for, among other things, great tolerance, and he is merely baffled by Silia's fury. Even when Leone explains his detachment in act 1 and urges Guido to adopt it, Guido seems not to understand a great deal, though he clearly dismisses the proposal because it offers too little (*Ah, troppo poco, scusa*). Then later, after failing to prevent the duel, he unexpectedly carries out his role as Leone's second with what looks very like his self-interest in mind.

But in acts 2 and 3, as Silia softens in the face of the implications of her rashness and Guido snugs himself into his conventionality, Leone reveals that he is not the model of detachment he had claimed. At the end he is capable of sending Guido to his death as his obligatory surrogate in the duel, and he does so not with disinterested mastery, but out of a desire to punish both Guido and Silia. In this way he profits from the social game, which he claims he watches with detached amusement while playing *his* game, by using it to serve passions earlier denied. By act 3, indeed, the easy, clocklike movement of the early acts tightens and strains as, ironically, the same rationality that had created the triangle and structured Leone's consciousness brings on the disastrous denouement.

Leone's image of the ballasted doll is one representation of the precarious equilibrium of a consciousness holding many elements in suspension. Sara's image of the feather in *Diana and Tuda* (1926) is another: "To maintain the spirit continuously in a state of fusion: to keep it from congealing, rigidifying," it is necessary that life be like a feather, rigid yet responsive to every breath of air.[13] Donata Genzi's metaphor of the theater in *To Find Oneself* (*Trovarsi,* 1932) is still another. All these figures illuminate the process explicitly addressed in "The Secret Notebook" of maintaining harmony "by the perpetual concourse of the elements that constitute the living being." In another passage borrowed from Séailles Pirandello goes on: "The spirit doesn't know where it comes from, how and what it is in its totality; but because it is alive, for this fact alone, it tends without pause to organize and concentrate in the unity of its current consciousness as much as possible of the images that wander about within it."[14]

For all its difficulties consciousness as Pirandello understood it is also an opportunity, perhaps the best of opportunities in the modern world. It is always a bit problematical to know how far to believe him as he made positive, constructive statements: so much of his energy went into destroying the world of words and laying a new foundation, for the individual at least, in things and *sincerità* that his more distant goal often disappears. But Pirandello's thought is completed only by his ideas concerning how the consciousness, once freed and freshened to function honestly, can enable the individual to shape his experience and in the process to create himself. On occasion he could be annoyed that he was called a pessimist! "I seem a devil destroyer who pulls the ground from beneath people's feet. But don't I, on the contrary, advise where they should put their feet when I pull the ground from beneath them? It's we, I say, who create reality, and it's indispensable that it works like this."[15] "My art is devoid of that pessimism that generates a distrust in life. Nor am I a negator since in the activity of spirit that torments me and animates my works there is a steady, spasmodic will to create life."[16] He attacked, he fulminated, he exposed, but only, he insisted, to destroy illusions, false gods, empty languages, derivative lives; and he did all this to clear the way for creation. Recent critics who find in his vision a subjectivism of despair ignore completely the positive aspect of his thought;[17] and when they offer Marxism as the way out of this condition, they are voicing their own hopes far more than Pirandello's beliefs.

Pirandello was perhaps at his most positive in his advice to his children. To Stefano in 1916, then a prisoner of war in Austria, he wrote encouraging him to study so that he might "master his world" and provide a "stronger and wider basis for his reality."[18] The aim to beguile the darkness with a self-generated universe is especially strong here. Actually, Pirandello never underestimated the powers of darkness, but acknowledging their potency and omnipresence did not prevent him from urging Stefano to give himself a form and to adapt himself to it without sacrificing those possibilities not encompassed by it. At bottom this advice stresses a highly deliberate selection among one's personal possibilities of what in a letter to his daughter he described as a sense of oneself so true that all subsequent elaborations have consistency.[19] The end of this self-creation remains theoretical, of course, an ideal for experience; but perhaps we get a glimpse of one form of it in the wealth of value that Pirandello in a self-congratulatory moment claimed for himself. In a letter to Marta Abba in 1930 he explained that instead of glory he had had "the richness of [my] spirit, the power of [my] mind, and the enormous faculty for feeling of [my] heart."[20] The claim is uncharacteristically complacent, but it puts the emphasis where Pirandello always intended it to be: on the interior life, its dimensions, its density, and its quality.

Yet uncharacteristic though the figure of Pirandello as preceptor seems, it enables us to understand a number of his unexpected enthusiasms. Despite his many years as a reluctant teacher of young women at Rome's Magistero, he persisted in at least a theoretical passion for youth because it was at the beginning of everything, unformed. The writer-protagonist of the late play *When One Is Somebody* (*Quando Si È Qualcuno,* 1932), in many respects a portrait of Pirandello himself, is said by Natascia, a young woman devoted to him, to be "sick with youth," by which she means that he is intoxicated with fresh possibilities and determined to resist being fixed by others in the figure of a national monument. Before the action of the play begins this rebellion has taken the form of his writing in a new manner and publishing the new work under the name of Délago (confused with Dédalo, or Daedalus). This new persona becomes the hero of the young and, paradoxically, the archrival in the public's mind of his own creator, who is never given a name. In fact, the action is a good deal more complex than that, involving as well the protagonist's unconsummated passion for Natascia's fiery sister, Verroccia, also young (that relationship is clearly suggestive of Pirandello's friendship with Marta Abba), and an equally intricate and ambiguous set of family relations. But the protagonist's movement toward fixity is the main issue, culminating at the end of the play when his final speech is magically incised in stone and he himself becomes the statue venerated by all. Theatrically, the satiric, often comically exuberant quality of that movement is deepened by the great man's ambivalence: he wants both to be young and fluid and to be somebody and fixed. Fixity, despite all his resistance to it, is an end quite normally sought: life wants it; the mind wants it. In the play the protagonist is at last constrained to it, but not until he has made a passionate apologia for youth.

Youth, moreover, is what initially attracted Pirandello to America, where new forms of life were being born: "Life, pressed by natural and social necessities, searches and finds new forms there. To see them born is an incomparable joy for the spirit." "This putrefying Europe," on the other hand, repulsed him. "[There] the dead persist in making life, crushing the life of the living with the weight of history, tradition, and custom. The solidity of the old forms obstructs, impedes, arrests all vital movement."[21] "England is by far the worst. . . . I met only one completely young man there—Bernard Shaw."[22]

In much the same way Pirandello's long and, in his biographer's phrase, "inexplicable adherence"[23] to fascism can be best explained in terms of his application to culture and society of his ideas about creation and self-creation. It bears recalling that he was the son of Risorgimento revolutionaries committed to ideals of independence, personal freedom, and national as well as individual destiny. As a student he associated himself with both radicals and socialists; then by the turn of the century he was capable of siding with both Giovanni Giolitti's moderate government and its leftist critics, while privately calling himself an anarchist.[24] But more constant than any of these associations was his insistence throughout his life that he was, in fact, apolitical, uninterested in and innocent about politics, in his word, politically "chaste."[25] Except for the period from 1923 to 1926, when he was most active as a fascist, this last claim seems to have been most accurate.

Yet in the years immediately after the war he was unmistakably drawn to fascism. It seemed splendidly destructive of the bourgeois structures that had led Europe through the war; it seemed to some—especially in the early coalition between the moderate fascists and the liberal nationalists— to recapture the betrayed ideals of the Risorgimento. But clearly most important for Pirandello was that it offered a hope for the future congenial to his thought. From the first Pirandello saw in Mussolini a man committed to the politics of things rather than words, facts rather than theory. Because Mussolini could say: "The world is as we wish it to be; it is our creation,"[26] Pirandello could see in him the tyrant-creator the world needed. In a famous interview article in *L'Idea Nazionale* (October 1923), on the first anniversary of the march on Rome, he said to Orio Vergani:

> Mussolini must be applauded by one who has always felt life's tragedy to be implicit in the fact that to have consistency it needs a form, but once it has the form, it begins to die. . . . Mussolini . . . reveals so clearly that he feels this tragic, double necessity in form and movement, and . . . wills that movement find restraint in an ordered form and that forms never be empty, vain idols, but receive life within themselves pulsing and trembling so that it is recreated from moment to moment. . . .
>
> The revolutionary impulse initiated by him with the march on Rome and now all the features of his government seem to me the proper and necessary actualization in politics of this conception of life.[27]

Because of this felt affinity Pirandello could call Mussolini "the giver of reality"[28] and adapt himself to fascism as a movement grounded in things and a just idea of social change. Of course his enthusiasm for the Duce did not last: it was not many years before he saw him as a "vulgar man" and a factitious leader;[29] but although he withdrew from the foreground of the fascist scene after a brief falling-out in 1927, he never renounced his connection with the party or the cause. The crowning irony of the whole story, of course, was that for all his lifelong hostility to the world of words, he was himself caught up in a web of words in the 1920s, both those of the fascists and his own as he talked and wrote about tearing down old forms and constructing a new life for the nation and the people.

Even in Pirandello's moments of blackest pessimism—when, for example, in a meeting late in his life with Sabatino Lopez he spoke of wishing to blow up the world[30]—he never entirely gave over his belief in the opportunity of consciousness. It was a gift as well as a curse, the one means of wresting an authentic if problematic reality from the flux of interior and exterior being. The self that is created may in the final analysis be only a metaphor for the intimate self that crouches unseen within us, as Serafino Gubbio explains at length,[31] and it must certainly be created day by day. But if composed honestly, it would be one's own, grounded in the things of one's being; and the more effectively and completely one brought the contributory faculties of intellect, imagination, and will into play, the "higher and vaster and stronger" the life created would be.[32]

Whatever the primary subjects of Pirandello's individual works, their deeper currents invariably bear upon self-creation. *Tonight We Improvise* (*Stasera Si Recita a Soggetto,* 1928) treats primarily, as we shall see, theatricality in experience. Yet against the background of that subject, Hinkfuss, the director-commentator, broadens his choruslike explanation of how theater works in experience to clarify how experience itself and the self are fashioned through a process identical to that which produces works of art.[33] *The Pleasure of Honesty* (*Il Piacere dell' Onestà,* 1917) is less explicit and analytic, but implicit in all of Baldovino's efforts to reconstitute himself is an interest in managing the materials of self to the end of self-creation. Late plays like *As You Desire Me* (1930) and *To Find Oneself* (1932) are explicit studies of self-creation.

Seen as a vast totality, indeed, Pirandello's work has most coherence as a long, many-faceted meditation on consciousness. The term "meditation" is Umberto Bosco's, appropriate because Pirandello's work offers no solutions or resolutions, and certainly nothing approaching philosophical system.[34] True to his convictions about reasoned systems, it illuminates facets of the processes by which experience and the self are composed, focusing now on these faculties and their mutual relations and now on those. Pirandello began roughly where the existentialists began—the affinity has frequently been noted[35]—with man adrift in an absurd universe. But where Sartre emphasized the importance of acts to self-definition, Pirandello stressed one's drive to live in fictions invented for oneself and then ranged over the whole gamut of processes by which these fictions are derived and sustained. Where Sartre sought to bring moral coherence to consciousness, Pirandello found a basis for morality only in the deepest truths of individual consciousness. For this reason Pirandello's major effort went to studying consciousness, pondering its endless drama of creating and uncreating. In an interview with Mario Missiroli in 1934 he came very close to saying this explicitly when he accepted Missiroli's description of the created world of his work as "the drama of modern consciousness."[36]

In the course of this long meditation Pirandello treated a wide range of subjects and registered a wide range of responses to them. No one of these responses is permanent: neither the work nor the career ever comes completely to rest. In a considerable number of plays and stories, for example, he fixed on the deceptions with which individuals construct a self to confront the world. Giustino Boggiolo of *Her Husband* (*Suo Marito,* 1911), convinced that his wife's literary fame is largely the result of his management of her work, locks himself in the bustling mediocrity of his petit bourgeois ambition, comic, grotesque, pathetic, decent, without a trace of self-perspective or understanding. Quacqueo, the decayed lamplighter of "Certain Obligations" ("Certi Obblighi," 1912), on the other hand, has long resisted learning the truth about his wife because he suspects that she has long betrayed him; when at last he does break in on her to explode the myth he has lived by, he discovers a far more exalted lover than he had expected and considers the old myth overruled by a new one, namely, to protect his superior from scandal and harm. Chiarchiaro, the accused "hexer" of "The License" ("La Patente," 1911), accepts that persona with tragicomic defiance by demanding a license as *jettatore* so that he can at least earn a living by allowing himself to be bought off. Then there are all those characters who have penetrated the deception and understood the game, the Cosmo Laurentanos and Baldovinos and Henry IVs, and to them Pirandello responded still differently.

Pirandello ranged over these evasions, adaptations, and rebellions, ruthless in his exposure, sensitive and sympathetic to the varieties of anguish and modest heroism at issue, profoundly understanding of the dynamic of each case, frequently lingering lovingly on the marvels of complexity that human beings create and live by. Adriano Tilgher was the first to see the deeper unity in all this variety, that the common crisis in this gallery of figures is that they are all stretched to the breaking point by the very choices and practices, the artifices for living, that have given them definition. Whether engaged in their myths or detached, they struggle with the drama of their individual consciousness, tracing myriad modes of self-creation and a human comedy of inexhaustible resources.

Behind these modalities of self-creation, these exercises in fashioning and refashioning the consciousness, of course, there is always the "mania to live" (*smania di vivere*), and self-creation must never be abstracted from this molten imperative. Yet the mania to live is different, more like a determination to resist annihilation than a constructive purpose. We see it clearly in Marco Lèuca of "The Difficulty of Living Like This," in the inchoate agony of his shame and consuming sexuality; it is fainter but no less important behind the frigid diffidence of Signora Lèuca in that voice that continuously tells her that she has not yet lived. But it is perhaps clearest of all in the numerous mothers in the stories and plays, women all driven not only to live but to give life to their children. For a remarkable number of these figures maternity is an obsession before which everything must give way: health, morality, husbands—even death, in *The Life I Gave You* (*La Vita che Ti Diedi,* 1923). Baldovino speaks of mothers as "irreducible constructions," by which he appears to mean creatures focused by drives that go to the depths of their being. Yet they are as a group merely extreme expressions of a kind of rage to be that animates all Pirandello's characters and that is always part of the drama of consciousness, potent if unformed.

The drama of consciousness to be met in Pirandello's work, then, is a kind of hundred-movement toccata and fugue in which the mind chases itself endlessly, now and then suddenly facing itself, always limited by the conditions of its own and the modern world's system. The signal value of describing the work and career as a long meditation on consciousness rather than as any of the abortive attempts at philosophy that have been proposed is that so described it clarifies a coherence that is not rigorously systematic or philosophical. The term "meditation" emphasizes openness and exploration, a probing of infinite possibilities. Once clarified, this open coherence predicates, it is true, certain relationships, between things and *sincerità, umorismo* and the intellectual faculties, flux and form, and consciousness and self-consciousness; but it insists on no absolutes.

The supreme importance of Pirandello's work and career resides in its pervasive recognition of the turn that twentieth century culture had taken in fixing on consciousness as its chief source of value. With the loss of traditional structures were also lost not only the building blocks of moral system and purpose, but the means by which individuals defined themselves and what they were about in the world. A title, a uniform, a function were no longer enough; society itself had become an arbitrary charade. And whoever looked beyond social role to assess personal, private quality could no longer trust to the Ten Commandments or the gentleman's code as guides to superior or inferior performance. There was no way to know what or who, at bottom, you were because all the conventional means of definition were worse than useless; in fact they complicated the search by generating illusions. Hence the resort to consciousness as the last authentic basis for self-creation.

That consciousness has become the major source of value in modern western society is by now a truism among leaders of thought. The work of Proust, Joyce, Eliot, Beckett, and Sartre, to name some of the literary leaders, is unified by nothing so conspicuously as a profound interest in consciousness as the stage on which the drama of the past and present is played out in confluences of memory, fugitive images, disjointed fragments of experience, often seen as a kind of stream. The metaphor of "stream of consciousness" is problematic chiefly because it projects the constituent elements of any experience on a largely two-dimensional "surface." Self-consciousness consists in floating or riding, so to speak, on this surface, adding to the perceptual flow from memory and imagination to some extent, but for the most part riding free, going where the flow leads. Pirandellian consciousness, by contrast, is multidimensional, more emphatically an "assembly" that is what it is as a result of an act of mind. We create it as an artifice for living, always aware that we are living with a construction both arbitrary and necessary. Yet consciousness in both metaphors stresses the modern tendency to see experience as an organization—always changing—of that surface or assembly. To be fully human is to be aware of that surface or assembly, of its continuities and discontinuities and its patterns or lack of them. A liberal education in our time has become a process of cultivating the consciousness, of filling it with the lore of human history and models of superior human behavior, with all that constitutes being human now. Our shibboleths are "self-realization," "self-fulfillment," "quality life," all terms that predicate the fullest, richest experience of oneself possible. Tourism, education in the humanities, literature: these are some of our major exercises for cultivating consciousness to the ends of self-definition and a perspective on experience that makes qualitative distinctions possible. With the possibility of making qualitative distinctions, self-creation becomes inseparable from creating values, and individual experience takes on coherence.

No one has grasped the implications of the shift from traditional structures to consciousness as a source of value more fully than Pirandello: from first to last it was his basic subject. No one saw more clearly than Pirandello, moreover, that the activities of creating and sustaining a self-image and deriving value were always personal and idiosyncratic, more often wracked by suffering or quivering with poignant comedy than triumphant. More than most, Pirandello was acutely aware of the chief pitfalls in the struggle toward self-creation.

He saw, for example, that because of the great difficulties of overcoming inauthenticity and disciplining oneself to *sincerità* the whole process of self-creation could easily be perverted to the end of sick self-absorption. This was his principal quarrel with the dilettantes. As early as 1893 in "Art and Consciousness Today" he had attacked those who study rather than live life, for whom "art consists in setting out thoughts with clean precision, in opening up the most delicate, most secret folds of feeling, all the causes and nuances of every sensation, in perceiving and savoring the perfume of life, and in going beyond. This spirit is a fugitive thing, a curious bee. This is modern dilettantism . . . , another expression of contemporary emptiness, which is also to be seen in egoism, moral exhaustion, a lack of courage in the face of adversity, pessimism, nausea, disgust with oneself."[37] Such dedication to a closed circuit of interests grows ever narrower because the governing principle is not self-discovery through the discovery of one's world, but continually surpassing the intensity of previous moments. As Pirandello said of the poet Ludwig Hansteken, individuals so dedicated end by "squeezing stones" in their efforts to do the impossible because only in the impossible do they find an excuse for their impotence.[38] The quintessential embodiment of this narcissism was for him, of course, D'Annunzio.

Hence self-creation could be perverted, and still more troublesome was that it could lead by steps perfectly consistent with its normal operation to spiritual paralysis. To work on the consciousness willfully, to shape, to give definition, to create, and to be self-conscious of that effort is to see into an abyss of arbitrariness. To create for the purpose of standing off the void, to devise artifices for living, to take up a part in a puppet show and know what you are doing: these are exercises in vanity, which, like the Medusa, can turn you to stone if you look at them. The most eloquent passage on these "moments of interior silence" occurs first toward the end of *Umorismo* and then again in the "The Secret Notebook" and renders powerfully the horror of getting just the right perspective on one's artifice for living.[39] Constructed relationships fall away; the structures of consciousness fall away. These moments are the opposite of living inauthentically, or with false structures, in that they consist in recognizing that finally all structures are false, or at least arbitrary. To live like this is to live with absolute *sincerità* and for a brief, desolate moment to pull the darkness around you. At such moments courage is indispensable, the courage to put one's mask together as best one can, the courage, that is, to create even when the taste of falsehood is particularly bitter.

In the course of Pirandello's long meditation on consciousness, he looked again and again, first on this facet of it, then on that. His brutal honesty forced him to argue that as a last resort for value and coherence consciousness offered, if used scrupulously, a firmer foundation in things, even if they were the elusive things of interior life, than religion or philosophy or conventional morality. At the same time this honesty forced him to admit that consciousness offered no absolute foundation. Consciousness is an imperfect opportunity, a curse as well as a blessing. But to choose it as a source of value and coherence is to choose to live, to choose to resist sinking into the surrounding darkness. Whatever its difficulties and perils, it is, according to Pirandello, all we have.

4

⦿⦿⦿⦿⦿⦿⦿⦿⦿⦿⦿⦿⦿⦿⦿⦿⦿⦿⦿⦿⦿⦿

IN THE GRIPS OF
ARCANE FORCES

IN THE COURSE of Pirandello's long meditation on consciousness he ranged over the full gamut of possibilities, from the experience of those locked so securely in their "artifice for living" that they have no self-perspective at all to those so detached from themselves and the human comedy that they are paralyzed by the arbitrariness they see on all sides. Moreover, he has illuminated this range in brilliant detail in the many consciousnesses inhabiting his stories, novels, and plays, in the accumulated overlays of figure on figure, from his most primitive Sicilian peasants to his most sophisticated humorists. In what follows we shall have to forego some of that detail to give adequate attention to certain matters not properly part of the process of structuring consciousness yet crucial as factors that condition that structuring. We have seen how "human things" are focused in consciousness to constitute the created moments of experience (or art). We must now look to those matters that bear decisively on the character of those created moments to give them their modern cast.

Of all the factors that condition consciousness none is more persistently present than the sense of arcane forces dominating and subverting the very process of conscious control itself. In the interview with Mario Missiroli in October of 1934 Pirandello distinguished between *No One Knows How* (*Non Si Sa Come,* 1934), his most recent play, and his previous work by arguing that where the previous work had dealt with consciousness and its makeup, the new play dealt with action and the slightness of our control over it. "How much is the will capable of in our life? Half the time we live in a dream, the other half in the grips of the arbitrariness of sensations. Rarely can a man explain his actions to himself, even in the most important of actions, those that determine his existence." In the play Romeo Daddi is in despair before the specter of everyone's life out of control.

"Life seems to him increasingly in the grips of arcane forces very few of which we identify and can dominate. The rest is mystery."[1]

The truth is that Pirandello had always been oppressed by a sense that life was driven by mysterious imperatives: his interest in lives almost if not entirely out of control is everywhere in his work. "Arcane" was one of his favorite words: he spoke of "arcane things," "arcane silences," "arcane tedium," and "the enormous arcane," all variants on that aggregate of influences that shape and direct our experience and yet lie beyond our control and understanding. Throughout his life he pondered the many shapes of these influences. Consciousness was not only affected by them; it functioned with a bedeviled sense that it could never escape them.

No One Knows How, Pirandello's last complete play, offers a striking summary of this interest because it pulls together materials from stories going back at least to 1902. Actually, the claim made by Emanuele Licastro that "And Two" ("E Due," 1902) is one of several sources for the play could as easily be made for any of the many stories in which characters seem impotent to direct their lives, stories like "The Sun Rising" ("La Levata del Sole," 1901) or "God My Master" ("Padron Dio," 1898), to take just two. More to the point is "In the Whirlpool" ("Nel Gorgo," 1913), the story from which the central action of Romeo Daddi's "madness" was taken. In this story Romeo's friends explain to Nicolino Respi that Romeo had seemed to sink into a desperation verging on madness when he became convinced that his wife, Donna Bice, a paragon among women, was capable of betraying him. Why he has become so convinced no one knows, but he has taken to staring into people's eyes at close range and mumbling about "abysses," and has somehow lost altogether what one of Respi's informants calls "the civility machine." Respi later gets a partial explanation for this behavior from Gabriella Vanzi, the Daddis' close friend, when she tells him that she and Romeo had recently had the briefest of encounters. An embrace, almost nothing, it had meant nothing, not enough to justify remorse, she insists. And yet it had demonstrated to Romeo that if Gabriella, a virtuous woman devoted to her husband, could suffer a momentary lapse, any one, even Bice, could do the same; and he strains himself to the breaking point with thinking about it.

But the encounter with Gabriella, Ginevra in the play, is only one of several reasons for Romeo's anguish: toward the end of act 1 he confesses to his wife and friends that as a boy he had killed another boy and had never told anyone. Pirandello has taken this episode from the story "Cinci" (1932), in which the boy of the title wanders into the country while waiting for his mother to come home and in a chance meeting with a country boy accidentally kills him in a boys' quarrel. The story is steeped in a desolate sense of estrangement: blank walls along empty streets, a blank face in a window, the indifferent fields, a meeting and a sudden quarrel, and all while no one is looking on. Before the afternoon is over even Cinci has almost forgotten what had happened. At any rate, this episode grafted onto Romeo's early life provides the background for his conviction that our lives are "in the grips of arcane forces." His desperation completely engulfs him when, in an attempt to mollify Ginevra's husband, Giorgio, for Ginevra's seeming lapse, he invents the story that Bice, his wife, had once called out in her sleep for Giorgio and startles Bice into revealing that she had in fact dreamed of Giorgio as a lover. His worst fears confirmed, Romeo provokes Giorgio into killing him, and with this act all four of the major characters have committed deeds they had never thought themselves capable of.

Although *No One Knows How* suffers from the overheated, casuistical style of many of the late plays, it is a powerful expression of Pirandello's belief that we have only the slenderest of holds on what we are. The play has only five characters, and its action consists of dialogue that turns on itself again and again, probing, examining details microscopically, scratching relentlessly at the flimsy fictions that each character has lived by until the fragile upper-class world of the present seems a chimera. Despite the fact that two of its acts take place on a terrace overlooking the sea, it is the most claustrophobic of Pirandello's plays. Romeo's insecurity shakes loose the ghosts of suspicions in the other characters, and with each tremor in the structure of loyalties binding the two central couples the emotional pressure intensifies. Questions of guilt, responsibility, and morality remain ambiguous; even the degree to which events have actually occurred is often unclear. Yet somehow the insubstantiality of the meandering search is never felt to be greater than the insubstantiality of the personal structures assaulted. We do what we have no intention of doing; we fashion a consciousness of ourselves and of our experience from thoughts, emotions, and sensations that almost immediately seem to belong to someone else. In Romeo's long reflection on consciousness in act 1 his key assertion is that it is unstable. "When you believe you have made yourself a consciousness and have established that each thing is this way or that, it takes very little to make you see that your consciousness was founded on nothing."[2] Like the young Pirandello in his first letters to his sister, Romeo feels himself lost in darkness, alienated from everything and everybody, including himself. He speaks piously of "navigating" through the unknown, of holding, as his friend Giorgio, a ship's captain, does, "to certain known things," but he finally recognizes that even the consciousness we fashion of things is uncertain. To live a conscious life, a life grounded in the values and coherences of consciousness, is to live with the tension of this insecurity.

The darkness is of course the same that Pirandello had been born into on the Sicilian headland called Chaos. He wrote of it all his life, and of the little interior light—the firefly—that creates a world for us by throwing a feeble circle of light around us. Perhaps the most searching and fully articulated commentary on the metaphors of darkness and light is to be found in the passages on lantern-philosophy (*lanterninosofia*), first in *The Late Mattia Pascal* and then in *Umorismo*. In the novel Anselmo Paleari, one of whose main functions is to bring philosophical commentary to bear on Mattia's situation, consoles Mattia during his forty days of convalescence by explaining that the darkness that follows his eye operation is only imaginary. We live with an awareness of enveloping darkness because we carry within us a little light that projects a circle of light around us and causes us to perceive everything beyond it as darkness. This is the light of consciousness, that aspect of our makeup that makes us different from trees by conferring on us the sad privilege of "perceiving ourselves live" (*sentirci vivere*). Called a firefly elsewhere, in Paleari's account this light is a little lantern (*lanternino*), "which causes us to see ourselves lost on the earth, . . . which projects all around us a more or less ample circle of light beyond which is the black shadow, the frightening shadow that would not exist if the *lanternino* were not lit within us."[3] In *Umorismo* this light becomes the spark that Prometheus stole from the sun and gave to man, which creates "all that shadow, the enormous mystery." In both passages Pirandello worries that all that lies beyond the light might be only a deception, something that seems to exist only because we create it. But whether outer or inner, or both, the mystery is real, dominated by arcane forces that tyrannize and torment.

In his fiction and plays Pirandello retained the outer-inner distinction despite his suspicion that the whole phenomenon was inner after all. A story like "The Victory of the Ants" ("Vittoria delle Formiche," 1936) is heavy with a sense of an outer world not merely indifferent but hostile. The unnamed protagonist has lost everything—family, property, position— everything except a shack on a small piece of land, where he lives off the little that the peasant who works the land gives him. His is a squalid existence, unredeemed except for the consolation that the beauty of the countryside provides. Then out of this same countryside come the ants, in long thin lines, in battalions, in hordes. They invade his house and occupy everything in it, and finally they invade even his person. He declares war on them and determines to set the anthill just a few steps from his door afire. When he does, however, during a windless period before rain, a sudden breeze comes up, setting the shack afire and finally setting him afire. As he is carried off to die in a hospital shouting "An alliance," meaning an alliance between the wind and the ants, he is thought to be mad; but when he dies with a smile on his lips, it seems possible that he has perceived a deeper kindness in the forces that have destroyed him. All in all, his is the story of a victim buffeted by a fortune so outrageous as to begin to be grotesquely comic.

"A Passing Touch" ("Una Toccatina," 1906), by contrast, deals with the mystery within, the mystery of what we are or think we are and the feeble hold we have on it. Cristoforo Golisch, a German who has lived in Rome since earliest childhood, meets an old friend, Benjamino Lenzi, on the street; he is appalled to learn that Lenzi has suffered a slight stroke, which has impaired his speech and causes him to drag one foot. Infuriated at the spectacle of this formerly robust friend reduced to childishness, he resolves that if death should ever touch him in this way—in passing, a light touch in anticipation of the great calamity to come—he would kill himself. Then, shortly afterwards, he too suffers a slight stroke, which deprives him of control of one side and which, more remarkably, causes him, without his realizing it, to forget his Italian and to speak German. As the doctor predicts, he does not kill himself: at first he seems to accept the improbable explanation that he has been stricken by an indigestion, then he seems to understand that he has had a stroke but believes that the paralysis will soon disappear. He joins his friend Lenzi in a park where they exercise their afflicted limbs in machines. One day they visit an old girlfriend, Nadina, who, deeply moved, treats them like the children they have become. Lenzi cries; Golisch speaks his Italian-German; Nadina, in the final image, kisses them on the brow and feeds them biscuits.

"A Passing Touch" is one of Pirandello's most masterful treatments of the instability of what we are, or think ourselves to be. One day hale and hearty, a well-known trencherman, a lion among women, a man among men with memories of a rowdy and heroic youth; then a "passing touch" and we are someone else, someone who speaks another language, who has forgotten almost everything, an idiot or imbecile child. And all this accompanied by the usual instinct for developing the self-preserving "deception for living." Here the arcane forces are inward, nearer than the wind or the ants, yet no less arcane or overwhelming for all their nearness.

In yet another variation on the general theme, in "The Fly" ("La Mosca," 1904) the arcane forces are both inner and outer, and the uneven struggle with them is again, as in "The Victory of the Ants," savage and brutal, culminating in screams of terror as the fly that has fed on cattle dead with anthrax brings Neli and his cousin Giurlannu to quick, ghastly ends. These forces are concentrated unmistakably in the insect indifferently cleaning his tiny feet as the cousins die in agony. But despite the title, they are also present in the accidental nick that the barber gives to Neli as he shaves him for his brief meeting with Luzza, his fiancée, and perhaps even in the exuberance that drives Neli to want to see Luzza while he is fetching a doctor for his stricken cousin. Certainly they are seen in the mad vengeance of the dying Giurlannu on the innocent Neli. The cousins were supposed to be married in the same ceremony. Now the dying man watches the fly feed on Neli's nick, suspecting that it could have been the very fly that inoculated him, and he says nothing. Had he dreamed it? His sudden fever? His silence about the fly? Instead of being married together, the cousins die together.

In this grim vision the fly encapsulates a nature at once squalid, vicious, and indifferent. It insists on a hazy connection between the mouldering cattle dead of anthrax and the dying men; it is an insidious enemy, little, black, deadly. Yet it is only one of the forces moving through the dark, cruel world of the story and no more important than the fatal cut, the muddle of human motives, and the web of circumstance. A world of hard work, of teeming animality, of love and its melting promises, of unexpected and unmerited agony and death: in this context Saro's screams as Neli dies echo the accents of Euripidean terror.

To be conscious that we live "in the grips of arcane forces" is to keep the mystery continuously present, to recognize that we see but a small part of it, and to acquiesce deliberately in that partial perception. It is to recognize, as Silvia Roncella does at the end of *Her Husband,* that life is an immense eddy, that "beyond the paltry necessities that men create for themselves other, dark, gigantic necessities weave through the calamitous currents of time."[4] It is to live with a consciousness that you are always in that eddy, afloat in a medium that is constantly changing, in touch with little more than touches you at any given moment.

Pirandello's conviction that these forces were not to be understood or controlled did not prevent him from believing that they could be possessed imaginatively. They must be entered as water is entered so that contact begins as sensuous contact. The writer must ingrain them in invented lives and actions, render them in particulars evocative of the obscurity beyond. Living the conscious life meant comprehending them through experiences of their manifestations. In the course of his long fascination with these forces Pirandello focused repeatedly on certain of these manifestations, as if for him the whole of the enveloping mystery was summed up in them. He never attempted to define them in an abstract way or to identify patterns within them, since by their nature they defy such precision, yet his treatment of them provides not just a heightened but an unmistakably clearer sense of them.

He saw these forces in tragicomic form in the intractability of human beings. In "Nenè and Ninì" (1912) we meet them in the obstreperous egotism of children. Nenè and Ninì have been left in the hands of their stepfather, Erminio Del Donzello, a rake-thin French teacher, ridiculed by his students and maligned by the neighboring women, all of whom assume that he, like all stepfathers, is cruel to his stepchildren. In fact, he is the soul of solicitude; it is the children who are barbarous: unmanageable, spoiled by the doting neighbor women, cruel without ever understanding cruelty. Erminio and his saintly second wife so exhaust themselves trying to tame Nenè and Ninì that Erminio finally dies, giving as his parting advice that his wife marry quickly because she will soon follow him. The children, bubbling with destructive health, prevail absolutely.

In "Competition for a Post with the Counsel of State" ("Concorso per Referendario al Consiglio di Stato," 1902) the intractability is largely a matter of Pompeo Lagumina's irrepressible animality. Pompeo is a large man, with large animal appetites; discipline comes hard to him. When faced with an examination on which his future with Sandrina depends, he goes to a convent in the mountains, now a kind of hotel, to study without distraction. The story consists of his torments as he struggles with gargantuan dinners, naps in the sun, parties and outings with his fellow residents, the *douceurs* of the women; in a word all that beckons to the flesh and is not study. He has been neglecting his work miserably when Sandrina and her mother unexpectedly arrive, discover him playing a lawn game with some of the young women, and break the engagement. He briefly entertains the idea of suicide, then rejoices that he will not have to study anymore and can become the padre priore of the festive "conventuals."

But the ungovernability of human nature can also take forms of unrelieved horror. "Puberty" ("Pubertà," 1926) offers a vision of humanity as a kind of molten stuff welling up and exploding. Dreetta, a girl experiencing puberty, is astonished by her own odors, perplexed by the changes taking place in her body, maddened by energies and impulses she does not understand, by turns amused, in tears, and enraged at the creature she is becoming. She hates living with her grandmother and dreams of her dying so that she can live with a cousin; more wildly, she dreams that an

Englishman or an American will appear and adopt or marry her. In the climactic scene with Mr. Walston, her English tutor, the sight of his exposed white calves incites her to hysterical screams. As he is ejected from the house, she calls to him from an upper floor to take her with him and then jumps to her death. What in another age might have been traced to witchcraft or possession Pirandello treats as an obscure violence just barely concealed in the most commonplace and innocent of figures. In these stories human nature seethes and churns with a secret, riotous life; like existence at large it is a tyranny unto itself. Although we can exercise control—indeed it is also human to try to do so, and to exaggerate our ability to do so—the wisest part of any control is in recognizing that it is always partial.

In the abundant criticism that sees Pirandello as an intellectual, cerebral artist, far too little attention has been paid to his profound interest in the hidden currents that shape and condition experience. Some of the critics who have stressed that interest have concluded that it led him to a serious commitment to the occultism fashionable in his time and of which he had considerable knowledge.[5] But occultism no less than rigorous philosophizing consists of reasoning about the hidden currents, if from special premises, and illuminating the surrounding darkness. Pirandello, on the contrary, consistently emphasized the mystery. Although it is true that the famous Pirandellian character is typically a man or woman reasoning passionately about an irrational condition, it is also true that Pirandello was as much drawn to the irrational condition as to his characters' reasoning about it and as much committed to rendering its swell and heave as to rendering the intricacies of character. In fact it is impossible to make a clean distinction between the characters and the forces that drive and shunt them about because these forces are as often inner as outer, as often in the intractable stuff of which human beings are made as in the wind and the ants. Pirandellian characters seen in gross are more frequently dominated by emotion than by the reason of a Baldovino or Laudisi of *Right You Are* or Leone Gala. They are a bustling, energetic crew, heroic in love, quick to take offense, aggressive in their cunning, imperious in their demands for justice and vengeance. Most fundamental of all, they are embattled, as Renato Simoni has argued, by a struggle against annihilation.[6]

The pressures of this "mania to live," in Massimo Bontempelli's phrase,[7] can be felt everywhere in the work. A story like "The Vigil" ("La Veglia," 1904) is a whirlpool of high emotion. Fulvia Gelli had left her husband for a lover, then the lover for Marco Mauri, while Marco had deceived Fulvia about his marriage so that she would consent to live with him. Now both her husband and Marco gather at her bedside in a death vigil before which all constraints of convention fall away. But the story is less about the inadequacy of convention to order human relations than about the fever to live that literally consumes Fulvia and Marco. In "Life Seen as a Nude" ("La Vita Nuda," 1907) the social surface is less turbulent and more ironic, but the passions driving the characters are much the same. Because the figure of Life in the sculpture that Signorina Consalvi has commissioned to commemorate her dead fiancé was initially to resemble her, she had insisted that it be clothed. But when she unexpectedly falls in love with the sculptor, she agrees that it be nude—crude, like life—and no longer resemble her. Beneath the polite surface of this almost Jamesian reversal, the pressure to live dominates all the pretty sentiment and nice decorum. Although Signorina Consalvi has no moment like the intoxication that Signora Lucietta in "The Rose" ("La Rosa," 1914) experiences at the ball at which she reenters society after two years of widowhood, she is propelled by the same hunger. Mattia Pascal speaks for all of them when he decides to start a new life in Rome: "After all, I had to live, live, live."[8]

This mania to live is in Pirandello's characters an inadvertent recognition of the menace of death in many forms. There is the living death of disuse, the slow, steady desiccation of youth and vitality that Signorina Consalvi and Signora Lucietta unconsciously acknowledge, or the inevitable capitulation to age, disease, and infirmity of the old men in "A Passing Touch." Then there is more simply but no less tellingly the ubiquitous presence of physical death.

Death is a commonplace in Pirandello's fiction and drama, leaping suddenly out of the dark, calamitous. Suicides, murders, children consumed by hideous fevers, young mothers ravaged by childbirth, the old noiselessly slipping into the mists. Pirandello wrote often about death because it forced his characters to moments of authenticity, to tear away masks and social veils and to reveal difficult truths. This is what happens in "The Vigil," when after all the posturing and rhetoric the two men, husband and lover, sit together at the bedside of the dying woman they have both loved. Everywhere death shakes situations into clarity. But Pirandello also wrote about it because it is there, the prime evidence of arcane forces waiting, covertly dominant.

The early "Visiting the Sick" ("Visitare gl'Infermi," 1896) is a long, detailed study of people in the presence of death. Gaspare Naldi has suffered a stroke after journeying two hours in the hot sun to tender his condolences to a friend whose child has just died; now he lies dying in a room in the friend's house as friends arrive and discuss the calamity in an adjoining room. The story deals with this vigil, with the elaborate attempts of those in attendance to recover the smallest detail of Naldi's collapse, with their half informed, half ignorant speculations on his status, with their windy efforts at philosophizing and poeticizing, with their rapt attention to each new event: a bowel movement, an injection, a movement in the good leg. Clear in all this, though unacknowledged, is their deeper fascination with and terror at the great mystery in their midst. Throughout Naldi's ordeal they are held by the thing, as if by a spell; with his death in the morning they disperse, happy to be alive, ready to take up their lives, somehow renewed. Death, perverse, sovereign, always indifferent, is the clearest, most absolute proof of the tyranny of the enveloping mystery.

Less clear but equally tyrannical is the peculiar annihilation that Ersilia Drei resists in *To Clothe the Naked* (*Vestire gl'Ignudi,* 1922) as she tries desperately to cover the confused welter of motives and impulses that characterize her behavior with an acceptable, coherent definition of herself. By the year of this play Pirandello was in his period of richest theatrical invention. Having won Italy's attention with *Right You Are* in 1917 and Europe's with *Six Characters* in 1921–22, in the next six years he completed thirteen plays, including *Henry IV* (*Enrico IV,* 1922), *To Clothe the Naked* (1922), *The Man with the Flower in His Mouth* (*L'Uomo dal Fiore in Bocca,* 1923), *Each in His Own Way* (*Ciascuno a Suo Modo,* 1928), and *Tonight We Improvise* (1928). In *To Clothe the Naked* the menace of annihilation comes not so much from arcane forces as from arcane processes that feed on nondefinition. The action of the play consists basically of Ersilia's search, past and present, for a persona, for what she calls "a decent little garment" to cover her "nakedness." At the outset she has tentatively accepted the hospitality of an aging writer because she hopes he will write a novel about her recent experiences in Smyrna, where her charge, the child of a consul, had been killed in a fall, the consul's wife had discharged her, and her fiancé had jilted her. All this had won her a kind of poignant fame through a newspaper account, and she hopes the writer will take that farther in a novel. But the three initial versions of these events—the writer's imagined version, the newspaper version, and her own—are only the beginning of her difficulties. With each successive disclosure the focus shifts and the events take on a new shape, and with the scenes dealing with the newspaperman, her former fiancé, and the consul, discoveries are made that throw everything into question. Laspiga, her former fiancé, now penitent, wishes to make restitution, until he learns that Ersilia had been the mistress of Grotti, the consul. Grotti is a maelstrom of motives:

he has come to Rome to correct the newspaper story and save face for himself and his wife, but he is still obsessively drawn to Ersilia, now more than ever because in his view they share the guilt for his child's death since the accident had occurred while they were neglecting him for their lovemaking. Only Ersilia insists that it was no one's if not life's fault because life would not allow her to take on a distinctive character, literally, "to consist in some way."

All this is by now fairly familiar of course in Pirandello's work, if not always so skillfully managed. What is different is Ersilia. Unexceptional, hysterical, by any standard clumsy in the extreme in her efforts to create herself, she brings a compulsive passion of great authority to the lies she tells and the errors she only half corrects. As she moves through quick-sands of compounded deceits toward the serenity of knowing at last that she must die unclothed, nude, she gives the profound muddle at the bottom of many lives a tragic resonance. Hers is an ambiguous reality, and finally she knows that it must be. The tremendous intricacy and pressure of motives and intentions and partial understandings and misunderstandings are in the end of no account because they are so often the rule.

Pirandello's fascination with the menace of annihilation and the tyranny of the arcane is everywhere in his work. It declares a primary condition in the making of a consciousness; it also passes inevitably into the related subject of living with this condition.

The Sicilian stories and plays are especially rich in details of the individual's uneven struggle with an obscure condition. In backwaters like Milocca, Montelusa, and Richieri, all locales that occur several times, the ignorance, superstition, and prejudice of Pirandello's more primitive compatriots link up with arcane forces to give this condition a distinctly barbarous, if frequently humoristic, definition. Pirandello was always deeply interested in and sympathetic to his characters' attempts to master this condition, and in these stories and plays particularly drawn to the native cunning that enables a Liolà or a Professor Toti of *Think about It, Giacomino! (Pensaci, Giacomino!* 1916) or a Cecè to manipulate their worlds to at least temporary advantage. But in Sicily as in Rome neither reason nor cunning is finally of any help. In a good many of his Sicilian primitives, indeed, what we find is not reason at all, but a kind of reason of unreason, a perverse, twisted logic a little like madness. When in "Set Fire to the Dross" Simone Lampo agrees to the eccentric zealot Nazzaro's urgings that he release the birds he keeps because imprisoning them puts him in mortal sin, he understands Nazzaro's invitation to put *fuoco alla paglia* (literally "fire to the straw") to mean that by releasing the birds he will be expiating his sins.

But Nazzaro has in mind a thorough shriving, and he actually burns Don Simone's grain, thus depriving him of his last material support. Even language is an impediment to system, control, and understanding. In "The Other Son" ("L'Altro Figlio," 1915) old Maragrazia is the victim of a logic that has nothing to do with logic. She has three sons, two in America who ignore her and to whom she nonetheless continues to write for help, one in her own town who has always stood ready to help her and whom she ignores because he resembles his father, a *mafioso* who had killed her husband's murderer and held her in bondage. Yet Maragrazia's obstinacy is not simply the result of stupidity: Pirandello sees it as a product of imperatives from a bestial past, a mentality of clay subject to earthquakes.

As a group the Sicilian stories and plays abound in strange and wonderful abuses of the mind. In "The Surprises of Science" ("Le Sorprese della Scienza," 1905) the scientific-minded populace of Milocca demonstrate with impeccable logic that it would be unreasonable to undertake urban improvements in lights, streets, sewers, etc., because science will soon outstrip current technology; hence Milocca remains an unlighted sinkhole. In "The League Dissolved" ("La Lega Disciolta," 1910) Bombolo, a Turk in provincial Montelusa, runs a so-called league, the function of which is to recover stolen cattle at a price that allows the league to pay the thieving peasants what the *padroni* should have paid them in the first place. When, however, with the achievement of a fair wage and the release of three key prisoners, Bombolo tries to dissolve the league because the reasons for it no longer exist, no one takes him any more seriously than they had taken his pious negotiations as agent for the league: the thefts of cattle continue, and Bombolo finally gives up and goes back to Turkey. In "The Little Red Book" ("Il Libretto Rosso," 1911) Rosa Marenga has already married three daughters with money she has earned by nursing foundlings; now she wishes to marry a fourth, Tuzza, though she has trouble getting credit because her milk is uncertain. At last she does get a little red book, the record of her credit; and as she, Tuzza, and the fiancé prepare for the wedding, the child, because he is not getting enough to eat, sucks his thumb until it becomes a monstrosity. When to everyone's surprise and chagrin the child dies, everything seems lost, until Rosa succeeds in getting yet one more little red book for yet another foundling.

In all these stories the mania to live—to choose, to act, to confront the enemy lurking in all things—is clear, but the resources available to those who would live are obscure, unreliable, even dangerous. Sicily, with its peculiar antiquity, its desperate poverty, its violence and decay, supplied a perfect context for these figures beating back the sea with ancient swords.

Pirandello found other qualities to admire and love in Sicily, in the painful dignity of the peasant father in "To Work!" ("Alla Zappa!" 1902) or that of the old Garibaldino in *The Old and the Young,* or in the health of Micuccio in *Sicilian Limes* (*Lumíe di Sicilia,* 1910) or that of Annicchia in "The Wet Nurse" ("La Balia," 1903). But more characteristically he saw Sicily as a land of embattled survivors in the grips of unknowns all around and within them. Their struggle could be funny, grotesque, poignant, bitterly painful, even contemptible, yet he always looked on it with, among other emotions, the deepest compassion.

Toward the tyranny of this condition Pirandello clarified a range of responses. At one extreme he could take a wild glee in the spectacle of human beings trying to walk through a swamp with dignity. It is dignity that prompts Professor Gori in "The Tight Waistcoat" ("La Marsina Stretta," 1911) to force himself into the too small swallow-tailed coat requisite for the wedding he is about to attend. He goes, in agony, and there rises to the occasion of the sudden death of the bride's mother and the attempts made by the groom's family to break up the marriage by bullying everyone into going through with the ceremony. After it is all over, as he stands holding the sleeve torn off at the height of his fury, he recognizes that he would probably not have succeeded had he not had the irritation of the tight waistcoat. He is comic, a model of bourgeois heroism, a source of reassuring delight. At the other extreme Pirandello could find an almost paralytic pessimism in scenes of injustice and suffering such as "The Fly" and "The Little Red Book" provide.

Perhaps the most common, certainly one of the most important, of the responses defined was rage. Despite his reputation for generosity and affection, Pirandello was scarcely a mild-tempered, mild-mannered man: he could be nasty with literary enemies like Croce; he was frequently exasperated by what he saw as pious deceit in the world around him. It should be no surprise, then, that a great many of his characters and narrators express outrage at the life they look into. Matteo Falcone, the brutish teacher in *The Outcast* who falls in love with Marta Ajala, is a caldron of molten bile, in his most characteristic gesture spitting at Palermo and its spectacle of life: "Worm that I am—to you, city of worms!"[9] But Matteo's hate goes far beyond poor Palermo, comprehending as well his physical afflictions, the grotesque comedy of his aging mother and aunt, each deluded that she is prevented from marrying by the other's refusal to die, the injustice of Marta's beauty and its power—in other words, the whole condition. When he is again repulsed by Marta, after following her to Alvignani's house, he pleads that he is not "the monster; the world is a monster, an insane monster that has made her so beautiful and me like this. . . . Vendetta! Vendetta!"[10] Matteo's fury is probably the most explosive in all of Pirandello's work, in quality and intensity like the outrage of the narrator of "The Trap" ("La Trappola," 1915), though without his ironic sense of defeat, since that wooer, by contrast, succeeds with the woman of his desires.

Rage as a part of seeing "life in the grips of arcane forces," accordingly, itself takes a variety of forms. Also more complicated than Falcone's passion is the impatient, ironic anger of Bobbio in "Bobbio's Hail Mary" ("L'Ave Maria di Bobbio," 1912). Saverio Bobbio, pharmacist and philosopher, suffers from toothaches. One day when a particularly severe one forces him to leave his country house and guests to return to the city, he stops at a roadside shrine and out of boyhood habit says a Hail Mary. The toothache passes. Humiliated that he is behaving like a superstitious woman in seeing a connection, yet a little ashamed at his ingratitude, he reviews the history of miracles from Saint Augustine to Montaigne, and as his skepticism rises, the toothache returns. But after trying another Hail Mary without success, he again proceeds to the dentist only to have the toothache pass again as he draws up to the door. Had he said a Hail Mary without noticing? Furious now, he has the dentist pull all his teeth: "I don't want these jokes; I don't want any more of these jokes. All, one by one, I'll have them pulled!"[11]

In some contexts the rage has a different coloration because it is directed less at the condition than at the creatures who imagine themselves its masters. Toward such vanity Pirandello could generate a fine fury. We see it in "The Imbecile" ("L'Imbecille," 1912) in Luca Fazio's detestation of the public men who complacently believe they run the world, and again in the portrait of Consigliere Ippolito Onorio Breganze, the priggish official in *The Outcast* who drives Marta from her job and hometown. We see a more ambiguous but extraordinarily powerful version of it in "The Destruction of Man" ("La Distruzione d'Uomo," 1921), in which Nicola Petix sees the middle-aged Porellas' many unsuccessful attempts to have a child as a symbolic expression of our irrational passion to reproduce ourselves. Signora Porella, forty-seven and grotesquely deformed in the last weeks of her sixteenth pregnancy, takes a daily walk with her husband, aged fifty: the eternal couple, vain, courageous, timorous, proud, almost comic in the fierce autumn wind. Nicola Petix, driven mad by their mania to add yet another child to the faceless multitudes already overrunning their tenement, one day intercepts them at a point where the Via Nomentana crosses the Aniene River—echoes of the Romans and the infinite tedium of history—and drowns the woman. Petix's hostility, the obverse of his anguished impotence, is of all of Pirandello's variations on rage perhaps the least qualified by compassion.

Taken together, these instances of rage and outrage give a general idea of an important part of seeing life "in the grips of arcane forces," hence an important part of the drama of consciousness in which this sense of life is constant and important. Rage is a dimension of the seeing, a part of fashioning an idea of oneself and of one's experience.

Like rage though sufficiently different to constitute a separate response to this condition is the alienation so frequently met both in Pirandello's characters and in numerous private statements. In a letter to his daughter, Lietta, in 1933 he wrote: "I don't know if I am fleeing life or life me. I know that I feel almost entirely 'detached.' The earth is extremely remote. Hence, not only you, little Lietta, even though from here to Chile is a good piece, but I from where I now look at all the things of life, I am much, but much more distant."[12] And so it is with many of his characters. In "Far Away" ("Lontano," 1902) Lars Kleen, the Norwegian sailor left in Sicily when he falls ill, is a central image of living in an environment that is always alien. After he marries and tries to settle down, he continues to feel alone and desperately clumsy among the Sicilians, ridiculed by his peers and the town children, "as if fallen from the sky." The story contains little of the sense of violent and destructive forces lurking in ordinary surfaces, compared with, say, "Cinci," but it conveys an oppressive picture of life out of control, moved quietly, secretly, by forces unseen and unknowable.

A more organized picture of alienation is contained in "The Wheelbarrow," a bitter, first-person account of the suffering that comes from feeling absent from oneself, completely detached from the life one is living. The speaker looks at his body, his wife, his four children, but he cannot feel that they are his; he sees himself fixed in a role, a job, an office, but he can never feel that the person he sees is himself. His therapy for the anguish of living in a continuously false position is to close himself in his office, seize his old dog by the hind legs, and walk her around like a wheelbarrow. It is a mad act, he recognizes, but it avenges him: on the dog, who, as she lies watching him work, knows how to live; and on life and its absurdity. It was stories like "The Wheelbarrow" that supported the figure of the existentialist Pirandello popular with critics after World War II.

From alienation it is but a short if decisive step to the nausea commonplace in the existentialist dialectic. Like alienation and rage, nausea is a response to the surrounding mystery frequent among Pirandellian characters of all ages. Didi of "The Long Dress" ("La Veste Lunga," 1913) is sixteen and at last allowed to put on a long dress for the journey to meet the middle-aged marchese she is intended to marry. As she looks out on the arid, desolate landscape and contemplates the meaning of the trip and the adult figures of her father and brother, she experiences a repulsion and ennui so violent and suffocating that she drinks off her father's medicine and kills herself. Gosto Bombichi of "The Sun Rising" is forty-five, tired of his life, his wife, and himself; he sees life as a ridiculous game of chance that he has lost. But when he takes his revolver and leaves a note telling his wife that he will be dead shortly after he has seen his first sunrise, he does not reckon with the forces that cause him, finally exhausted from walking, to sleep soundly, as he always has done, straight through the sunrise and his appointment with death. Both disgust and self-disgust are overruled by a constitution too healthy to be concerned with philosophy or pessimism.

But Pirandello's best-known treatment of nausea occurs in the short play *The Man with a Flower in His Mouth* (1923) from the story "Death Is upon Him" ("La Morte Addosso"), originally "Night Cafe" ("Caffè Notturno," 1918). The action consists of a chance meeting late at night in a railway coffee shop between a traveler trying to get home to his family and a man who we presently learn haunts public places and seeks out the company of strangers. The men talk, idly at first. As the talk is dominated by the second man, one of the most powerful images in modern literature of man's desolation before death unfolds. The night wanderer speaks of his fascination with strangers, of how he spends his time watching people, in shops, salesgirls tying packages, always strangers, and of how in this way he attaches himself to life, like a climbing vine—"to the life of strangers, around which my imagination can work freely . . . until I succeed in putting myself inside. . . . I need to attach myself by way of my imagination to the life of others, but I do so without pleasure and without taking any great interest in it; on the contrary . . . so as to feel the vexation in it, to be able to judge life foolish and vain."[13] He speaks of the "anguish in the throat" that is the "savor of life, the taste that cannot be satisfying because life . . . is so greedy for itself that it doesn't allow itself to be tasted."[14] Then with a series of numbingly swift disclosures he fills in the picture of his situation, of the cancer, the "flower" on his lip concealed by his mustache, of his wife who scratches the sore and tries to kiss it so that she may die with him, who even at this moment is watching him from just around the corner, of the apricots now ripening and so delicious that they distract him from killing himself. The vision is chilling, a gasp of horror amid the routine sights and sounds of a railway cafe; at its center the defiant disgust of the man with the flower in his mouth.

To live with a consciousness of the mystery in so much of what determines life is to live with both the mystery and the full gamut of responses to it. Yet even these responses are only part of the story. Beyond the outrage, disgust, and crippling alienation Pirandello was also moved to a profound wonder; at its most delicate and finely wrought, a wonder very like piety. Most frequently he found this wonder in utterly commonplace events and surfaces, in actions in which outward stability and normalcy contain deeper dramas of staggering power and beauty. The early story "The Three Darlings" ("Le Tre Carissime," 1897) traces a baffling picture of waste in a world that scarcely notices it. The narrator, a young painter without means, assists at close range at the elaborate, pathetic, and unjustly unsuccessful efforts of three sisters to win husbands. Although they are intelligent, full of life, and unusually attractive, men who should hardly expect to do so well pass them by. At last they move away and the painter sees less of them, then finally nothing at all as they gradually marry and begin to have children. In the course of this unexceptional progress through courtship, an elusive disparity is clarified between the young women, rare in their power to create value, and the world that is only obliquely aware of them. What is most remarkable is that no one seems to notice and no one complains, not even the young women. The outward signs of bourgeois solidity are at all points present, and apparently that is all that anyone expects or wants.

Pirandello was acutely sensitive to the undercurrents of such domestic drama: he found a yawning, aching pathos in the image of human beauty moving through middle-class living rooms and gardens, moving and then gone, like the painting of the sisters that in the story is sold and lost. Throughout his career he turned to quiet scenes to express it: scenes of family life, of meetings between friends, of casual conversations in bars or in railway cars, of men and women in the course of routine labors. In "If" ("Se," 1898) two officers who had formerly served together meet by chance in a terrace bar, and one tells the other of his disastrous life since they had last seen each other, of how he was not sent to Udine or Bologna, as they had expected, but had remained in Potenza, of how that had set the course for a marriage that ended in his killing his wife, who had also married because of a chain of events that could easily have led another way. Steadily the terrace bar fills with an oppressive sense of the chanciness of any life: whatever you look at could easily have been different—a different wife, a different career, a different stage for it all. "The Raven of Mizzaro" ("Il Corvo di Mizzaro," 1902) is a kind of folk parable about a raven who has had a bell tied to his neck by a shepherd and whose flights with ringing accompaniment puzzle and amaze the peasants. Like the others, Ciché interprets the ringing as the sounds of spirits, until finally he captures the raven and then resolves to make it into a pet for his children. But nothing is so simple or so sure: as Ciché drives his cart homeward the raven frightens the donkey, who breaks into a mad dash, killing himself and Ciché. Thereafter the ringing is heard again, and again it puzzles and amazes the peasants thereabouts. "In the Evening, a Geranium" ("Di Sera, un Geranio," 1934) is one of several brilliant stories about age and leaving life. Very short, it deals with an old man dying, reduced to almost nothing, and the way his mind visits the things in the nearby garden and finally fixes on a red geranium. His delight at the bloom crystallizes the inexpressible beauty of the life he is leaving. "In the evening," he meditates, "sometimes in the gardens some flower suddenly bursts into flame like this; and no one can explain the reason for it."[15] And in fact there are no explanations: the beauty and perversity and torment of life "in the grips of arcane forces" are alike mysterious, parts of a moving spectacle far deeper than its surface motions suggest.

Pirandello's last published story, "A Day Passes" ("Una Giornata," 1936), is essentially a vision of a life led with a consciousness of its wonder. The story traces the speaker's surrealistic movement through one day, from his tumbling off a train just before dawn in a strange station through his various efforts to hold on to the outward signs of life in his meetings with people who seem to know him; to his contacts with a beautiful woman now extending her arms to embrace him, now gone; to his fugitive memories of hard work now very nearly forgotten; to a last scene with children, his children, and then his children older with their children. "Is my life finished already?" he asks as he looks at his aged figure in a mirror and feels himself sliding into frailty. Pirandello's management of grand effects with astonishingly simple means was never surer, nor his vision steadier. But the life that seems here like a day, with all its uncertainty and anguish, ends in neither anger nor nausea, however valid these responses may sometimes be, but in the tremendous compassion with which the story's speaker looks for as long as he is able at his, by now, old children. Compassion embraces all else. As a summary expression of Pirandello's perception of the underlying mystery of human life, "A Day Passes" catches both the mystery and the temper of the consciousness that has acquiesced in it.

5

●●●●●●●●●●●●●●●●●●●●●●●

RELATIVITY AND
THE FICTIONS OF
THE SPIRIT

FROM PIRANDELLO'S earliest letters to his sister Lina to the end of his life his sense of a world out of control, or nearly, traced in large part to his conviction that all knowledge and values were subjective, hence relative. "The world itself has no reality unless we ourselves confer it," he was to say repeatedly[1]: it is in continuous flux, and within that flux the individual seeks a fugitive coherence by naming, abstracting, fixing or seeming to fix, devising tricks and illusions that give the appearance of coherence. But our acknowledgement that reality is subjective, thus relative to the individual, does not free us from a responsibility to the world, neither to the exterior world of action and others nor to the interior world of consciousness. We must construct reality with *sincerità,* which, though it does not change the essentially subjective character of the process, leads to a creation and self-creation of a reflexive, highly complex kind. Painfully aware that all such efforts were arbitrary yet necessary to give substance and shape in the moment to what was continously changing, Pirandello saw a continuous awareness of relativity as no less important than our continuous sensitivity to the arcane forces in experience.

This perception of relativity extended, of course, to virtually everything: sensation, judgment, institutions, morals. Much of the extraordinary confusion of modern intellectual life traced, Pirandello argued in "Art and Consciousness Today," to the relativity of all standards.[2] But as Joseph Wood Krutch pointed out some time ago, it was largely relativity as it affected identity and the principal agents that define it that mattered most. A treasured conviction—that each of us is an inviolable "I," at some level irreducible—"dissolved," in Krutch's term, and with it every traditional way of deriving civilized systems.[3] Pirandello pondered this dissolution from first to last, always acutely aware of its profound implications for modern sensibility, always convinced that the only way to deal with it was to face it honestly. In *Umorismo* he addressed at length the vagaries of self and the indeterminacy of the consciousness, memories, and experiences that serve to define the self.[4] In the early fiction these vagaries are not the central, intense preoccupation that they were to become in the plays, but they are prominent, in Marta Ajala's discovery in *The Outcast* that after all she has never loved any of the important men in her life, or in Fausto Bandini's passage from madness to wisdom in "When I Was Mad" ("Quand' Ero Matto," 1902), when he learns that everyone sees a different world and that not to see it for oneself is not to see oneself. Of course the elusiveness of identity has been a concern in the comedy of all ages: we see it in bold form in the many variants on transformation, disguise, and ritual discoveries of long lost relatives. But where in traditional comedy the Antipholi of *The Comedy of Errors* and Ernest of *The Importance of Being Earnest* are bemused and stunned in the presence of transformations or undisguisings because they are convinced they have an identity that somehow has been misplaced, in Pirandello characters are baffled by their discovery that they have no fixed character or personality at all. As the protagonist of Pirandello's last novel was to learn, they could be one, none, or a hundred thousand.

Pirandello readily acknowledged his intellectual debts in this matter. By 1900, the year he published "Science and Aesthetic Criticism" ("Scienza e Critica Estetica"), he had read and reread Alfred Binet's *Les Altérations de la Personnalité* (1892) and was studying psychology.[5] In Binet he had met the idea that personality consisted of a collection of elements continuously combining and recombining, that one lives with a suitable combination of them, and that society for reasons of convenience encourages one to. Such ideas were in the air, of course, extended and popularized by books like Giovanni Marchesini's *The Fictions of the Spirit* (*Le Finzioni dell'Anima*, 1903). Perhaps fundamental to all others was Bergson and his comprehensive vision of change and interpenetration in all life; he is notably present in a passage like the following from *Umorismo*: "Life is a continuous flux that we seek to arrest and to fix in stable and determinate forms, within and outside of us.... These forms ... are the concepts, the ideals with which we try to keep ourselves consistent, all the fictions we create, the conditions, the states in which we aim to stabilize ourselves. But within ourselves, in what we call the spirit ... the flux continues, indistinct, flowing under the banks, beyond the limits that we impose as we compose a consciousness for ourselves and construct a personality."[6] In this view variability and instability are fundamental. What most sharply differentiates Pirandello from Bergson and the others who might be cited as his intellectual sources is that his major effort went into not restating these ideas, but into studying their consequences for the quality of life in his time and devising ways of living with them.

Even in the early work the kinds of insecurity, bafflement, anguish, and shock attributed to relativity, and particularly to the relativity of self, cover a broad spectrum of experience. In "Prudence" ("Prudenza," 1901) the narrator is thirty-four years of age; out of sorts with himself, his graying beard, and his mistress, he decides to have a haircut and shave. As the barber unaccountably makes mistake after mistake, the narrator begins to lose himself to another man in the mirror until finally, after the barber has shaved both his head and his face, he can no longer recognize himself. Furious, he returns home and there his mistress also fails to recognize him and, to his delight, drives him off, a free man at last. "The Best of Friends" ("Amicissimi," 1902) likewise stresses the comedy of disappearing identities. When Gigi Mear is embraced one morning on his way to the office by one who presents himself as an old friend from Padua, dragged to his home for lunch, and subjected to a long discussion of Gigi's family, he is shaken to his foundations to realize that he recalls neither the man's name nor the man. Whatever once existed between them—and it is considerable for the "old friend"—has vanished completely for Gigi. Helpless and embarrassed, Gigi finally takes his courage in his hands and asks the man's name, but the "old friend" refuses to tell him and, mightily amused, leaves. In both of these stories the trusted outlines of self and personal relations fade into unintelligibility at the slightest touch of circumstance.

Other stories from before the war sound a graver, more distressing note. "A Voice" ("Una Voce," 1904) is the painful tale of a young, blind marchese who has fallen in love with his deceased mother's companion, a young woman named Lydia who has ministered to him unstintingly. In his sightless world she becomes for him a salvation, an effective lifeline to the world through her beautiful voice. What he does not know is that she has kept from him the evidence that his blindness can be cured because she is convinced that if he sees her, though she is physically handsome, he will no longer love her. He loves the voice, not the woman he would see; with sight his world and all the people in it would be different for him. In an agony of guilt Lydia finally admits that she wants the marchese blind and dependent, an admission that of course contains the recognition that even the most important of human bonds, love, loyalty, and devotion, rest on the flimsiest of foundations. Even what a mother is to her young son can change drastically, as Stefano Conti explains in "A Portrait" ("Un Ritratto," 1914), a story of how at age seven he learned that his mother had been previously married and had had another son. With that discovery his "true mama," that mama of whom they say there is only one, died for him, and his mother thereafter was another. In "Response" ("Risposta," 1912) the narrator comments on his friend Marino's distress with a long analysis of the variability of identity. Marino is in love with Signorina Anita, but is poor and unable to ask for her hand. Signorina Anita is also poor and has recently been asked in marriage by Commendatore Ballesi, sixty-six, an old friend of the family who already supports her mother. At Anzio, where Signorina Anita is trying to adjust to the shock of Ballesi's proposal, Marino walks on the beach with her and resists an opportunity to make love to her. After he has left her, Nicolino Respi, a sportsman and ladies' man who had once saved Signorina Anita from drowning and had bitten her in the process, joins her and takes full advantage of her vulnerability. Marino's disillusion at Signorina Anita's behavior, the narrator explains, rests on his error in thinking she is the same Anita for all persons. On the contrary, the intelligent, sensitive Anita whom he loves has very little, if any, connection with the Anita of the flaring nostrils who secretly remembers Respi's bite. She is those two, and still many others; what one sees of her at any moment is only a very small part of what she is.

In these stories the insecurity of recognizing the insubstantiality of self is already important. We are phantoms clutching at masks, as Ignazio Capolino clutches at the eyeglasses that give him a new dignity when he goes off to the Chamber of Deputies in *The Old and the Young.* We are different for everyone who sees us and knows a part of us, and different even for ourselves as we meet and respond to others. The consciousness in which we are continuously creating our idea of ourselves and of everyone else is a caldron overflowing with possibilities, full to the superfluity that Simone Pau in *The Notebooks of Serafino Gubbio* finds fundamental to man's melancholy estate. Pirandello speaks of it with unusual directness in his letter to Stefano of 5 March 1917, where he discusses the many possibilities for being that Stefano contains, and urges a prudent adaptation to them.[7] Elsewhere he dwells at length on the difficulty of this adaptation and the instability of the consciousness itself.

To be fully cognizant of the relativity of all experience involves first recognizing the variability of consciousness. Consciousness is a "discord of voices," a hub of perceptions, images, opinions, experiences, memories exposed momentarily to the wakened intelligence but shading rapidly into the enveloping mystery of the past and present. In *The Old and the Young* there is a remarkable scene in which Francesco d'Atri, an aging minister with a distinguished, heroic past, experiences extreme detachment as he wanders from room to room late at night. He has asked to see his wife, the young and beautiful Donna Giannetta, on her return from the theater, yet he has almost forgotten why. He is about to see Giulio Auriti, and he can scarcely recall the terrible revelation he is about to make to him. He hardly recognizes the old man with the badly dyed beard he sees in the mirror, yet he knows that that is one of the Francesco d'Atris within him, one who would like to sit in a corner by the fire, who has nothing whatsoever to do with the young hero, the distinguished public man, the cuckolded husband now profoundly attached to a child that is not his, or the many others. Amid the late-night exhaustion, with the nurse weeping from her failed efforts to calm the colicky baby and Donna Giannetta dozing as her husband has his serious talk with her, what the narrator calls the "senile disarray of [d'Atri's] consciousness" becomes briefly a model of consciousness in Pirandello, more flaccid and less disciplined than Donna Giannetta's, which we see immediately afterwards and which in its youthful determination holds to a narrower idea of itself, a better-defined fiction, but which for the same reason is less authentic.

The obverse of recognizing the instability of consciousness, of course, is recognizing the absolute necessity of self-conscious pretense (*la finzione consapevole*). From the teeming possibilities within we must choose a form, or mask; we must create a self, conscious always that it is a fiction, and only one of the many that may be operative in the life of an individual at any one time. To be fully cognizant of relativity is to live with this openness, to nourish it, and to recognize further that even what seem to be the limits of consciousness at any given moment are not, that they shade into reaches of the self present and important but lost to view.

From Pirandello's earliest work, then, relativity was fundamental to his understanding of consciousness and inseparable from the process of creating "fictions of the spirit." Before the war it was an important component in his broad vision of the human condition and a primary source of the insecurity of that condition, but no more prominent than other components in that vision. During the war, as his work underwent a progressive narrowing of focus, it became a central issue that quickly came to dominate the work of the postwar years.

The war years were very difficult for Pirandello. Antonietta's condition continued to worsen; indeed he waited until 1919 to place her in a sanatorium only so that Stefano could be home to support him in that painful step. Stefano, meanwhile, was a prisoner in Austria; Fausto, the younger son, was finally released by the army to his father's care because of illness; and Lietta, the daughter, was sent to Florence to live with her Aunt Rosalina because of Antonietta's desperate sexual jealousy. During these years Pirandello continued to work at a fearsome rate, teaching at the Magistero, producing an enormous quantity of fiction—some of it his best—and at last returning to play writing.

From his earliest efforts at play writing, only *The Vise* (*La Morsa*, 1892) and *The Reason of Others* (*La Ragione degli Altri*, 1890) survive; but he had never entirely given over writing for the theater. Between 1910 and 1915 he wrote three plays, including *Sicilian Limes*, the first of the plays done by Nino Martoglio's Sicilian troupe. Martoglio, the leading figure in Sicilian theater, had been urging him since 1906 to write for him. They had collaborated on a highly successful play, *The Air of the Continent* (*L'Aria del Continente*, 1915), for which Pirandello would take no credit, and they would collaborate on others; in 1913–14 they had discussed numerous film projects. Then in 1916–17 Pirandello wrote the four Sicilian plays, *Think about It, Giacomino!* (1916), *Liolà* (1916), *Cap with Bells* (*Il Berretto a Sonagli*, 1917), and *The Jar* (*La Giara*, 1917). In all this his governing ideas were essentially what they had been in 1900. But a subtle change in manner had begun to appear: the scale on which issues like relativity were treated steadily enlarged; the highly cerebral quality with which he was soon to be, and has since been, identified, clearly emerged. As he became disenchanted with drama in Sicilian and began writing plays in Italian,[9] a new emphasis on probing analysis declared itself, most notably in *Right You Are* (1917).

But in fact an increased attention to the manifold intricacies and ironies of relativity and the extraordinary complexity of creating fictions of the spirit was already evident in the fiction of the war years. "The Dream's Reality" ("La Realtà del Sogno," 1914) explores once again the profound disparities among the many selves that lurk within, but emphasizes a kind of analysis that is new. As the young wife, raised by a savagely jealous father, tries to justify her extreme embarrassment in the presence of men other than her husband and then to defend herself from her husband's friend's charge that excessive embarrassment is usually a sign of a sensual nature, there is simply more discussion than in the earlier stories. Moreover, when the young wife, having dreamed that the friend has made love to her, tries to avoid him, faints, and then in her husband's presence throws herself at him recklessly, the event is simply thrown open to inquiry. How real was the dream? Who was at fault? What could the husband do? Which woman was she?

A still richer example of the way the commentary of, say, *The Late Mattia Pascal* yields to deliberate analysis is the 1915 novel *The Notebooks of Serafino Gubbio*. The story of Serafino, cameraman and voyeur, an intelligence so detached from the world he observes that by the end of the novel he has lost his voice and simply records, is itself a quite abstract image of modern consciousness at one extremity of its range. But the parablelike structure of the action is only part of the book's mechanism for analysis. More prominent because more consistently before us is the analytic posture of Serafino's mind as he evolves the first-person narration while committing his consciousness of events to notebooks. In the course of the book all the important characters come to him and attempt to explain themselves, and his unique position in events as camera eye gives him an especially full sense of the content of the unfolding drama. In all that he sees and hears he is particularly sensitive to the different, highly relative versions of persons and events composing the real and yet always unreal world of the Kosmograph Studio. Of the crucial Mirelli affair, for example, he assembles a collage of conflicting accounts. He had known Giorgio Mirelli and his grandmother and sister in Sorrento and had followed as closely as he was able the story of Mirelli's infatuation with Varia Nestoroff, a model who has since become an actress, and his subsequent suicide when Nestoroff took his sister's fiancé, Baron Nuti, as her lover. Along with what he imagines to have been Mirelli's version of these events, he hears a sketchy account from his Neapolitan friends and can easily imagine the version of Mirelli's grandmother and sister, reduced by the disaster to misery. All are drastically different from what he understands from Nestoroff, when they meet at the studio, to be her version.

Serafino sees Nestoroff as a bedeviled femme fatale tortured by her own wickedness, a victim of her helplessness and power. As Douglas Radcliff-Umstead observes in his shrewd study of the book, she suffers acutely from an identity crisis[10]; yet she knows what drives her and she both embraces it and recoils from it. Men are her enemies because they never see more of her than her elegant body; she moves from one love affair to the next both to avenge herself on men and to define herself as only her encounters with men can fugitively define her. She had avenged herself on Mirelli and inadvertently driven him to suicide, Serafino concludes, because he had seen her only as a painter sees figures. Yet her cruelty in that, as in other affairs, causes her to suffer, and she tries to flee the destructive amalgam of creatures she is, indeed wishes to die, oddly enough in Serafino's presence. In fact, she does die while he watches and photographs.

Baron Nuti, too, is drawn so that as much as possible of his character hovers in unresolved suspension without reducing his outline to a blur. When he comes to Serafino with yet another version of the Mirelli affair, he defends what Serafino calls his "metaphor for himself" by insisting that he had seduced Nestoroff to show Mirelli that she was unworthy to be his wife. "Who is he?" Serafino queries as he ponders this rationale:

Ah, if each of us were able to detach ourselves for a moment from that metaphor of ourselves that we are inevitably impelled to form from our innumerable conscious and unconscious pretences and the fictional interpretations of our acts and sentiments, it would be immediately clear that this *him* is *another,* another who has nothing or little to do with him, and that the true *him* is the one who is screaming within, his guilt, the intimate being often condemned for a whole life to remain unknown to us! We wish at all costs to save, to keep upright that metaphor of ourselves that is our pride and our love. And for this metaphor we suffer martyrdom.[11]

In the same way Serafino probes and dissects each of the major figures in the novel, discovering at the center of each not a core but a kind of cave of winds filled with the "discord of voices" discussed so many years before in "Art and Consciousness Today." Carlo Ferro, another actor and Nestoroff's current lover, sees Serafino's idea of "constructing oneself" as a way by which others throw up stalking horses; he sees no connection between that and his Sicilian concepts of manliness and heart. Doctor Cavalena, the scriptwriter called "Suicide" because all his scripts end in suicide, lives not only in his own fiction, but in his wife's mad fantasies of his affairs with other women. Even Luisetta Cavalena, the kind of young woman in Pirandello who is often spared his analysis, lives a romantic dream that enables her to transfer Nuti's delirious ravings for his former fiancée, Mirelli's sister, to herself and to see the broken, pathetic Baron as an object of love. The winds blow and the voices howl and, most remarkable of all, a drama transpires that seems to have coherence. But the final effect on the watching Serafino is to reduce him to silence.

The artistic step from the meditating, highly sophisticated, always compassionate narrator exemplified by Serafino, passing events through the laboratory of his mind, rendering the world as that mind experiences it, to plays like *At the Exit* (*All'Uscita,* 1916) and *Right You Are* was apparently not difficult for Pirandello. He seems to have turned from the methods of fiction to the methods of drama without more than a passing notice that his work in drama was what he then thought a brief parenthesis.[12]

But the implications for his future as he began to represent analyses in the form of characters experiencing themselves and talking about that experience were immense. *At the Exit* is the first play conceived as a parable and treated so that at least some of the characters are constantly analyzing it. The action deals with figures "at the exit" of a cemetery, figures dead but clinging to their lives through one last vanity before leaving the world. Chief among them is a philosopher who reasons about the others, examining the vanities that control them. The fat man who lingers to see his unfaithful wife killed by her lover, the lover who with the fat man's death reluctantly moved out of the shadows to become the "man," the child eating a pomegranate: they are all caught up in a world at once vaporous in its insubstantiality and volcanic. Only the philosopher does not leave it, and he suspects that he may never because his vanity of searching for coherence is a vanity without end.

The dialectical, casuistical manner in embryo in *At the Exit* emerges full-blown in *Right You Are*. Indeed, the differences between the play and the source story, "Signora Frola and Signor Ponza, Her Son-in-Law" ("La Signora Frola e il Signor Ponza, Suo Genero," 1915), reveal clearly the opportunities afforded by the dramatic form for a finely articulated, highly dynamic treatment of the relativity of selfhood. In the story the contradictions and paradoxes of the mutually exclusive accounts of why Signora Frola never sees her daughter, Signora Ponza, except from the dark courtyard below her top-floor apartment are all held in the mind of the narrator; the pathos, the ironic humor, the baffling wonder of these circumstances are communicated by his voice. In the play these circumstances are given an existence in a theatrical present with the result that Pirandello is able to reveal more of their intricacy and density as the characters themselves, more authoritatively than is possible to a narrator, declare their versions of the "reality."

It is likely that when Pirandello described this parable (a term he frequently used for the play) as a "great deviltry,"[13] he had in mind the dazzling suitability of the action for representing the ambiguity of selfhood. In the play we first hear from Signora Frola that Signor Ponza keeps his wife locked up out of morbid possessiveness; then from Signor Ponza that he does so to indulge Signora Frola's mad delusion that his second wife is actually her daughter, his first wife; and then again from Signora Frola that it is his delusion that she is mad and that her daughter is his second wife. This triple turn of the story is rendered in three successive scenes in the dizzying first act. It is at once a bewildering, comic, and painful demonstration, vibrant with the poignancy of Signora Frola, the desperate intensity of Ponza, and the humorous bafflement of the busybody neighbors. But in the second act Pirandello goes beyond the short story by representing a contrived meeting between Signora Frola and Ponza, an agonizing encounter after which Ponza claims to have feigned the madness he is accused of to humor her madness. Then in the final act a veiled Signora Ponza is herself brought in to declare that she is both the first and the second Signora Ponza. Moreover, all this is qualified by the presence of Lamberto Laudisi, a raisonneur who continually insists on the impossibility of one truth and concludes each act with the ironic laughter that is yet another and perhaps the superior response to this "great deviltry."

Altogether, *Right You Are* provides a brilliant illustration of this crucial moment in Pirandello's career, when his increased attention to relativity as a cardinal principle in consciousness and self-consciousness and his increased use of drama began to determine the direction of his work. The idea of relativity was by no means new, it bears repeating, but the deliberate, painstaking probing of it and, more important, the highly textured representation of what it means to the quality of life are new. Pirandello had long asserted the necessity of fictions in the process of self-creation, but he had not previously pondered so intently the implications of living with fictions created with a full awareness that they are fictions. Moreover, he had not achieved, either in his fiction or in his plays, the particular treatment of consciousness achieved here. Here for the first time the action articulates itself so as to mark the stage-by-stage layering of awarenesses that is the full state of consciousness induced. The innovation involved is important. As Richard Gilman has pointed out, in this play Pirandello has adopted the *pièce bien faite* so that it generates a new kind of theatrical power.[14] That power is the drama of consciousness in the process not merely of being extended but of acquiring a new way of functioning.

Pirandello's fullest treatment of relativity and the fictions of the spirit came a few years later in *Henry IV*. The action of this masterful inquiry into selfhood is designed to set forth both the intricate implications of relativity for modern consciousness and a brilliant image of the spiritual desolation brought by it. Henry is an Italian nobleman, otherwise unnamed, who had fallen from his horse and hit his head during a masquerade pageant. In the pageant he was playing the Emperor Henry IV of Germany, he who had fought with Pope Gregory VII in the eleventh century, tried to replace him with an antipope, and kneeled for forgiveness in the snow in a famous act of contrition outside a castle at Canossa, where Gregory was the guest of Henry's enemy the Marchesa Matilde of Tuscany. In hitting his head the masquerader had settled into the fixed delusion that he was the historical Henry IV.

The play begins twenty years later when Henry's nephew Carlo Di Nolli brings a doctor and certain old acquaintances to his "castle" to assist in his cure. Unknown to them, Henry had some eight years before come out of his delusion, but decided to persist in the appearance of it. Now, confronted by Donna Matilde Spina, a woman he had pursued many years before and who had played the Marchesa Matilde of Tuscany in the pageant, her lover, Belcredi, an alienist named Doctor Genoni, the nephew, and his fiancée, Donna Matilde's daughter, who seems the figure of her mother twenty years before, Henry is first inclined to play with them from the advantaged position of his persona. As he does, however, he is irritated to the point of revealing his pretence to the actors hired to support him in his madness, then made furious when the intruders shock and terrify him with ghostly images of the past. In his anger at their incomprehension and insensitivity he kills Belcredi and, to protect himself from prosecution, seals himself forever in his fiction.

Throughout, the heroic world of Henry contrasts with the pedestrian world of his visitors. From their first appearance the visitors quarrel and bicker and humiliate each other. Belcredi is coolly, sourly superior to what he calls the puerilities of putting on costumes and the unscientific science of Doctor Genoni. Donna Matilde is scathingly belittling to him: she wonders why he has come and accuses him of lacking imagination and feeling. "It's always like this," her daughter Frida complains. "For every nothing there's a discussion"; yet she too whines that everything is so strange here, and frightening. Their scenes together stress the meanness and triviality of their lives.

Yet the visitors not only sharpen a contrast between their world and the grandeur and coherence of Henry's; their mission, so to speak, supports an elaborate structure of commentary on both. The theme of identity is present from the beginning, introduced first in the interview between Henry's "councillors" and Bertoldo, the new man hired to replace a recently deceased councillor. To calm Bertoldo's anxieties because he has mistakenly prepared himself in the story of Henry IV of France, the old hands assure him that precision is hardly necessary in playing one's part: they have no fixed identity; they are names of the period; they have form but no content. The most important feature of their preparation, they point out to the visitors later, is the costumes they wear. Even Henry, indeed, dyes his hair badly and uses obvious daubs of rouge on his cheeks to emphasize the theatrical surface without which identity is always fluid and elusive. In the visitors' scenes together, moreover, the questions of who Henry was, what he was like as a young man, and who he is now, as well as who they were and are, are foremost. Donna Matilde is fascinated by the blurring of her present and past selves, the portrait of herself as a young woman in which she looks more like her daughter now than herself. Belcredi dwells upon the changes in all of them while Henry has remained fixed.

This instability of character is also notable in the ambiguity of the motives that have brought them to Henry. In some sense they have all come to save him from his madness, to assist in his cure; and at the end of act 1 and the beginning of act 2 they think they have caught him at a moment when he is ready to shake off his delusion. But some of them, especially Donna Matilde, have come to save themselves too, while still others are simply swept along by Henry's fiction, curious to see what it means to them, eager to be titillated by it.

Like the identity theme, the theme of salvation is present from the beginning. On the literal level it would seem to consist in curing Henry, in briefly entering his fictive world and leading him out. But Henry makes clear that in entering his world his visitors are merely passing from a larger world of illusion, what they consider the real world, to his smaller one, no different but clearer. Salvation, more deeply, is not just a question of Henry's sickness, but of everyone's, and not simply of leading Henry out of his nightmare, or even of leading ourselves out of ours, but of coming to terms with the larger condition of which the situation of the play is a heightened analogue.

In the play the visitors engage in the game that Henry has laid out, the same game of fictions they have always played, but now Henry's version of it. Some, like the councillors, play it for laughs and profit. Belcredi, to whom I shall return, plays it out of cynical boredom, while Donna Matilde plays it because it excites and moves her for reasons she does not understand. Some, like Di Nolli and the Doctor, play it to end it, in the firm belief that Henry is sick and that what he will be returned to is health. Then beyond all these Henry himself plays it with utter seriousness and complete self-consciousness, to fill a void, to create meanings and coherences where there are none. In act 3 Henry explains carefully why, when his mind had cleared eight years before, he had chosen to persist in his so-called madness.

I reopen my eyes bit by bit, and at first I don't know whether I'm asleep or awake. But, yes, I'm awake. I touch this and that; I turn to see clearly.... Ah!—as he says (indicating Belcredi)—away, away, with this masquerade costume! this incubus! Let's open the windows; let's breathe life! Away, away! let's run out! (suddenly arresting his outburst) Where? To do what? To have myself pointed out by everybody, on the sly, as Henry IV, no longer like this but arm in arm with you, among my dear life-long friends? . . . And look at my hair . . . I've made them gray, here, as Henry IV, do you understand? And I didn't even notice! I comprehended it in a single day, all of a sudden, reopening my eyes, and it was terrifying because I understood immediately that not only my hair, but everything had become gray like this, all in ruins, finished, and that I would arrive with the hunger of a wolf at a banquet already cleared away.[15]

Then a few moments later,

I am cured, signori, because I know perfectly that I play the madman, and I do it here, quietly. Your trouble is that you live your madness in great agitation, without understanding it or recognizing it.[16]

Cut off from his past by twelve years out of time, then, and yet settled in what his reawakening had forced him to see clearly as a fiction, he deliberately chose the fiction, what Belcredi calls his "conscious" madness. In act 2 he had explained to his councillors, who were staggered by the discovery that he was no longer mad, that to be mad is to see with a mind that disintegrates conventional structures because it constructs with an unconventional logic; in other words, to be mad is to penetrate to the inescapable relativity of all structures and values, to live with a heightened awareness of the arbitrariness of what is real and true.[17]

Yet having decided to carry on the masquerade, Henry does so with a most acute ambivalence. He wants the beauty and fixity and coherence of history, all of which he confidently recommends to his councillors in act 2; but he also rebels at the inauthenticity of his recreation. He has had enough of make-believe; it annoys him.[18] Although he can still show a gentle solicitude for his old servant and carry on, as he dictates to him at the end of act 2, almost as if performing a religious exercise, he feels a profound contempt for the deception beneath it all: it "nauseates" him.[19] This ambivalence is the key to Henry's profundity and the sine qua non of a new and distinctly modern authenticity in experience.

To a large extent the action of the play has been designed to clarify Henry, to define his hoax and to explain his relations to it. But the play does more than simply explain Henry: it also celebrates him as the tragic figure par excellence of our time, the twentieth-century scapegoat figure who sums up in himself the terrifying insecurity of self-consciously living a life based on lies, a life that he knows to be a fictional expression of the self he cannot otherwise find.

Henry is eminently suited for the role of scapegoat. Even before his accident, according to Donna Matilde and Belcredi, he had been inordinately serious and often emotionally exalted, as if in anticipation of the heroic mold he was to choose to cast himself in. At the beginning of the play's action he has been outside the normal world for twenty years and outside time and life as they are normally perceived for twelve. Moreover, he has no other name in the play: he *is* Henry IV. But more than anything else, his status as scapegoat is defined by Pirandello's choice of the role of Henry IV of Germany and the rich analogy that the historical Henry's condition offers to his own.

Critics have paid too little attention to Pirandello's choice of Henry IV of Germany. Earlier, in *The Pleasure of Honesty,* he had used the story of Saint Sigismondo to extend and sharpen his definition of Baldovino. Like Sigismondo, Baldovino had committed crimes against his family and heritage, had played the penitent, and had become a martyr and saint. In the story of the German Henry, Pirandello fixed on that period in Henry's life when his conflict with Pope Gregory VII was at its height. At that time Henry was most emphatically both the rebel defying the central figure of order in the Middle Ages and the penitent unable to live without that order. He waged war against Gregory, he conspired against him, he even tried to supplant him with another pope; and yet he also kneeled in the snow outside Canossa and begged his forgiveness. Pirandello used these traits in the historical Henry to sharpen the image of modern anxiety in his scapegoat hero. Like him, the modern Henry rebels at the structures of his world, the world of words: he knows them to be fictions, and they sicken him; yet he too cannot do without them because he also understands their value. Rebel and penitent: both the historical Henry and his modern impersonator are torn apart by these conflicting sides of their nature, tormented by essentially the same tension.

In act 1, before Henry has revealed that he is playing at his role self-consciously, he attempts in a fit of rage to throw off his hair shirt and "with an almost ferocious joy begins to tear it off."[20] Then, as his councillors intercede, he is "suddenly penitent, almost fearful," and as he allows them to put the hair shirt back on him, he says to Doctor Genoni and Donna Matilde, dressed as the Abbot of Cluny and Bertha of Susa, "Pardon . . . yes, yes . . . pardon, Monsignor; pardon, Madame . . . I feel, I swear to you, I feel the whole weight of the anathema."[21] At this point, of course, the anathema is the historical Henry's excommunication. By act 2, when we have learned that the modern Henry has self-consciously chosen the fiction, that he is a man both inside and outside his role, the anathema also becomes his monumental sense of the basic ambivalence of his condition. In the composite Henry consciousness and self-consciousness burn like a flame that on the one hand torments and on the other sustains what Pirandello felt the only mode of being available to thoughtful, twentieth-century man. Henry's grandeur and misery is that he embodies that peculiarly modern condition so completely.

Like all scapegoat figures, Henry is finally alone. He is impatient with his councillors for not having understood the game they have been playing so long with him, furious with the visitors who bend every effort to rationalize his madness but comprehend nothing of their own. Most of all he detests Belcredi, partly perhaps because of his position as Donna Matilde's lover, but chiefly because his is the least tolerable of the responses to the condition revealed. Belcredi is the mocker in the world of the play, the spoiler. His chief weapons are laughter and irony, and with them he sustains his idea of himself by ridiculing the folly of others. More clearly than any of the others, he has no particular commitment to any world. He is willing enough to play at the masquerade ("I don't mind"); then when he becomes annoyed, he indicts it as an insufferable puerility. What makes him Henry's chief antagonist is that his contempt is not just for this masquerade, but really for all masquerades, all life. His great fault, which finally intensifies Henry's anger to the point that he kills him, is that he lacks compassion. Pirandello paces Belcredi's assault on Henry in act 3 so as to strengthen by stages the probability of Henry's taking violent action against him. But the deeper reasons for the murder are thematic: Belcredi is, in fact, the villain in Henry's world, and the play must end with Henry locked into that world.

Henry IV is Pirandello's great statement about the place of relativity in the self-conscious life. He was to treat it elsewhere, and very effectively, in *The Pleasure of Honesty, The Game of Parts, Each in His Own Way,* and the novel *One, None, and a Hundred Thousand,* but he would never again develop so richly expressive a vehicle for it. At other times and in other moods he would see other alternatives for consciousness than self-creation through fictions of the spirit. Under the severest pressures of analysis even fictions consciously recognized as such became impossible, and he would feel himself driven to an extreme detachment and to alternative modes of being that I shall take up later. But consciousness as a structure composed of fictions always remained his major concern because consciousness structured in that way, he was convinced, was at the center of most lives. Even those like himself who occasionally swing to extremes of detachment and spiritual paralysis of the sort we have seen something of in Serafino Gubbio—even they, he conceded, swing back and "each reassembles his mask as best he can."[22]

6

⦿⦿⦿⦿⦿⦿⦿⦿⦿⦿⦿⦿⦿⦿⦿⦿⦿⦿⦿⦿⦿

THE THEATRICAL MATRIX
OF EXPERIENCE

PIRANDELLO'S fascination with relativity as a prime factor in the shifting configurations of experience never diminished. He continued to ponder it, testing it in one context after another, turning it like the polyhedron that had earlier served as an emblem of experience because it never revealed more than a fraction of itself at a time. His fundamental aim was always the same: to trace out its exfoliations and register its influence on the quality of contemporary life. Yet his interest in relativity, even the heightened interest that can be met during the war years and beyond, was only one of a set of interests reflected in the work of that time. The sense that experience was "in the grips of arcane forces" continued strong, though perhaps a bit less strong than earlier. Along with relativity, the idea that experience was at bottom theatrical, dominated by theatrical processes and forms, became a central preoccupation. Indeed, the plays after 1917, those often described by terms like "dialectical," "cerebral," "abstract," consist in large part of an analytical representation of the twin issues of relativity and theatricality.

We have already seen something of the theme of theatricality in *Henry IV,* in its secondary emphasis on makeup, costumes, and theatrical trappings. Pirandello's fullest and most brilliant treatment of it had appeared a year earlier in *Six Characters,* which I shall return to presently. For a more balanced treatment of theatricality and relativity, one that in full measure details their often symbiotic relations, we should first turn to the later play *Each in His Own Way.*

Although *Each in His Own Way* has always held an important place with Pirandello's critics, it has never enjoyed the success it deserves in the theater. The truth is that it is a difficult work to produce, and difficult largely because of the problems of playing one action on the stage against a second, a framing action, among the spectators in the theater. The conception is brilliant. In the stage action we meet the situation from *The Notebooks of Serafino Gubbio:* a young artist, here named Giorgio Salvi, has committed suicide after discovering on the eve of his marriage to the actress Delia Morello that she had taken his brother-in-law-to-be, Michele Rocca, as her lover. We learn of this situation because a quarrel has taken place between Doro Palegari, who had defended Delia Morello's action by claiming that Morello had seen that the marriage would be a mistake and wished to drive Salvi off, and his friend Francesco Savio, who had argued that she had done it for spite against Salvi. This quarrel with its comedy of reversed opinions provides the episodic structure for the action on stage. Pirandello's theatrical innovation here is that this stage action—the triangle of Salvi-Morello-Rocca and the quarrel about it—is duplicated in a framing, ostensibly "real" scandal involving a recent young suicide named La Vela, the actress Amelia Moreno, and Baron Nuti: in fact, the stage action is a *drame à clef* for this scandal, and the surviving "real life" figures, Moreno and Baron Nuti, are present in the audience for the presumed first night and appear in the entr'acte scenes.

The Palegari-Savio quarrel is designed to reveal a whirligig of changing opinions. It opens the play at a party at the Palegari house with a series of vignettes presenting first a "subtle young man" and an "old man" who quite simply declare the utter relativity of all judgments, then two young women whose bafflement underscores the impossibility of knowing anything for sure, even oneself, and finally Diego Cinci, who will serve as a kind of raisonneur. Cinci defines consciousness for the young men as "the others in us" and explains how it enables us to feel comfortable about our actions. After this choral preparation, the action proper begins with Donna Livia Palegari's entrance and her discussion with Cinci and the others of the previous night's quarrel between her son Doro and Savio. She fears the duel that must follow, and perhaps even more the possibility that her son had defended Delia Morello because he too is in love with her. Diego Cinci objects, insisting on a human complexity that Donna Livia would reduce to simplistic moral categories. He claims, as Doro had, that Delia Morello can be legitimately defended and even admired; and he supports this claim by arguing the ambiguity of all human motives. In the normal course of things, he insists, human beings have the greatest difficulty sustaining a clear and consistent character.

But no sooner has this support for Doro's position been advanced than Doro himself comes in and announces that he has changed his mind and now holds Savio's view, to be joined instants later by Savio who announces the contrary, that he now believes as Doro had. Like Bergson's jack-in-the-boxes, Doro and Savio quickly quarrel again, prompting yet another duel. Then, as soon as these new positions have been taken, Delia Morello arrives to thank Doro for his earlier defense of her, and flattered and moved, Doro acquiesces once again in the role of defender. But as he reveals to her the nature of Savio's attack on her—that she had wished to dominate Salvi and, especially, that she had wished to drive him to despair for not presenting her to his mother and sister—she is so profoundly shaken that she admits that even she is unsure of why she has done what she has done. With this further reversal the ground seems cut from beneath all opinions, and the act ends.

Immediately follows the first choral intermezzo, which takes place in the theater's corridors. In his directions for this episode Pirandello speaks of "distancing" and "driving" the public that has just witnessed the "first plane" of the work in the stage action to a second plane and ultimately to a third. The second consists of the diffused and in part improvised discussion of the first act by critics and spectators. The third emerges when these spectators learn that the stage action is a *drame à clef*. In fact, Pirandello had already initiated these discriminations in the introduction that precedes the opening act, where he had suggested that the performance begin in the street in front of the theater. Newsboys could sell specially printed newspapers announcing the opening of a new Pirandello play dealing with the famous scandal involving the deceased sculptor La Vela, Amelia Moreno, and Baron Nuti, and then Moreno and Nuti could themselves make brief, frenzied appearances. The spirit of all these directions is suggestive, leaving a considerable margin to producers, but by the end of the intermezzo the three planes are clearly in place, separate yet intricately related.

Act 2 takes place in Francesco Savio's house, where he is preparing for the duel, which by now nonplusses everyone. Savio's friend and second, Prestino, maintains some coherence by holding stubbornly to the crude forms of the duel's ritual. But Diego Cinci plunges matters into deeper obscurity by dilating further on the vagaries of experience and the fluidity of character. He admits that he admires Delia Morello for having confessed to her confusion: in acknowledging that she may have acted out of spite and vindictiveness, she had brought on the complete collapse of the superior person she had thought herself. Cinci himself had offered a stunning example of character in such disarray in his act 1 recollection of the night his mother had died, when exhausted by nine nights without sleep, he had been distracted by a fly drowning in a glass of water and had not noticed his mother's passing.

As raisonneur, indeed, Cinci's chief function is to relate the abundant evidence of relativity in the characters' opinions and attitudes to the deeper difficulty of maintaining personal definition. When Prestino protests that understanding that difficulty should call forth compassion and not laughter, Cinci agrees and points out that compassion is especially appropriate when the persona defined in externals does not completely obscure the interior self straining for definition. "Yes—if you look like this . . . within your eyes, like this!—no—look at me—like this—naked as you are, with all the miseries and uglinesses that you have within—you like me—the fears, remorses, contradictions!" The imperative, he goes on, is to be conscious of both your interior and exterior selves, and of their interplay. "Detach from yourself the little clown that you fabricate with your fictitious interpretations of your acts and feelings and you will see suddenly that it has nothing to do with what you are or could be truly, with what is within you and you are aware of, what is a terrible god if you oppose it."[1] Too often we resist that imperative and submit to the exterior, theatrical persona out of some sense that we are responsible to it; we resist departing from it as if that were a profound disloyalty. But the created exterior persona is only a *pulcinella* or *pagliaccetto,* a form devised to confer definition. In the world of roles and choices, of work, love affairs, and families, these elements of action supply theatrical materials at one and the same time imperfectly expressing interior life and indispensable to that expression. (Both the repeated use of the word *pagliaccetto* and the commentary itself recall the moment in 1934 when Pirandello was informed of the Nobel Prize and asked by photographers to pose for a considerable time at his typewriter. During this staged scene he had typed again and again the word *pagliaccetta* ("clown show"), filling a page with it.[2])

The most stunning support for Diego Cinci's commentary within *Each in His Own Way* comes in the second choral intermezzo. Shortly after Cinci delivers the passage cited above in act 2, Delia Morello arrives and talks to Savio in another room, while Michele Rocca presents his defense of himself to Cinci and Prestino. When Morello returns and she and Rocca face each other, yet another facet of this affair reveals itself as they acknowledge a still deeper truth than any so far advanced: that they were originally and still are powerfully, obsessively, attracted to each other. It is an explosive moment: earlier versions of what had happened fade, prior conceptions of character collapse, and submerged selves surface to take charge as Delia Morello and Michele Rocca go off together. Then in the second intermezzo, which follows immediately, all the demonstrated relativity and ambiguity of this plane is yoked to the "real" world of Amelia Moreno and Baron Nuti as they go up on the stage, quarrel with the actors and theater officials, then duplicate the discovery of the stage action by admitting their profound attraction for each other and going off together. In repeating almost verbatim the scene from the stage action, the scene creates a dazzling moment. As soon as Baron Nuti joins Moreno on stage, he calls out, as Michele Rocca had, "Amelia, Amelia. . . ."

> *A general commotion among the spectators, who can hardly believe their eyes in finding before them, alive, the same characters and the same scene witnessed at the end of the second act; they convey their emotion by, other than their facial expressions, brief, subdued comments and exclamations.*

Spectators' voices. —Oh look!—There they are!—Oh! Oh!—Both of them! They're replaying the scene!—Look! Look!

La Moreno. (*To her companions. Frenzied.*) Take him away! Take him away!

The Companions. Yes, let's go! Let's go!

Baron Nuti. (*Taking hold of her.*) No, no! You must come with me!

La Moreno. (*Freeing herself.*) No! Let me be! Let me be! Murderer!

Baron Nuti. Don't repeat what they made you say!

La Moreno. Let me be! I'm not afraid of you!

Baron Nuti. But it's true, it's true that we must punish each other! Didn't you hear? By now everyone knows! Come away! Come!

La Moreno. No, let me be! You're cursed! I hate you!

Baron Nuti. We've drowned, truly drowned in the same blood! Come! Come!

> *He drags her off left, followed by a great many spectators and noisy comments:* —"Oh oh!—It can't be!—It's incredible! Terrifying! —Look at them there!—Delia Morello and Michele Rocca!" *A good many other spectators remain in the corridor, following them with their eyes and making roughly the same comments.*

A Foolish Spectator. To think that they objected! Objected—and then they did the same thing as in the play!

The Capocomico. Exactly! And the leading lady had the nerve to assault me on the stage! . . .

Many Spectators. It's incredible! It's incredible!

An Intelligent Spectator. But no, gentlemen: it's entirely natural! They saw themselves as if in a mirror and they rebelled, especially at their last action.

The Capocomico. But they've repeated precisely that action!

The Intelligent Spectator. Exactly. And that's entirely right! They were forced to do, here in our sight, involuntarily, what art had anticipated.[3]

The passage demonstrates that the inchoate emotions of the "real" characters have been clarified for them by the theatrical figures, that the "real" persons find purpose and a cue for action when prompted by theatrical models. In the scene, of course, the theatrical structures imitated are literal theatrical structures, while the play as an imaginative totality proposes a metaphorical relation between subjective life and the "theatrical" forms of action that help it to definition. But the dependence of the one on the other is clear, and the need to recognize that dependence is crucial to the conscious life. Like the spectators in the play, we are forced to see that we define what we are only as we theatricalize; we impose an invented coherence on the welter of subjective life only as we behave like characters in a play.

Moreover, the story does not end there, with the achievement of a fugitive coherence through theatrical forms: there is presumably a third act in the stage action that we have not seen and that contains all that happens to Delia Morello and Michele Rocca afterward. When the actor who plays Diego Cinci is asked what the third act contains, he answers, "Things, things, *signori....* And afterward ... —after the third act ... things! things!"[4] *Each in His Own Way* ends with the announcement that it will not proceed into the further mystery of these "things"; that is, it ends with an entirely just and appropriate state of irresolution.

Of Pirandello's works after the war and in the 1920s *Each in His Own Way* is perhaps best illustrative of the way the focus of his vision had changed. Essentially it was the same vision of his earliest letters, of people lost in darkness, creating their worlds and themselves from the shadows thrown by the flickering light of consciousness. But by this time it had become a more selective and more concentrated vision of that condition, altogether a narrower gauged articulation of it. Like relativity, theatricality was by no means a new interest for Pirandello; we meet a shrewd analysis of its relevance to self-creation as early as "Dishonesty of Feeling in Art" (1890). But, like relativity, it became increasingly central to the analytic probing of these years, not simply as an idea but as a prime determinant of the quality of experience.

Pirandello's intensified interest in relativity and theatricality accounts, in part at least, for his new attention to drama. As critics never tire of pointing out, the affinities between his vision and dramatic form are obvious.[5] Yet even as he searched the many ways theatrical structures serve self-creation, he also continued to be fascinated by the surfaces of life as it is lived. Characters speaking for themselves and colliding with ideas and values different from their own inevitably declare the relativity of what they are, while characters playing at social games and shaping their experience in terms of rituals and traditional forms inescapably reenact the theatrical basis of experience. In his essay of 1935 arguing the preeminence of Italian theater Pirandello could speak of theater as a "form of life itself," "a true and proper 'act of life.' "[6] At all stages of his career he professed that self-creation was essentially a continuous making and unmaking, a movement toward form, but above all always a movement.

Altogether, then, the shifts in emphasis and the concentration on drama to be seen in this period were perfectly consistent with what had gone before; yet they also made for important differences. The rigorously analytic manner of these plays opens up the issues of relativity and theatricality in a new fullness of detail. As I have already suggested, this new manner can in part be traced to Pirandello's personal life during the war: to judge from his letters to Stefano, his desperate problems with his children and Antonietta apparently drove him to a greater inwardness and a closer study of subjective processes. At the same time he continued to read and study and talk, and continued to develop as a result of books read, of ideas and arguments absorbed, and of his reflections on all these. We have, of course, only fragments of the content and glimpses of the process of this development, but it will be useful to dwell briefly on what we have for any light it can shed on Pirandello's perception of theatricality.

Of all the intellectual experiences that influenced Pirandello during these years probably the most important was his encounter with Adriano Tilgher. Scholar, expositor of contemporary culture, drama critic, Tilgher was Pirandello's first important interpreter and continues to be his most influential. In even his first reviews of Pirandello's plays, of *Think about It, Giacomino!* in 1916 and *The Graft* (*L'Innesto*) in 1919, he saw with great clarity that the locus of the plays was the consciousness; in his first summary consideration of Pirandello in "Theater of Mirrors" ("Teatro dello Specchio," 1920) he explained as no one had before the tensions and convolutions of "watching oneself live." But for all his enthusiasm Tilgher had trouble initially with the plays themselves, even through *Six Characters* in 1921, because they seemed to him never to lead to solutions or resolutions. To use Elder Olson's terms, Pirandello's actions were neither "causative," that is, designed to set forth a series of episodes linked by cause and effect and to take the characters to the end of something, nor "didactic" in that they traced out arguments, but "descriptive" in the sense that they set forth and defined a condition.[7] Not until Tilgher's review of *Henry IV* in 1922 did he sufficiently appreciate this purpose to articulate for the first time the famous life-form formula, and by then he and Pirandello were fast friends. By 1921 Pirandello was admitting in a letter that he was "very grateful" to Tilgher and that *One, None, and a Hundred Thousand* contained a "great many of the things [he] had read recently in [Tilgher's essays]";[8] Tilgher was calling Pirandello the visionary artist of their generation.[9] They even collaborated on a play, *Diana and Tuda,* though by the time it was published in 1926 they had grown apart, and when it was produced in 1927 Tilgher attacked it. This estrangement harked back to 1924 and Pirandello's movement toward fascism. In 1925 Tilgher joined Giovanni Amendola on the Roman daily *Il Mondo,* where he took a stand against fascism. At about this time he apparently came to believe that he had largely created the mature Pirandello. Certainly by 1927 Pirandello was twitting Silvio D'Amico in a letter for seeming to accept Tilgher's claims about his crucial influence and pointing out that the ideas at issue had been clear in his stories and novels many years before he had known Tilgher.[10] As late as 1940, a year before his death, Tilgher was saying that "it would have been much better for Pirandello if he had never read [my essay]. It is never especially good for an author to acquire too clear a consciousness of his inner world. . . . My essay fixed Pirandello's inner world in terms so clear and . . . well defined that Pirandello must feel himself imprisoned within them."[11]

Whatever the final truth in this matter, it is reasonably clear that the claims on each side had some foundation. Before Tilgher Pirandello had many times given imaginative expression to the ideas that Tilgher saw as the cornerstones of his work; indeed Tilgher admitted as much when he alluded to the "inner world" that presumably preceded their encounter and used earlier stories to document his exposition of Pirandello's ideas. At the same time it is true that during these years Pirandello undertook an unprecedented analysis of relativity and theatricality and their place in the processes of consciousness and experience, an analysis that appears to have been crucially sharpened by Tilgher's exegesis.

The life-form formula was central. Having first appeared in Tilgher's review of *Henry IV* on 20 October 1922, it received its first full-scale examination in his chapter on Pirandello in *Studi del Teatro Contemporaneo* (1923). There he explained the "fundamental dualism" as follows:

On one side there is the flux of life, blind, mute, obscure, eternally unstable and restless. . . . On the other there is a world of crystallized forms, a system of constructions that attempt to channel and embrace the rumbling flux within itself. . . .

Most men live sunk in fixed and immobile forms not even distantly suspecting that beneath them a dark and raging ocean churns and boils. But in some few . . . thought separates itself from the forms in which the warm flux has coagulated and sees them for what they really are, that is, constructions entirely provisional, ephemeral, contingent, fleeting, fragile, beneath which the stream of life as it is in itself purls and bellows, beyond all human illusion and construction.[12]

The main problem is to determine to what extent this and other expositions of the idea influenced Pirandello. Here, by citing such earlier stories as "The Trap" (1915) and "Candelora" (1917), Tilgher seems to concede that the formula had some kind of prior existence in Pirandello, though later he would claim that the formula was substantially his and that he had merely taken a few suggestions from Pirandello.[13] Even when his claims were most extravagant, however, it is difficult to deny his claim that Pirandello repeatedly explained his work with reference to the formula, and always with terms very like Tilgher's. Accordingly, it is difficult not to conclude that Tilgher affected him. And even if he was affected only to the extent of being prompted to greater clarity, that greater clarity might account in some large measure for his intensified interest in theatricality.

Certainly the life-form formula is quintessentially theatrical. Flux, tension, change: these are the conditions of life, or as Pirandello put it more precisely in the letter to Silvio D'Amico, of the movement that is in eternal conflict with form within life.[14] Forms are what we need to bring clarity and a semblance of stability to the welter of experience. They are the roles we play and the masks we assume and then put aside; they are the social games of courtship and marriage and duty that bring meaning to the enveloping mystery. The struggle between form and movement is at the heart of the idea that experience is fundamentally theatrical. All this is obviously important in Pirandello, and some of it probably owes something to Tilgher. The great problem with Tilgher is that he equated the famous formula and its implications for conscious life with the whole of Pirandello. When in *La Scena e la Vita* (1925) he said that Pirandello had only one string to his bow, he was quite simply wrong.[15]

Moreover, Tilgher's importance, however great, should not obscure that during this period Pirandello was also influenced by others. He was much attracted, for example, by the pantheatricalism of Nikolai Evreinov, who believed that life for all living things was a kind of continuous theatricalization. Pirandello produced two of Evreinov's plays in the Arts Theater, which he and ten of his friends organized with state support in 1925, and in 1929 he referred to his "friend Evreinov's" book to support his argument that theater "before being a traditional form of literature [was] a natural expression of life."[16] Antonio Gramsci discussed this influence as early as his *Quaderni dal Carcere* (*Prison Notebooks,* 1926–37).

In addition, Pirandello was clearly sensitive to the innovative and experimental work going on around him. Through friends like Anton Giulio Bragaglia, on whose periodical *Cronache d'Attualità* he collaborated, he came to know the work of Giorgio De Chirico and the futurist painters and met F. T. Marinetti and his avant-garde colleagues. Although he never wrote any of the "theatrical syntheses" characteristic of futuristic experimentation in the theater, he did write the scenario for a ballet entitled *La Salamandra* (Massimo Bontempelli wrote the music) for the Futurist Pantomime Theater in 1928. Moreover, his close friendship with Bontempelli, Rosso di San Secondo, and others drew him near to the center of the activity often described as the Theater of the Grotesque. He produced their work in the Arts Theater, and he wrote an important review of Rosso di San Secondo's *Marionette, Che Passione!* (1918). As Gaspare Giudice has shrewdly observed, even where it is not possible to trace a clear influence from this work, it is possible to see that the example that these young men offered Pirandello probably prompted him to innovations he would otherwise not have tried.[17]

Still more elusive was the influence of various actors on him. Pirandello made no secret of the fact that a good many of his most important characters were designed to the models of Ruggero Ruggeri, Paola Borboni, and Marta Abba. Indeed, he said again and again that his usual procedure in constructing plays was to follow the imperatives of character.[18] The paradox in this is unavoidable. Despite his profound convictions about the instability of character, he nonetheless began with it, inventing his actions to reveal it and, when these actions were dramatic actions, often conditioning the whole process by having a specific actor or actress in mind. Hence Henry IV, Leone Gala, Angelo Baldovino, and the Father in *Six Characters* owe a great deal to what Pirandello perceived as the expressive capability of Ruggeri; and in the same way all the tormented young women of the later plays owe much to Marta Abba.

Altogether, Pirandello's conception of character and its relations to action, and in drama, the relations of both character and action to the actor who gives them expression, provides yet another way to understand theatricality in his thought and work. In the story "The Tragedy of a Character" ("La Tragedia d'un Personaggio," 1910) he suggests his practice as a writer of fiction by treating fancifully the process by which he selects characters for stories from the crowds that present themselves during his regular office hours for them on Sunday mornings from 8:00 to 1:00. The way the characters materialize may owe something to the occultism of which he was knowledgeable, though it is doubtful that the debt went beyond a debt in metaphor. What is important is that to begin with there are only the characters, like the Doctor Fileno who beseeches the author to save him from the unsuitable novel in which the author had met him; when the author has accepted one, he next invents the action that gives the character life. As a playwright Pirandello's practice was much the same, except for the presence of the actor, who also conditioned the action as it was invented.

But perhaps Pirandello's practice as a director enables us to see most clearly how character functions as the epicenter, so to speak, of the action. From what we know of Pirandello as a director, he apparently gave virtually all his attention to the actors, and his basic advice to them was that they "sink into [their] characters" (*calarsi in un personaggio*), enter the characters so completely that the characters become the artistic rationale for everything done. Although the characters might be unstable and ambiguous—the likelihood in Pirandello was that any character would be—the actors should dispose themselves to possess that particular instability and ambiguity. They should avoid any dependence on the prompter (Pirandello finally banished prompters from his theater); they should make the characters laws unto themselves and in this way the laws of the action. As a director and playwright, finally, Pirandello saw action as the medium that gave character expression: the one could not be effectively separated from the other. But character was first, even if it lived only in its theatricalization.[19] In his "Loose Sheets" ("Foglietti") he said, "It's necessary that being take place, that it create for itself its appearance—the world."[20] The passage, as Claudio Vicentini has pointed out, seems a borrowing from Bernardino Varisco, a writer he used elsewhere: "Being only realizes itself in determining itself. It only exists as form of happening."[21] Hence actors must begin with character to give their impersonations integrity, but they must always see impersonation as a happening, in terms of its details: suitable readings, appropriate tone and gesture, congruence of energy. Although characters have existence prior to their plays, they have life only in the images that a Ruggeri or a Marta Abba gives them.

Pirandello's quite sudden concentration on writing plays, therefore, was entirely consonant with his intensified interest in theatricality. Life *is* theater. Just as characters live only in the theatrical form the actors give them, so we live only in the roles we play. In a rare moment Pirandello was personal about all this in the advice to his daughter alluded to earlier: "Seek and find a certainty in yourself, my Lietta, and clutch it so that it does not get away. You will not be able to find it if you don't create it for yourself. Accordingly, search for nothing that does not come from you. A sense of yourself, of your life; let it be a sense of something through which you can give yourself substance, certainty."[22] The advice is a simplified version of what we find in the plays, and its emphasis is uncharacteristically on "certainty"; but essentially the burden is the same. Life is a perpetual movement between the shapes of consciousness and the forms that give these shapes meaningful definition.

But life was still more than that for Pirandello: it was that movement as it is observed by consciousness, held in the gaze of its self-seeing eyes and as far as possible controlled. Experience is a continuous process of self-creation accompanied at all points by the fullest awareness that the process itself is essentially theatrical. We think, therefore we act, therefore we are. And the quality of our experience is mediated by the richness of the consciousness that produces it.

Perhaps the fullest, most intricately analytic study of self-creation is the late play *To Find Oneself* (1932). Its external action is extremely simple. Donata Genzi, a famous actress, has come to the seaside villa of a childhood friend for a month of much needed rest, and there she meets, among others, Elj Nielsen, a young painter. One day on a rash impulse she and Elj go out on Elj's yacht in a heavy sea; they are wrecked, and Elj barely manages to preserve them until they are picked up. Returned to shore, they go at Elj's insistence to his beach house where, isolated for twenty days as Donata recovers, they fall in love. They agree to marry, but they differ over what Donata should do about her career and immediate commitments. At last Donata decides to return to the theater, provisionally, so that Elj can have an opportunity to understand her better. Then during the first night of her return Elj leaves before the end of the second act, repulsed by her exposure of herself before others. He goes back to the beach house and the sea. She, perceiving the enormous distance between them, decides to give him up and accepts with greater understanding the life that the theater offers her.

The focus of these events is on the exposition that they make possible of Donata's self-conscious self-creation. Donata is initially drawn to Elj because she feels she has no self: she is an actress and not a woman, a vessel for

many others but no one in her own right. Moreover, she is her impersonations with complete self-consciousness; that she never loses herself in her
roles is affirmed by the fact that she never closes her eyes, even when she is
kissed on stage. Elj, by contrast, is as unself-conscious as Pirandello can
make him. He despises the stage, society, and sport, anything that involves
conventions and roles; he loves the open sea and living on impulse. What
Donata comes to understand is that she does not wish to lose herself in a
wholly instinctive, unself-conscious self. To do so is to surrender what
little freedom one has to the tyranny of others and conditions. She comes
to recognize that the personal uncertainty and unfixedness that she had
always felt as an actress while playing at being someone else are, after all,
natural.

> Thus this bafflement of mine is natural: this anxiety. . . . There isn't,
> truly, there can't be any certainty. . . . The will, yes, the will to make
> a life, the need to give it substance in some way, as best as possi-
> ble . . . ah, yes, as best as possible. Because it doesn't depend on us
> alone: there are the others—circumstances, conditions, those who
> are closest to us and can oppose and obstruct us; you're no longer
> alone at the center of all this uncreated that wishes to create itself and
> does not succeed: you're no longer free! And so . . . the place where
> life is created with freedom is, instead, the theater.[23]

Hence she chooses the self-conscious self-creation of the theater, living
with her eyes open. It is never perfect, never complete, but it is less
fragmentary, less vague and indeterminate than permitting others to define
you. Elj and the alternative of "spontaneous movement" that he represents
are unsatisfactory.

To Find Oneself concludes with a scene-within-a-scene that serves as an
emblem of experience as theater. As Donata meditates on the events of the
evening and removes her stage makeup before a large mirror, she is drawn
once again into the scene in which, after playing badly for two acts, she
had rediscovered herself as an actress. For two acts, in Elj's presence, she
had "seen into the abyss," that is, she had played her character with so
acute a sense of its arbitrariness that she had been unable to commit herself
to it. Then she had caught fire and "everything [had become] clear, . . .
secure, secure . . . life, but so full, so full, and so easy."[24] With this recognition the other actors materialize, and she begins playing again the scene
in which she affirmed in the play that she was loved. Supported by the
actor-phantasms, she admits that now, acquiescing in theatrical convention,
everything is possible, that she is capable of everything. More specifically,

in this moment and with the freedom available only to those who live self-consciously, she is choosing love. All this, moreover, with the awareness that "this is true . . . and nothing is true. The only truth is that we must create ourselves, create. Only in this way do we find ourselves."[25]

Unlike the best of Pirandello's plays, *To Find Oneself* is a didactic structure designed for the most part to execute an elaborate commentary on Donata's self-consciousness. The play's excitement comes largely from this exposition, and except for the final scene-within-a-scene, it rarely embodies the full tension of theatricality as a lived dimension of consciousness. In the scene-within-a-scene, by contrast, Pirandello represents the symbiosis between theatrical means and consciousness with a stunning sense of immediacy. As Donata finds love through a theatricalization of it, by turns she engages in and withdraws from the theatricalization much as the consciousness rides with and withdraws from itself in self-consciousness. As that happens, the actor-phantasms, the mirror, and the enactment that is at one and the same time interior and exterior fuse brilliantly in an image of consciousness as it creates. Although brief, the scene is a superb example of Pirandello's sure authority with nonrealistic resources.

The striking fact is that he turned to such resources so rarely. In a career as a playwright that resulted in thirty-one full-length plays, eleven short ones, and one long fragment, Pirandello departed from theatrical realism only in the two short plays *At the Exit* and *I'm Dreaming (But Maybe Not)* (*Sogno* [*ma Forse No*], 1929), in the dramatic fragment *The Mountain Giants* (*I Giganti della Montagna*, 1934), in the scene-within-a-scene in *To Find Oneself*, and in the three so-called theater plays, *Six Characters, Each in His Own Way,* and *Tonight We Improvise.*[26] Taken together, this work hardly supports the claims that theater historians have been making since, that in his nonrealistic work Pirandello broke new and important dramaturgical ground for the subsequent drama. *At the Exit* is little more than a fablelike fantasy, while *The Mountain Giants* is an allegory, inconclusive because incomplete; both plays are cast in nonrealistic veins well worked by Pirandello's day. In fact, only the theater plays, the scene from *To Find Oneself*, and perhaps *I'm Dreaming (But Maybe No)* attempt a nonrealistic dramatization of consciousness.

By the 1920s, of course, the decade of these efforts, the theatrical world had seen many nonrealistic experiments in subjective drama, some of them highly successful and influential. But no one—not the expressionists, or the surrealists, or in Italy, the futurists—had undertaken anything so intricate and carefully integrated as Pirandello was to try. The fact is that what Pirandello did was neither extravagant nor remarkably different from the experiments of his nonrealistic colleagues. It was simply better. Some part of that superiority can doubtless be credited to Pirandello's rich invention and literary tact, but part of it traces to his deliberateness of purpose, a deliberateness produced by decades of study and thought. By the period of these plays Pirandello's understanding of consciousness was settled: his conception of it may still have left a great deal of room for the unknown and arcane, but it was complete and coherent. From that coherence came the superior integrity and greater authority of these plays. In them for the first time consciousness is seen not as a kind of railroad switching yard with random impulses and loosely related impressions coming through like trains run amuck, but as a kind of desperate human engine operating under great pressure; it functions according to laws and within the limitations imposed by these laws, and it has definable if elusive purposes. Of course the supreme example of this work is *Six Characters*.

Six Characters has proved difficult for readers and critics largely because it resists what *To Find Oneself* lends itself to readily, a relatively easy translation into ideas. Despite its look of allegory or parable, it is in fact neither. On the contrary, it can best be described, perhaps, as a surrealistic expression of a tension, but of a tension experienced so that the details of its articulation are far more prominent than any of the ideas implicit in it. This is the tension we meet in Pirandello's first reference to the subject when in a letter to Stefano he speaks of six characters who pursue him, show him their wounds, and insist that he write a novel about them, while he chases them away.[27] Tilgher also appears to have identified it in his account of the play's debt to futurism: "*Six Characters* . . . is the strongest attempt made . . . to realize scenically an entirely inward state of spirit, to discompose and project on the stage the planes and various phases of a continuously flowing process of consciousness, according to a method similar to that by which the futurist painters discompose light and planes."[28] Unfortunately, Tilgher then found that purpose wanting because it did not provide a resolution by moving to what he called "universal values."[29] Actually, Pirandello is perfectly explicit about the nature of this dramatic action and is himself the most helpful commentator on its density.

It is strange that so few critics have taken notice of his remarks in the essay written in 1925, "How and Why I Wrote *Six Characters in Search of an Author*" ("Come e Perché Ho Scritto *Sei Personaggi in Cerca d'Autore*"). His explanation is not simple, but it goes straight to the heart of the matter by establishing that the play is about characters in search of but not finding an author and accordingly not finding the life-as-form an author could give them; it is about, in other words, impulses to life refused. "I wanted to show six characters in search of an author. The drama does not succeed in being represented precisely because the author they are searching for is lacking; instead, what is represented is the play of their vain attempt, with all that it has about it of the tragic because these six characters have been refused."[30] A little further along he describes the action of the play as "the drama of being in search of an author, [of being] refused."[31]

Now a great deal of the confusion about the play traces to a failure to understand this as a purpose to create a dramatic tension and not to mount an argument. Pirandello's explanation, for example, that he had originally rejected the characters because he could not find their "particular sense of life" or "universal value" has misled some critics into concluding that he was mainly interested in the process of artistic creation. But to settle for that is to ignore that ultimately he did find a "particular sense of life" and "universal value" in the circumstance of characters searching and being refused. He even goes so far as to describe the activity of searching while being refused as tragic, and as we shall see, he used this term to characterize the painful necessity of struggling between the extremes of movement and form. In the essay he reverts to his usual account of how the "life germs" or "vital germs" become characters who then need the "form" of a dramatic action to live, who need, in other words, to be theatricalized. As he put it as early as 1921 in a letter to Tilgher, the life of the six characters is "infused but not yet expressed, not yet 'constructed.'"[32] He accepts them for this play only when he sees that their universal value here consists in the act of their searching for an author who will put them in a play and thus enable them to live and in their not finding this "coordinating spirit." To put this another way, Pirandello has here described an action that while containing a great many of the issues that have long interested him, positions its characters between being, with its impulses to live in a form, and form itself; he has created an image of life as a play that never quite gets put on. It does not matter that it is a painful play: it *is* the play of these characters.

To begin with, it is very important that the characters have come not to narrate—they, and especially the Father, are contemptuous of mere words—but to play out their story, to reify their lives in the only way available to them or to any of us, as action. They are different from the members of the theater company because they are narrowly held to the limited series of events that the playwright had devised for them before abandoning them. Unlike the actors, who, as the Father explains in act 3, can change and for whom even the events of their lives can change as these events are forgotten or seen with different eyes,[33] the characters cannot change. The Father is particularly sensitive on this point because he wishes desperately to free himself from the definition that the Step-Daughter and the given events of their story impose on him, an unjust definition, he insists, which leaves him "suspended," "in pillory." But all the characters are similarly fixed, and Pirandello underscores this fixedness in the stage direction amplified in the version of 1925 to include the suggestion that the characters wear light masks.

> *This will reinforce the deep meaning of the play. The* characters *should not appear like* phantasms, *in fact, but like* created realities, *unchanging constructions of the imagination, and therefore more real and consistent than the inconstant naturalness of the actors. The masks will help give the impression of faces devised by art and fixed immutably in the fundamental emotional expression suitable to each character, such as* remorse *for the* Father, vengeance *for the Step-Daughter,* disdain *for the Son,* suffering *for the Mother (she with fixed wax tears in the ashen paleness of her eyes and along her cheeks such as one sees on the painted statues of the* Mater Dolorosa *in churches.*[34]

The characters are to be understood, therefore, as different from human beings because fixed, but cognate creations in that like humans they hover between the impulse to have form and theatrical form itself.

Six Characters is about living in this state of suspended animation. Its power and excitement trace primarily to the image of the characters searching, struggling, held in a kind of dynamic incompleteness. That is not to say, of course, that their encounter with the actors does not occasion a good deal of commentary: it does. But the comments on words and the multiplicity of selves and the eternal struggle between movement and form and the elusiveness of truth and reality serve rather to focus and deepen the central image than to define it. That image is essentially defined by the characters' encounter with the actors and their attempts and failure to find in the Manager the "coordinating spirit" who will give them life in a theatricalization of their story.

The series of disclosures in act 1, after the Father's first line, "We are here in search of an author," traces a dizzying descent first into a sphere of incomplete realization and then into a volcanic domestic situation. As the Father and the Step-Daughter rapidly piece together the past that has led to their present anguish, they show themselves to be under tremendous pressure to live their drama. The Father, while recognizing the multiple selves that huddle within him, wishes to actualize through living it a more adequate version of his moral nature than his Step-Daughter's idea of him and the events of their story allow. The Step-Daughter, meanwhile, bursts with eagerness to play the meeting with the Father at Madame Pace's so as to live the full dimensions of her nausea: "I'm dying, I tell you, of the mania to live it, to see it, this scene."[35] These imperatives invest these two characters with a conspicuous intensity. But even the Mother and Son, though far more passive, are capable of great intensity when aroused.

Throughout the play this intensity contrasts sharply with the hazy flaccidity of the actors. In a letter to Ruggeri in 1936 concerning a projected production of the play, Pirandello reiterated the emphasis of his additions to the version of 1925: "It will be necessary to avoid the error that has always been committed of making the characters appear like shadows or phantasms instead of as superior and more potent beings because 'created realities,' forms of art fixed forever, immutable, almost statues in contrast with the mobile naturalness, changeable and almost fluid, of the actors."[36] And within the play the characters themselves recoil from the disparity between their sense of themselves and the theatricalized versions of them proposed by the actors. Even as the Manager assigns the roles, the Father perceives the falsity: "I no longer know what to say to you. . . . I already begin . . . I don't know, to hear as false, as if they were other sounds, my own words."[37] The Step-Daughter laughs outright at the actors' impersonations. Throughout the play the characters keep screaming for truth—"The truth! The truth, *signore!*"—while the Manager keeps reminding them that the theater can produce only a limited truth. A great deal of the represented action of the play consists of this struggle: the characters on the one hand demanding to live completely, the actors on the other almost foppishly acquiescent in compromise. Moreover, the energy generated by that opposition is experienced directly by us, mediated, as Gino Rizzo has shrewdly argued, by no interpreting voice.[38] The tension produced by the characters' failure to achieve some kind of rapprochement with the actors is at the heart of the play's power.

That Pirandello's conception stressed the concreteness of this action, of the characters "in search of an author" and "refused," is supported by his revisions of the play. Despite such passages of Tilgherian analysis as that in "How and Why I Wrote *Six Characters in Search of an Author*," in which he expounds on the "immanent conflict with vital movement and form" and numerous passages of commentary within the play itself, the changes to be found in the definitive version of 1925 all serve to solidify the surface of the action. Long speeches are broken up or eliminated; stage directions are amplified; awkward choral speeches like the Step-Daughter's speech on the theater at the beginning of act 2 in the first version are set into the action less conspicuously; important moments like the concluding image of the Manager leaving the theater are opened up. In the first version of the conclusion the Manager, left on stage as the others carry off the dead child, simply screams in exasperation that he has lost a whole day. In the final version once he is alone he instructs the electrician to turn out the lights and then complains when they go out that he might at least leave him enough to see by.

> Suddenly, behind the rear curtain . . . a green reflector is lit, which will project, large and clearly outlined, the shadows of the characters minus the Boy and the Little Girl. The Manager, seeing them, will scurry off stage, terrified. At that instant, the reflector behind the rear curtain will go off and on the stage the blue night light seen before will come on. Slowly from the right side of the curtain will come first the Son, followed by the Mother with her arms extended toward him. Then from the left side the Father. They will stop half way onto the stage, remaining there like bemused forms. Lastly, the Step-Daughter will come forth from the left, and she will run toward one of the stage stairs. On the first step she will stop to look at the other three for a moment and then will break into a coarse laugh; then hurrying down the stairs she will run through the theater, stop once more and laugh again as she looks at the other three, then she will leave the hall and even from the lobby her laugh will be heard.
>
> Shortly after this the curtain will fall.[39]

These additions to the closing image intensify the sense of chasm that lies just beyond the represented action of the search and the failure to find an author. The action is not only unresolved, as so many Pirandellian actions are; it is played against a future that is felt acutely as a blank. Life as a play that never gets put on, life as a state of suspended animation between a mania to live and a theatricalization that even before it is achieved is known to be inadequate, is vexed further by the sense that it is played in anticipation of a future like an abyss. This facet of the action, however abstract in the telling, is also in the image and part of the play's extraordinary immediacy and directness.

Altogether, the dramatic action that Pirandello has devised here is his most masterful embodiment of his vision of life as theater. The device of bringing a group of dramatic characters face to face with a theatrical company and then having them experiment with playing the drama that for the characters is their life provides, among other things, numerous opportunities to show figures standing apart from their lives and commenting on them. In the course of these commentaries, as the characters review and mull over details, we see them contemplate their lives as theatricalizations. When they are asked to stand aside so that the actors can take their parts, they object, as we have seen, to inaccuracies and distortions. At other times they ponder with fascination and horror the details that fix their experience, details like the Mother's scream at finding the Step-Daughter in an embrace with her husband. As they review the theatrical progress toward the scream, they underscore how theatrical detail gives substance to the event.

> The Father.... All our passion must culminate in her final scream!
> The Step-Daughter. It's still in my ears! It drove me mad, that scream!
> —You can represent me as you wish, *Signori;* it doesn't matter!
> Even dressed, provided that I have at least my arms nude—only
> my arms—because, look, being like this (*she approaches the Father
> and places her head on his breast*), with my head resting like this and
> my arms around his neck like this, I saw a vein pulsing here in my
> arm. And then, as if only that living vein horrified me, I shut my
> eyes, like this, and buried my head in his breast! (*Turning toward the
> Mother.*) Scream! Scream, mama! (*She sinks her head in the Father's
> breast, and with her shoulders pointed as if to ward off the scream, says
> again in a voice wracked with pain*): Scream, as you screamed then!
> The Mother. (*Rushing to separate them.*) No! My daughter! My daughter!
> (*And after having separated her from him.*) You brute. She's my
> daughter. Don't you see she's my daughter?[40]

Now in much the way this passage positions inner promptings and external event so that the whole dynamic by which impulse struggles to expression is kept before us, the play as a whole generates an acute consciousness of experience struggling, without success, to complete itself in theatrical form.

Pirandello's final major treatment of theatricalization as the indispensable matrix of experience is the third of the so-called theater plays, *Tonight We Improvise.* Here the subject is introduced even more explicitly than in *Each in His Own Way.* The action begins on what is in that play the second plane, that of the audience talking among themselves and then responding to the director Hinkfuss, who, entering through the theater, goes up on the stage to prepare the audience to participate in an improvised theatricalization. In fact, this is a simple pretext, since *Tonight We Improvise* is an almost wholly written text, but it enables Hinkfuss to review Pirandello's principal ideas about the symbiosis of movement and form. His purpose, Hinkfuss insists, is to orient the audience, to position them with respect to the process by which a text, here the story that is to be the basis for the improvised play, is brought to life through theatricalization, and in this way to enhance their participation in it. His function, he boasts—though the actors will later dispute his claim—is to bring inert texts to life through theatricalization. By doing so he creates *his* work, and with each successive performance that work becomes yet another creation. At the end of this extended preparation he introduces the actors who are presumably to improvise a play from the outline provided by Pirandello's story "Farewell, Leonora" ("Leonora, Addio," 1910).

What is new in *Tonight We Improvise,* and what sets it off from *Each in His Own Way* and *Six Characters,* is its emphasis on creation as a confused collaboration. As explained by Hinkfuss, the actors bring movement to the fixed outline of the story, which Hinkfuss compares to a sculpture: they theatricalize it and in that way create experience. Their efforts, depending on your point of view, are helped or hindered by the director and his backstage aides. What is most important from our point of view is that the creation at issue be seen as the product of many individuals at once contending with each other and yet cooperating, quarreling, taking and giving offence, sulking, and rebelling, even as they are all propelled forward by the events of the outline story. Moreover, we are in a position to see that this image of Hinkfuss's actors making a play is mirrored both in the efforts of Pirandello's actors to theatricalize his text and in those of the characters in the "improvised" play to perform scenes from operas, especially *Il Trovatore.* Seen as a totality, then, *Tonight We Improvise* consists of interpenetrating theatricalizations: Pirandello's actors are performing the written script of a play in which actors "improvise" a play in which the characters in turn put on amateur versions of opera. The ensemble of these efforts is disorderly, even clumsy and inept, and it is held together by the purpose of giving form to experience that would otherwise remain a chaos of contending voices. The action reveals not simply that the process of creation, scenic or otherwise, is messy, but that messiness, hence precariousness, is intrinsic to it. Actors putting on a play can serve as an emblem of the process by which experience is created through theatricalization; but actors improvising a play stress the dominant quality of that process, its chanciness, the wonder that the play ever gets put on at all. The further implication, of course, is that all this is true not simply of what Hinkfuss calls scenic creation, but also of self-creation.

Of the trilogy of theater plays *Tonight We Improvise* is the most loosely structured. The distinctive planes of theatricalization do not collide in it as in *Six Characters* or *Each in His Own Way:* they overlap and dribble into each other. The actors' awkward first steps into improvisation, as when, for example, the mother mismatches the suitors with her daughters, or the actors break into the action to object or complain that something has been changed or omitted, or the sisters and mother appear surrealistically in the long scene between Mommina, the prosecuted sister, and her mad Sicilian husband who, stepping out of his role of the husband and speaking as the actor, protests that they are not literally there: all this strengthens the sense of indeterminacy in the action, even as excursions into *Il Trovatore* sustain an obbligato of overwrought intensity. When the actors rebel and drive Hinkfuss off, their gesture marks merely a further stage in a process that sporadically threatens to become wholly anarchic. But it never does. Hinkfuss returns and the collaboration resumes with Hinkfuss's promise that texts may be provided, as the actors are demanding, though not an author or indeed anything that might hobble spontaneity. This temporary truce between director and actors affirms that creation will continue, always open and uncertain, like an improvised performance, and always governed by the theatrical matrix.

Finally, understanding the place of theatricality in experience serves, like understanding the other dimensions of consciousness, to bring imaginative depth and density to self-creation. To live with a full awareness of the theatricality of experience is to accept the perpetual tension between the impulses to live and theatrical forms, to acquiesce in the fact that the role you play is never entirely your own and never completely adequate to the self of your consciousness. Settling for this compromise does not compromise *sincerità:* it is in the nature of *sincerità* that it comprehends the necessity of partial measures; but it recognizes the ironic heroism of playing a role at all, a heroism caught wonderfully by Chiarchiaro of "The License," the character who demands that he be licensed as a "hexer" because that is how people insist on seeing him. To live with these awarenesses is to clarify the extremely delicate exercise of sustaining the tension between the immediate, with its flawed opportunities for living, and everything the mind brings to bear on it.

Perhaps Pirandello's finest brief treatment of the discipline of this exercise is the relatively late story "A Little Wine" ("Un Po' di Vino," 1923). It is the story of an encounter between the speaker, a nondrinker who has accompanied a visiting friend to a squalid tavern, and an old man who, assisted by a younger servant, is seated at a nearby table and served a quarter liter of wine. The old man is so cadaverous and immobile that the nondrinker cannot resist thinking of him as dead, or almost—he does not even disturb the flies that settle on him; finally, out of compassion the nondrinker offers to serve him some of the wine that stands before him untouched. At this the old man explains his position. He does not drink the wine standing before him because it is not real wine, genuine, though he would consent to a little of the stronger aleatico that the nondrinker's friend is drinking. The whole exercise of drinking, he explains, consists in taking a very small quantity of genuine wine, enough to stimulate one to a discreet vitality. Too much and reality changes, and he might bring disgrace on his family; too little and there is no stimulation at all. Moreover, he must take Costantino, his servant, into account. Costantino cannot drink at all because it could kill him, partly because of physical problems, but partly too, it is strongly suggested, because he has the heavy responsibility of a large family. He must not know even a measured vivacity, and the old man must not tempt him: some people, like the nondrinking speaker, are not up to "stimulation." Hence the old man cultivates, in deference to decorums and the needs of others, an austere equilibrium. If he drinks at all, he limits it so that he is stimulated but always under control; otherwise he simply comes to the tavern, like an almost dead man, to contemplate his sadness, his memory of vivacity and genuine wine, in the ritual of sitting with a glass of "fake" wine before him.

The nice tension between genuine and fake wine, between genuine vivacity (always within measure) and the memory of vivacity, between the tenuously sustained life within the old man's mind and the all but dead shell of his body: all these illuminate the discipline of consciousness as it watches itself live. As it watches, of course, the pressures of other awarenesses are also felt, of the ubiquitous presence and force of the unknown, of the relativity of all things; and even these do not exhaust the expressive power of the figure of the old man in his situation. In one moment these dimensions of consciousness constitute the imperatives of a pessimism verging on despair, in another they trace the exercise of consciousness as a begetter of values. The values in question all turn on savoring, not necessarily with pleasure, what it means to be human, to live with the fullest possible awareness of what is transpiring at all times, even as one moves toward the theatricalization known in advance to be inadequate. The humility to accept, the courage to persist, the charity to love a world of shadows and to commiserate a world of lies: these values are always parts of Pirandello's pessimism. They give a solidity to characters bedeviled by the recognition that they are phantoms; they give to Pirandello's vision a solidity often missed by those ready to conclude that identifying phantoms was his exclusive purpose. When Pirandello says that life is theater, he does so not to demonstrate once again that life is a dream, but to gauge the value of living the life that is a dream. In that difference we see the essential difference between modern consciousness and its antecedents.

7

●○●○●○●○●○●○●○●○●○●○●●

PIRANDELLO: THE ONE
AND THE MANY

IT IS A CURIOUS commentary on Pirandello's life and career that the many faces that he in true Pirandellian fashion revealed to the world as teacher, writer in various genres, fascist, humorist, and family man never seriously obscured the figure of the essential man and artist. All his life he was repulsed by the dishonesty and inauthenticity everywhere in the world around him. The violence evident in his meeting with Sabatino Lopez, when he claimed himself ready to blow up the world,[1] is not different from the somewhat posturing outrage of his earliest letter to his sister Lina. Seeking that modicum of clarity and coherence remaining to one for whom *sincerità* had become a last standard, he found it in a conception of consciousness by which consciousness itself becomes the sole source and nucleus of value. This conception was at the center of everything he did and appeared to be.

For Pirandello the process of self-creation was tragic as he understood that term. In the letter to Silvio D'Amico already cited he wrote: "For me life is tragic because it must obey the two opposed necessities of movement and of form—fatal necessities. . . . If life were to obey only one of them, movement exclusively, it would never have substance. To have substance it must obey the other necessity, it must give itself a form. Yet, form imprisons movement, while movement wears out and demolishes forms. Hence the perpetual, mortal succession of movement and form, in continuous conflict, which is in fact life."[2] The definition is abstract, somewhat Tilgherian, yet entirely consistent with Pirandello's specific uses of the word "tragic." Tragedy consisted for him in this "perpetual, mortal succession" of movement and form, this "continuous conflict"; to be more specific, it consisted in living in irresolution or a state of suspended animation. In the article on *Man, Beast, and Virtue* (*L'Uomo, la Bestia e la*

Virtù, 1919) he described the situation of his protagonist in even that farcelike action as tragic because he is forced to live a life that he never feels his own.[3] Not only is Professor Paolino surrounded by the bad faith of a world like a menagerie, he also promotes bad faith by sustaining grotesque fictions like the virtue of his mistress, a sea captain's wife who must seduce her own husband to legitimize her unborn child. In numerous comments on *Six Characters,* as we have seen, Pirandello saw the tragedy of the characters in the fact that they could not find a "coordinating spirit," or author.[4] Tragedy consisted in living with this tension and torment. Self-creation could wrest fugitive unities and coherences from the flux, but it could not alter the continuously volatile nature of the process.

Of course Pirandello's conception of tragedy was highly idiosyncratic. It shared with the traditions of Sophocles, Shakespeare, and Racine certain traits of vision by emphasizing the irremediable insecurity of human life and positing that suffering can lead to value. But in Pirandello's works even these similarities are often more apparent than real; like his great literary contemporaries he had relatively little interest in traditional tragic grandeur. If the drama of consciousness resembles in some respects the precariousness of Macbeth's descent into the abyss of his being, in some of his works this precariousness is accompanied by a strong sense that after all the characters are going to land on their feet. Such a sense is clear in *Man, Beast, and Virtue* and "The Tragedy of a Character," both of which Pirandello associated explicitly with tragedy. And even such powerful works as *Six Characters* and *Henry IV* suggest affinities with traditional tragedy without ever entirely reproducing its dynamics. The fact is that Pirandello's view of tragedy was largely limited to the instability created by the movement-form dynamic and for this reason too narrow to do full justice to his extended treatment of the drama of consciousness.

On the contrary, Pirandello's long meditation on consciousness reveals a range of attitudes toward it that considerations of tragedy can only obscure. To judge from the work itself, we find that for long periods he would settle into the ironic pessimism of *umorismo*. In this mood he could be playful, deeply appreciative of the comic grotesqueness of humanity, and full of awe before the heroism and wonder of human beings. At other times he would move to a deeper pessimism verging on despair, to the extreme bitterness, for example, of "The Destruction of Man." And at still other times he would register an extreme detachment, as in the letter to Lietta quoted in chapter 4: "I don't know if I'm fleeing life or life me. I know that I feel almost entirely 'detached.' The earth is extremely remote.

Hence, not only you, little Lietta, even though from here to Chile is a good piece, but I from where I now see all the things of life, I am much, but much more distant."[5]

In each of these distinctive moods or phases, the state of spirit sounded has the appearance of a kind of resolution or resting place, often even a reasoned response to the storms of change and uncertainty. At given moments in Pirandello's career, in fact, some critics have concluded that he abandoned exploration and description in favor of searching for an answer to the crisis of his time. But these were stances or solutions pondered seriously for a time and then abandoned. Pirandello's honesty would never permit him to settle for less than the total truth of experience; and since the world was always vaster and more complex for him than the mind with which he attempted to grasp it, any answer to its riddle was always less than comprehensive. And so he moved on, probing further, after World War I focusing intently on the implications of relativity and theatricality, still later stressing other interests. His long meditation on consciousness is the story of all these stops and detours; in their multiplicity we find the essential man and artist.

To fill out still further the figure of the one Pirandello as it coexists with the many, I wish now to examine the more important of these temporary pauses, and I shall begin with his movement through *umorismo* to extreme detachment because the components of this position have already been discussed in part. As we saw in chapter 2 *umorismo* was Pirandello's first carefully reasoned response to his condition, and it continued to the end of his life to be a major refuge. But it was not sufficient to all needs and seasons. Although the playful irony of *A Place in Line* (1902) was still to be met as late as stories like "The Turtle" ("La Tartaruga," 1936), it sometimes gave way to a cooler, distinctly more distanced perception, still playful in part, but heavier with tragicomic resignation. This is what we find in "My Wife's Husband" ("Il Marito di Mia Moglie," 1903), in which Luca Leuci, reduced to helplessness by a disease that is killing him, watches his wife and best friend as they minister to him. With a sad but comic understanding he projects his situation forward to the time when he will not be there and when they, he knows, will have married; his anger and sympathy and gratitude define an acquiescence that is always under control, but moving away from the immediate world. This increased distance from the world begets something like voyeurism in "The Light from the Other House" ("Il Lume dell' Altra Casa," 1909) and *The Man with a Flower in His Mouth* (1923), a voyeurism that grows progressively darker and more bitter as it becomes more remote. In its extreme form, it becomes a detachment by which the perceiver can master anything but which dims the outlines of human experience until they virtually disappear.

Extreme detachment as a response to the world appears first in clearly articulated form in Pirandello's candidate to lead the Italy of 1909, his scholar Paolo Post, with whose name he actually signed articles in 1896 and again in 1909. In the later articles, entitled as a group "From Afar" ("Da Lontano," 1909), he proposed as Post's chief qualification to be leader his capacity to see everything from a great distance, as if through a reversed telescope. Indeed, Doctor Post is the developer of "the philosophy of distance" (*la filosofia del lontano*), an identical twin to Doctor Fileno of "The Tragedy of a Character," who puts telescopes to the same use and who also has a philosophy of this title, and a first cousin to the speaker in "The Remedy is Geography" ("Rimedio: La Geografia," 1922), a man who disciplines himself to handle troubles close at hand by thinking about remote places. All these figures retain a good deal of the ironic fun of *umorismo*, yet all virtually abandon *umorismo*'s fundamental sense of contradiction (*il sentimento del contrario*) for mastery through distance. Even Federico Berecche in "Berecche and the War," whose passion seems to set him off sharply from Paolo Post, has his Post-like moment one night as he looks at the stars and contemplates how this world and its great war must appear from a great distance. As a teacher of history he can imagine what his counterpart a thousand years hence will say of it all:

> In a thousand years . . . this atrocious war that now fills the entire world with horror will be condensed into a few lines in the story of man, and there will be no sign of all the little stories of these thousands upon thousands of obscure creatures who are now being carried away by it. Each one of them will have gathered the entire world into himself and will have been eternal at least for a moment in his life, with this earth and this sky twinkling with stars in his spirit and his home a long way away and his own dear ones, his father, mother, wife, sisters, in tears and perhaps still uninformed, and his children intent on their games, remote, remote.[6]

The passage is long and full of the sadness of the vanity of human wishes and the extraordinary poise that comes with the god's-eye view.

For an example of the withering chill that at other times is the price paid for the sovereignty of this outlook we must turn to Silvia Roncella of *Her Husband* and her last night with her dead child. She too looks at the moon and stars, and she too is moved by them to see the human comedy steadily and whole. I have already quoted a small piece of this passage to illustrate the sense of man lost in the surrounding mystery so essential to Pirandello's vision. But Silvia is moved to more than awe and disdain at the "fatuity of men" as they "wander immersed in the immense vortex of life"; she also sees "other dark gigantic necessities standing out in profile within the beguiling flow of time, like those great mountains there in the enchantment of the green, utterly silent lunar dawn."[7] And as she dedicates herself to these ferocious, terrible, arcane necessities, she achieves an impressive, if gelid control, a little like that of Costanzo Ramberti, who sees himself dead in "The Illustrious Deceased" ("L'Illustre Estinto," 1909). It is not a perspective that Pirandello consistently recommended; it is quite simply one of the extremes among what he might have called the solaces of distance.

What looks less like a healing attitude and more like a self-consciously derived solution to the problems of human life, and what such discerning critics as Arminio Janner, Giovanni Calendoli, and Douglas Radcliff-Umstead propose as Pirandello's answer,[8] is his periodic interest in what they call pantheism, but what is more accurately a giving over of the struggle altogether in favor of sinking into the flux and nature. We see an early version of it in "When I Was Mad" (1902), the story of Fausto Bandini's discovery that he had been mad during all those years when he had housed a great many selves, most of them imposed by others. To be mad is to lose oneself among the chaos of selves within, to see neither oneself nor the world for oneself. With this recognition Fausto's sense of himself as an individual begins; he gives up reasoning, that is, accommodating the perspectives of others, and he becomes "wise." His state of being approaches something like pantheism on the night when, wandering outside the villa where his beloved sister-in-law awaits burial, he learns that his wife has a lover. As he dismisses all conventional responses to the betrayal, a dismissal that will later certify another kind of madness for the others, he is acutely conscious of the clouds and the wind and the vast mystery surrounding man's petty imperatives. He does not identify himself with this nature, yet perceiving it in this way he embraces the nonreasoned, nonstructured, almost prerational acquiescence that we shall see is central to Pirandello's so-called pantheism.

But "pantheism" is not a fortunate term for this response. Even in later, fuller treatments of it the term emphasizes a worship of God or the life-force in all things, while Pirandello was more interested in a kind of acquiescence, a way of sinking or settling into nature or the flux, that resulted in a passive, outer-directed mode of self-definition. In "Sing the Epistle" ("Canta l'Epistola," 1911), a story always cited to support the argument for pantheism, Tommasino Unzio, the former seminarist called "Sing the Epistle" because that was as far as he got in his preparation for the priesthood, settles into an attitude very like nature worship. For him too wind and clouds are crucial: the wind continuously moving, agitating, driving the clouds and leaves; the clouds, recently water, soon to be water again, constantly changing form. Before the "spectacle of nature" he feels himself little by little possessed by an "absentminded melancholy": "All the illusions and deceits and pains and joys and hopes and desires of men seem vain and transitory to him before the feeling prompted by the things that remain and prevail over them, unmoved. The individual affairs of men seem almost cloud-phenomena in the eternity of nature."[9] He becomes enchanted by tiny, delicate things, and the more fleeting the thing the greater his tenderness for it. Hence his fatal response to Signorina Fanelli's pulling out and chewing on one of his favorite blades of grass. Yet here too Pirandello was primarily interested in Sing the Epistle's attitude not because it led him to see in nature myriad manifestations of God, but as an alternative to the perpetual effort of marshaling the consciousness against the flux:

> To have no consciousness of being, like a stone, like a plant; to no longer recall even one's own name; to live for the purpose of living, without knowing about it, like the animals, like the plants, no longer with feelings or desires or memories or thoughts, no longer with anything that might give sense or value to one's life. There, stretched out on the grass with his hands behind his neck, watching the clouds in the blue sky, dazzling white clouds, puffed up with sun, listening to the wind making a noise like the sea in the grove of chestnut trees, and hearing in the voice of the wind and noise, as from a great distance, the vanity of all things and the anguishing tedium of life.
>
> Clouds and wind.[10]

The term "pantheism" does not get at the special character of this engagement in nature. For Sing the Epistle, "tired of the burden of his stupid flesh," his new-found peace is not so distinctly a form of worship, though it is also that, as it is a giving over of himself to clouds and wind, to a kind of blissful passivity that asks very little and rejoices in it.

One of Pirandello's fullest treatments of this alternative to an active, creative consciousness is found in his last novel. Begun as early as 1912 though not completed until 1925, *One, None, and a Hundred Thousand* has often been regarded as a definitive recapitulation of Pirandello's views;

indeed Pirandello himself encouraged this view of it.[11] But if it is his most intense exploration in fiction of the decomposition of self, it is far less a study of the reconstruction of self through life worship. Although its protagonist's acquiescence in clouds and wind is an altogether probable outcome of the agony of analysis that constitutes most of the book, the representation of this acquiescence is contained in relatively few paragraphs at the end.

Vitangelo Moscarda's difficulties begin when his wife points out to him that his nose bends slightly to the right. He had never noticed this fact, and the discovery shakes him to his foundations because it forces him to see that he has always been a different Moscarda for his wife than he has been for himself: in fact, he has been her "Gengè," someone he does not even recognize. What is more, this discovery forces him to see that he is as many different selves as there are people who develop an idea of him. In other words, he is the one Moscarda who bears his name and whom he sees in the mirror, yet he is no one, since even he finds the figure in the mirror a stranger, and at the same time he is a hundred thousand in the variable gazes of all those who perceive him. The discovery paralyzes him for a time, then sets off a series of events that on the one hand almost destroy him and on the other lead to his salvation.

The novel is chiefly devoted to a painstaking analysis of Moscarda's vision of relativity. As he attempts to do something about some of the persons he is for others, especially about Moscarda the usurer, son of his father the banker, Pirandello exploits every opportunity to have him dig and dissect, with the result that the book abounds in commentary: in the book's serial publication in *Fiera Letteraria* (1925) it had the subtitle *Considerations of Vitangelo Moscarda, General on the Life of Man and Particular on His Own, in Eight Books.* Yet with each effort to change the various personae by which he is known, he only succeeds in demolishing them and earning a reputation for madness. Finally, deserted by his wife and friends, held in contempt by the community, and believed incompetent by all, he gives his money away and withdraws to a hospice for beggars where he completes the process of deconstruction.

Yet even as Moscarda blunders toward decomposition, he ponders the problem of reconstruction (in that same serial publication book 2 had had the title "Reconstructing Oneself"). Like Sing the Epistle, he too has his moments with clouds and wind: chapter 9 of book 2, entitled "Clouds and Wind," begins with the passage just quoted from the story "Sing the Epistle": "To have no consciousness of being, like a stone, like a plant!" etc.[12] By the beginning of book 4 he can feel that he has destroyed all his extraneous selves, the community usurer, his wife's Gengè, all of them, *finalmente*. By the final pages of the novel he feels himself afloat in the flux there seen as a swollen, overflowing river, and he has learned to stay afloat and swim. But the case for pantheism in all this is clear only in the final few paragraphs of the book, where something very like pantheism is present: "No name," he reflects,

> no memory today of the name of yesterday, of the name of today, tomorrow. If the name is the thing, if a name is in us the concept of each thing outside of us, and without a name there is no concept and the thing remains within us blind, indistinct and undefined, then what you carry among men each of you etches like a funerary epigraph on the forehead of the image that appears before you. . . . It's suitable for the dead, for he who has finished. I am alive and have not finished. Life doesn't finish. And life knows nothing of names. This tree—I breathe and tremble with a new quickness. I am this tree. Tree, cloud; tomorrow book or wind: the book I read, the wind I drink. All outside, vagabond.[13]

Then follows a long paragraph in which he describes the sights and sensations around the hospice and how he goes out each morning to experience them anew, one by one, as they are. "In this way only am I able to live now. To be reborn moment by moment. To prevent thought from beginning to work within me again, and within to refill once more the emptiness with vain constructions."[14] In the final paragraph the city, the emblem of the constructed life, is opposed to this passivity: even as Moscarda dies in each moment, he is reborn "alive and complete, not in himself, but in everything outside himself."[15]

"Pantheism" seems to me a misleading term for this state because it obscures the negation of thought and conscious effort so central to it. As an alternative to the active, creative consciousness of a Henry IV, Moscarda's serenity is a fluid state of nondefinition that enables all shaping influences to come from without, a renunciation of the responsibility to organize oneself in favor of a prerational openness to the details of the world. Moreover, critics have perhaps been too hasty in seeing it as an altogether desirable state, supported by Pirandello as a preferred way of dealing with the so-called tragic structure of experience. As Gian-Paolo Biasin has pointed out, there is very little reason to stress it as a positive position or to see it as more than a metaphor for an alternative to contemporary life.[16] It is important to recall that at the end of the book Moscarda is living in a hospice, outside the community of human beings, alone. He is full of joy, it is true, but he is also something of a freak.

A much more attractive and authoritative image of Moscarda's life worship is to be seen in Cotrone, the Prospero-like magician from Pirandello's last work, the long dramatic fragment *The Mountain Giants* (1932–36). Although criticism has rarely associated Moscarda and Cotrone, Cotrone in fact provides an elaborate commentary on a prerational fertility of spirit very like Moscarda's passive receptivity, though without the secondary traits suggesting pantheism. Most of this commentary occurs in act 2 of the fragment, when Cotrone explains who he and the phantasms called *scalognati* are, after the arrival of Ilse's company of actors at the remote villa and the exposition of their mission to perform the play of the poet who had died for love of Ilse. Yet even in his first speech in act 1 Cotrone had set himself and his *scalognati* against reason and had located their world in an atmosphere of twilight.

In act 2 Pirandello's analysis of this mode of response is far more detailed and abstract than anything to be found in the stories and novels. The *scalognati*, a term that means the unfortunate or rejected ones, are impulses to life, the life that hovers on the frontiers of experience, the life of dreams, music, prayers, and love, here objectified in fireflies around the villa.[17] They are "germs" or "larvae" of the order of being of the characters in *Six Characters*, with definition, but before theatricalization, before the formalizing thought of an author; they are truths that the consciousness has never seized, never made conscious, and in this sense "rejected." Cotrone orchestrates them, calling them forth from the "secret areas of the senses" and "caverns of instinct," "dissolving" them into "phantasms" or "evanescences" or "shadows that pass," producing in that spectacle a kind of life worship like that of the long-livers in Shaw's *Back to Methuselah*. In this way he and the *scalognati* become "masters of nothing and everything"[18] and achieve a state of bliss that at one point he describes as "a continuous heavenly drunkenness."[19] This state of having nothing and everything he associates in another passage reminiscent of *One, None, and a Hundred Thousand* with the status of beggars, those "highly cultivated people . . . with rare tastes, who have been able to reduce themselves to that condition of exquisite privilege which is mendicancy."[20]

Cotrone and his *scalognati*, then, give still further definition to the alternative to an active, creative consciousness seen in simpler form in Sing the Epistle and Moscarda: they clarify a mode of experiencing that is prior to the activity of Ilse's company of actors in that they are what the actors ultimately give form to. Yet they must be sharply distinguished from art:

they are more akin to the spirit unbound than to anything so studied as poetry or drama. Ultimately, of course, they are, along with Ilse's company, brutally rejected by the giants of the mountain, those "fanatic servants of life" who savagely disrupt the play and kill Ilse; in fact, in act 1 Cotrone had explained that he and his crew had chosen to live at the remote villa because of the savage population's contempt for them.

If all this is still somewhat inconclusive, the truth is we cannot know exactly how the play would have treated the *scalognati* in the final act. In Stefano Pirandello's account of what his father had told him of it on the night before the night he died, the emphasis falls on the artists and the giants' rejection of them, largely ignoring Cotrone and his crew. We can only guess that Pirandello's final judgment of them perhaps resided in what he understood by the "ancient saracen olive tree" that was to be central to the final scene and in which, he told Stefano, he had found the solution to the artistic problems of the play's conclusion; but it is vain to speculate on what he meant by all that.

The fact that *The Mountain Giants* was apparently to conclude with Ilse's death and her company in disarray suggests that Cotrone and his *scalognati,* for all their gossamer insubstantiality, represented a more durable alternative for Pirandello than art. If so, and if the play was intended in part to be yet another treatment of the attractions of passively going with the flow, I must hasten to point out that this too was not a view Pirandello held continuously. Periodically throughout his career, and increasingly in the last decade, he saw it the other way around, finding the possibility for unity and heightened value not in passivity but in a consciousness quickened by that power of imaginative beholding that he found chiefly in art.

Of course Pirandello had always put a high value on art. In "Art and Consciousness Today" he could say as early as 1893 that "art is so to speak the pulse of life, that art follows and reflects life in every movement and emanation."[21] As we have seen, moreover, he always insisted that the processes of artistic creation were identical to the processes of self-creation, except that art was disinterested, fixed, and free of irrelevancies.[22] In other words, Pirandello always associated artistic imagination with the integrative function of consciousness, in large part with the power of humoristic perception, or the power to hold contraries in suspension. In its most highly developed form artistic imagination involved a special type of this perception that saw life emblematically.

It is the power of beholding of this second kind that offers yet another perspective on creative consciousness. Very simply, seeing life emblematically consists in gaining a kind of dominion over the flux by encapsulating its tension, texture, and detail in images, usually dramatic images or metaphoric actions. Pirandello manifested this special power himself relatively early in stories like "A Horse in the Moon" ("Un Cavallo nella Luna," 1907) and "Flying" ("Volare," 1907). In the first the terrible rite of passage from youth to adulthood is caught in the story of Ninò and Ida, young newlyweds celebrating their wedding in a country house by the sea. When they are left alone, he fat and nervous, she very young and "wild," they run across the fields to watch their families' carriages going off and happen on a dying horse and a swarm of ravens waiting to devour him. Ida is beside herself with grief for the animal and insists that they try to help him; Ninò, exhausted and feverish, suddenly feels very ill himself; Ida goes off leaving Ninò to watch a moon terrifying with overtones of madness come up. When she returns, she becomes hysterical at the moon, her sick and perhaps dying Ninò, and the horse, and cries out to her father to take her away. As a whole the action is an emblem of the world projected in all its mystery, focused in the couple's passage from innocence to experience, but expressive of a condition much wider than that of youth. In the second story, "Flying," Nenè, a young woman whose ailing mother and sister have become dependent on her, reads her destiny in the figure of a bird that, though attacked by worms, does not leave its cage after the door has been left open. Refusing to be so consumed by the polite world of gainful employment for young women, Nenè takes to the streets. This story too converts the world into a single, extremely dense image.

Pirandello's practice during the next two decades traces a steady movement toward fiction of this kind. Stories like "Night" ("Notte," 1912), "Ciaula Discovers the Moon" (1912), "Breath" ("Soffio," 1931), "Someone Is Laughing" ("C'è Qualcuno che Ride," 1934), and "A Day Passes," (1936); novels like *The Notebooks of Serafino Gubbio,* with its highly self-conscious treatment of cameras and technology, and *One, None, and a Hundred Thousand* with its story of Moscarda's symbolic withdrawal: all these reveal a deepening interest in actions conceived as emblems. But the importance of this mode of imaginative beholding in Pirandello's thought is most evident in the so-called myth plays of the last decade. Between 1925 and 1936 Pirandello completed, among other works, *The Festival of Our Lord of the Ship,* (*Sagra del Signore della Nave,* 1925), *Diana and Tuda* (1926), *The New Colony* (*La Nuova Colonia,* 1928), *Lazzaro* (1929), *The Fable of the Changeling,* (*La Favola del Figlio Cambiato,* 1932), and the long fragment *The Mountain Giants.* All this work reflects an effort to convert experience into what many critics have called myths, to transpose the surfaces of life into images expressive of their governing principles. Certain of them attempt still more by addressing abstract problems like founding a new society (*The New Colony*), or the relations between art and life (*Diana and Tuda*), or finding a religion in and for life (*Lazzaro*). *The Mountain Giants,* despite everything one might say about the case it makes for passive acquiescence, was clearly designed to say something about the relations among the artists, Cotrone, and the giants in a parablelike action. Pirandello had used the term "parable" (*parabola*) to describe plays before, most notably for *Right You Are (If You Think So)*. But where *Right You Are* and *Six Characters* and *Henry IV* achieve a parablelike status, even they do not suggest the self-consciousness with which Pirandello later strove for this kind of mastery. In his later work he cultivated seeing the world emblematically with a deliberation that sets that effort off as yet another exercise in perceiving and experiencing, an exercise analogous to Doctor Paolo Post's detachment and Moscarda's life-worshiping acquiescence.

That many critics have found yet another solution to the problems of living in the myth plays and in the attention they give to self-conscious artistic seeing is understandable in view of Pirandello's clear preoccupation with this matter in his last decade. But the truth is he finally rejected all answers, formulas, and resolutions in favor of the position that consciousness, all we have as a source of value and unity, is by its nature never fixed. We live in a continuous state of tension, he continued to assert through all the phases of his meditation, with the elements of our world in suspension; from our heightened sensitivity to the process of making and unmaking ourselves and our worlds we create value.

One frequent source of failure in Pirandello criticism is to see him as a problem solver, a kind of Italian Bernard Shaw who identifies problems and then proceeds to indicate solutions derived from a clearly articulated philosophy. Pirandello was an artist of a wholly different kind. Like Shaw, he was an intellectual, and that trait more than anything, perhaps, has prompted the wrong expectations about him; but he was an intellectual whose principal use of the mind was to discover the ultimate futility of thought. He insisted that intellect was always present and important in human experience: it could not be suppressed momentarily, as Croce argued, in favor of instinct; yet it could not do more, finally, than complicate one's sense of helplessness. It was a kind of bandmaster of consciousness, comic at times in his too-tight uniform, angry at other times at the puerility of the music he was helping to make. Although Pirandello always gave a prominent place to it in his vision, he rarely credited it with the power to solve problems. To see him as a problem solver, indeed, is automatically to see him as a failed problem solver.

The prominence of intellect in Pirandello and the attention it drew to his notorious cerebrality, moreover, point to a second source of failure among his critics: to see him, in the useful terms of Archilochus, as a hedgehog, who knows one big thing, rather than as a fox, who knows many.[23] Pirandello was acutely sensitive to and irritated by the reductive descriptions proposed for him by critics, and particularly by that which fixed him as a dilettante casuist. In a well-known letter to Domenico Vittorini in 1935 he complained bitterly of "the many Pirandellos in circulation in the world of international literary criticism, lame, deformed, all head and no heart, erratic, gruff, insane, and obscure, in whom no matter how hard [he tried, he could not] recognize himself even for a moment."[24] His bitterness here summed up a lifetime of simplistic dismissals, of which the most common and the hardest to bear was that he was essentially a critic lacking in humanity and warmth. This attack gained force with the appearance of *Right You Are* in 1917, and it has not been abandoned to this day. Even Silvio D'Amico, who commented on it and Pirandello's dismay at it in 1920, was, to begin with, a partisan to it,[25] as, with slight qualifications, was Tilgher. Pirandello's chief detractors, of course—Croce, Italo Siciliano, and their ilk—were to compound the case by arguing that he was not only narrowly cerebral but also incompetently so.[26]

The chief irony of Pirandello criticism is that even his friends, supporters, and passionate devotees contributed to the view that he was a thinker rather than an artist. He first won the reputation that made him a major figure in world literature not in Italy but in France. The birth of that reputation can be dated with unusual precision from the famous production of *Six Characters* at the Pitoëffs' Théâtre des Champs-Elysées beginning on 10 April 1923. But the Pirandello who emerged from that triumph was, as Georges Neveux, one of his leading apologists, described him, "the greatest prestidigitator of the twentieth century, the Houdini of interior life,"[27] the wit in a world of masks and mirrors, the master of the dialectic of relativism. This French Pirandello was the first one taken seriously by the world of letters, and for the most part it was he who profoundly influenced the course of twentieth-century drama in France. For the generation of Neveux, Jean Giraudoux, and Jean Anouilh, the term "Pirandellisme" meant "pure intellectual game,"[28] and Pirandellian structures meant characters seen as a layering of roles. In the work of Anouilh, for example, we see most of Pirandello's characteristic traits, but all sounded to a depth where they are either amusing or touching: Anouilh nowhere penetrates to the anguish of the Pirandellian vision. When, in another statement from 1935, Pirandello complained that he was vulgarly perceived as a "literary expert fortunate in having taken up a beguiling, carping tone, almost a juggler of ideas,"[29] he was not so much lamenting the unfairness of his detractors as the limitations of many of his supporters. Only after World War II, with the generation of Camus and Sartre, and, later, Ionesco and Genet, did this so-called French Pirandello give way to a darker, more pessimistic, more potent figure.[30] And only with Samuel Beckett was he joined by a major commentator on modern consciousness, one who does not see it as a drama at all, but a landscape dimly contiguous with the past, suspended in time, marking out its hours by listening to its own voice against the void.

Beckett stands squarely in the line of Proust, Svevo, and Pirandello: from his earliest writings his work treats the mind talking to itself and through its talk creating its life. The centerpiece of that work is still the trilogy of novels consisting of *Molloy, Malone Dies,* and *The Unnamable,* novels in which he moves from the parables-in-diptych that constitute *Molloy* progressively inward until in *The Unnamable* the "I" that narrates dissolves altogether. In *Molloy* Beckett presents the stories of one man trying to visit his mother and a second, his opposite, searching for but not finding him, and treats them in such a way as to turn each over again and again, in both parts advancing each slowly while keeping the whole of the respective searches, or most of them, continuously prominent. The method imitates the normal functioning of consciousness, the way it doubles back on itself as it constructs. Altogether, the story is very simple, but by combining and recombining its strands in imitation of the way it takes shape in experience, in the mind, it becomes complex. *Malone Dies* traces another journey, this time into the self and into the creation of self by way of writing or creating a discourse in stories. The dying of the title consists of gradually losing control of this process as the self disintegrates. With *The Unnamable* the movement inward is completed as the "I" who is the narrator dissolves entirely. Here the distinction is even clearer between the narrator, or the consciousness that narrates, and the narrated self or selves. As the various created fables peter out, the narrator has less interest in the selves they define than in the deeper self, or as it turns out, selves, that compel the consciousness to create. These include Worm, who would be happy to keep to an unconscious status quo except that a head grows out of his ear, and the "they" within who, like maniacs or hyenas, insist on a discourse. Beckett brings this account to no closure; like Pirandello, he settles for the unresolved openness of "going on." In the trilogy as everywhere in his work he believes himself in a cul-de-sac where the essential condition is one of waiting.

This examination of the dimensions and laminations of consciousness is the constant subject of Beckett's work. Even the recent, extremely short plays, rarefied and lyrical though they are, consist essentially of images of the consciousness and its major resource, language, holding off the void. But where Beckett frequently focuses his drama and fiction at the deepest levels of consciousness, where the "I" behind the "I-that-has-some-definition" lives, Pirandello more frequently treated the drama of created selves, the surfaces of the perceptible world. The difference is perhaps some measure of the distance between Pirandello's generation and our own.

All these many Pirandellos, in any case, the caricatures provided by critics as well as the many faces and voices legitimately to be met in the work, are best assimilated to an underlying unity by seeing that his constant subject was consciousness and that his life and career represent a long study of the crisis of consciousness in his time. Pirandello's response to the cultural disintegration of that time was to find in consciousness, for better or worse, a source of value and coherence, for him the only remaining source. Traditional structures had lost all authority and survived only in the dishonesty and inauthenticity of those who pretended that nothing had changed. Authenticity of experience could be achieved only by admitting this loss and then facing honestly the difficult truth that the self and its experience are created, from moment to moment, in the face of impenetrable mystery, and under conditions always relative and always insubstantial. Pirandello's work represents an extraordinary effort to examine those conditions and to represent the differences in quality of life that they produce.

At the heart of the many Pirandellos with their many interests and assertions, then, was Pirandello the man and artist intent upon conveying this vision to his fellows. In the letter to Vittorini quoted earlier he described himself simply as a man who wished to say something to other men;[31] in the article quoted earlier in which he protested the charge that he was a "juggler of ideas" he recoiled in exasperation: "I who have used up my life, a life rich if in nothing else in energy and feeling, only to find a language to speak as a man speaks to other men . . . [to know others] as they really are in their secret selves."[32] This Pirandello is elusive, it is true: he speaks always with an acute awareness that the relativity that subsumes all human efforts at definition and fixity applies to him as well as to others, but he is nonetheless there in the fundamental continuities of his work.

Briefly, what he seems to have been saying again and again, in many forms and by way of many voices, is that we are all locked in the strange casing we know as our bodies looking out on a world we can know very little. But we can know how little we know, and we can know that our experience consists of combining that little with a talent for creating forms, structures, and coherences all of which we desperately need to give us a sense that we are living and that our lives have stability. We can know, in other words, that we create ourselves, and in knowing that, we can undertake that creation with honesty.

Self-creation is a little like managing the famous horses of Plato's *Phaedrus:* you must let them run, yet you must hold them in check. Just so you must engage in the world with a healthy respect for its imperatives, taking what it gives you and using it with a lively awareness of the conditions by which you create. Although you are always limited to these conditions, you are free to create or not to create, free to live, despite many difficulties, honestly and with dignity. Pirandello counsels the courage to be free and to live honestly, to seize each moment with the greatest possible sensitivity to its fullness. Life can be terrible, funny, outrageous, embittering, he showed in a world of characters and stories, but it is also so beautiful (*così bella*), he added in that same letter to Vittorini in which he complained of being misunderstood. And the people who live it are wondrous to behold. To the extent that we are capable of facing the conditions of our lives and savoring that wonder, to that extent we are capable of winning the full measure of our humanity.

NOTES

INTRODUCTION

1. Matthew Arnold, "Sweetness and Light," *Culture and Anarchy: The Works of Matthew Arnold,* 15 vols. (London, 1903), 6:13.
2. For discussions of the philosophy of mind I have relied chiefly on Gilbert Ryle, *The Concept of Mind* (New York, 1949); D.C. Dennett, *Content and Consciousness* (London, 1969); Jerry A. Fodor, *The Language of Thought* (New York, 1975); and Hayden V. White, *Tropics of Discourse* (Baltimore, 1978).
3. George Bernard Shaw, *The Collected Works of Bernard Shaw,* 30 vols. (New York, 1930—), 10:112–14, 127.
4. Ibid., p. 102–3.
5. Ibid., p. 103.
6. Ibid., 16:208.
7. Ibid., p. 209.

1. A WORLD OF WORDS

1. Luigi Pirandello, "Informazioni sul Mio Involontario Soggiorno sulla Terra," *Saggi, Poesie e Scritti Varii,* ed. Manlio Lo Vecchio-Musti, *Opere di Luigi Pirandello,* vol. 6, I Classici Contemporanei Italiani (Milan, 1960), 1065.
2. Luigi Pirandello, "Lettere ai Familiari di Luigi Pirandello," ed. Sandro D'Amico, *Terzo Programma* 3 (1961), 281. This letter is dated 31 October 1886. All translations are my own.
3. Pirandello, "Lettere ai Familiari," p. 283.
4. Gösta Andersson, *Arte e Teoria: Studi sulla Poetica del Giovane Luigi Pirandello* (Uppsala, 1966), p. 89.
5. See Pirandello's "Fleeting Things" from *Troubled Joy, Saggi,* p. 485.
6. Pirandello, *Saggi,* p. 492.
7. Gaspare Giudice, *Pirandello* (Turin, 1963), p. 154. Note especially Pirandello's hostility toward D'Annunzio on this score in the letter of 3 June 1902 to G.A. Cesareo, "Lettere di Pirandello al Cesareo," ed. A.M. Dotto, *Nuovi Quaderni del Meridione,* 5 (1967), 475: "You will be coming into the field with your *Francesca da Rimini* against

an adversary who doesn't fight, unfortunately, with the same weapons that you use, and whom everyone has reasons for raising to their shoulders and holding aloft because the artifice that he has popularized and caused to pass for art is so easy and so convenient. Woe to all those who must work seriously at art, and therefore 'Viva D'Annunzio!' I think that this is the only reason for the continuing favor of this distinguished swindler."

8. Pirandello, *Saggi,* p. 874.
9. Ibid., pp. 919–25.
10. Ibid., pp. 1018–19.
11. See Gian-Paolo Biasin's searching analysis of the term "coscienza" in the context of Italo Svevo's *La Coscienza di Zeno* in Biasin's *Literary Diseases: Theme and Metaphor in the Italian Novel* (Austin, 1975), pp. 86–99.
12. Luigi Pirandello, *Novelle per un Anno,* [ed. Corrado Alvaro], *Opere di Luigi Pirandello,* vols. 1 and 2, I Classici Contemporanei Italiani (Milan, 1956–57), 2:734. The editorship for this and the other volumes of the *Opere* (with the exception of volume 6) is unspecified, but it is known to have been the work chiefly of Corrado Alvaro, Silvio D'Amico, and Manlio Lo Vecchio-Musti.
13. Pirandello, *Saggi,* p. 880.
14. Mathias Adank, *Luigi Pirandello e i Suoi Rapporti col Mondo Tedesco* (Bern, 1948), pp. 67–79.
15. Antonio Gramsci, *"Letteratura e Vita Nazionale,"* *Opere di Antonio Gramsci,* 9 vols. (Turin, 1947–54), 6:50.
16. Pirandello, *Saggi,* p. 849.
17. Ibid., p. 855. See Pirandello's "On the Usual Question of Language" ("Per la Solita Quistione della Lingua," 1895), *Saggi,* pp. 855–61, his answer to Pietro Mastri's response to his article. Note also the title of the lost play *Facts That Are Now Words* (*Fatti che or Son Parole,* 1889), Sandro D'Amico, "Itinerario di Pirandello al Teatro," *Veltro* 12 (1968), 83.
18. Luigi Pirandello, "Come si Scrive Oggi in Italia," *La Critica,* vol. 2, no. 33 (15 Sept. 1895), 784. See Carlo Dionisotti, *Geografia e Storia della Letteratura Italiana* (Turin, 1967), pp. 87–102, for an excellent discussion of literary Italian.
19. Pirandello, *Saggi,* p. 367. This essay is published with the title "Un Critico Fantastico."
20. See Mario Puppo, "Illuminismo e le Polemiche sulle Lingue," in *La Cultura Illuministica in Italia,* ed. Mario Fubini (Turin, 1957), pp. 222–32.
21. In chapter 27 of *Storia della Letteratura Italiana* (ed. Maria Teresa Lanza, 2 vols., Milan, 1956), entitled "La Nuova Letteratura,"

Francesco De Sanctis discussed at length the rivalry of the new literature and the older tradition of rhetoric and declamation. The first he associated with a new, more natural, more genuine interior life, the second with artificiality and superficiality. Throughout his exposition of the contention the phrase "things and not words" is central. Toward the end of the chapter he hailed the establishment in his time of a new, more authentic interior life for Italians. Later, in the essays on realism, he would be more tentative.

22. See Pirandello's review of Niccolò Tommaseo's novel *Fede e Bellezza* in *Roma Letteraria,* vol. 6, no. 22 (Nov. 1898), 521.

23. Ibid. See also Pirandello's "Subjectivism and Objectivism in Narrative Art" ("Soggettivismo e Oggettivismo nell'Arte Narrativa," in *Art and Science (Arte e Scienza,* 1908), *Saggi,* pp. 201–5.

24. Pirandello, "Teatro e Letteratura" (1918), *Saggi,* p. 987.

25. *Maschere Nude,* [ed. Silvio D'Amico], *Opere di Luigi Pirandello,* vols. 4 and 5, I Classici Contemporanei Italiani (Milan, 1958), 4:65. Pirandello's defense of Leopardi occurs in "Blind Leopardi" ("Leopardi Cieco"), *Roma Letteraria,* vol. 8, no. 3 (10 Feb. 1900), 51–54.

26. "Pirandello Interviewed," *Living Age,* 331 (1 Oct. 1926), 81. Pirandello's view of D'Annunzio is also especially clear in the essays on Verga, in which he plays him off against Verga.

27. Pirandello, *Saggi,* p. 417. See also the second lecture on Verga, "The Discourse Given at the Royal Academy of Italy" ("Discorso alla Reale Accademia d'Italia," 1931), *Saggi,* pp. 394–95, and "Dialectality" ("Dialettalità," 1921) *Saggi,* pp. 1169–72.

28. Pirandello, *Saggi,* p. 391.

29. Pirandello, "Renunciation" ("Rinunzia," 1896), *Saggi,* p. 1018. Pirandello used this passage more than once during these years. See also "Spoken Action" ("Azione Parlata," 1899), *Saggi,* p. 984, and his review of G. A. Cesareo's *Francesca da Rimini* (1905), *Saggi,* p. 945.

30. Pirandello made this argument in various places. I am here quoting from "Illustrators, Actors, and Translators" ("Illustratori, Attori e Traduttori," 1908), *Saggi,* p. 221. The full passage reads as follows: "The world is not limited to the idea that we can make of it: outside of us the world exists for itself and with us; and in our representation of it, therefore, we must commit ourselves to realizing it as much as is possible for us." An earlier statement, virtually identical, appeared in "Sincerità e Arte," *Il Marzocco,* vol. 2, no. 5 (7 Mar. 1897), 11v.

31. *The Outcast* was written in 1893 and first published with some changes in serial form in *La Tribuna* in 1901. The second edition was printed in a single volume by Treves (Milan) in 1908. The third

and definitive edition was published by Bemporad (Florence) in 1927.

32. Pirandello, *Umorismo,* in *Saggi,* p. 153.
33. Pirandello, *Saggi,* p. 184.
34. Pirandello, review entitled "Men, Women, and Puppets" ("Uomini, Donne e Burattini"), *Le Cronache Letterarie,* vol. 3, no. 98 (3 Mar. 1912), 17.
35. Quoted by Giudice, *Pirandello,* p. 388.
36. Pirandello, "Per un Libro di Novelle," *La Fanfulla della Domenica,* vol. 27, no. 3 (15 Jan. 1905), 2v.
37. Pirandello, "The Secret Notebook of Luigi Pirandello" ("Il Taccuino Segreto di Luigi Pirandello"), *Sipario,* vol. 7, no. 80 (Dec. 1952), 7. Apparently, there is no way to know precisely when the various parts of the "Secret Notebook" were written.
38. Pirandello, *Saggi,* p. 901. The appendix is entitled "On the Aesthetic Rationale of Words" ("Per le Ragioni Estetiche della Parola").
39. Pirandello, *Saggi,* p. 1169.
40. Ibid., p. 341.
41. Ibid., pp. 958–59.
42. Pirandello, "Sincerità e Arte," p. 11v.
43. Pirandello, "The Secret Notebook," p. 6. Claudio Vicentini, *L'Estetica di Pirandello* (Milan, 1970), p. 67, points to a probable debt to Capuana, who never tired of insisting that the work composes itself.
44. In "Novellas and Novella Writers" ("Novelle e Novellieri"), *Nuova Antologia* 207 (16 June 1906), 667, Pirandello wrote: "I have a high esteem for the talent of Papini, but I note with displeasure in him a frenzy that becomes increasingly violent to show himself original at any cost. Now one cannot be original by an act of will: either one is or one is not. Whoever wishes by an act of will to be original will succeed in being eccentric, strange, extravagant, and nothing else."
45. Pirandello, *Umorismo, Saggi,* p. 81. For the same passage in "Irony" ("Ironia") see *Saggi,* p. 993.
46. See Pirandello's obituary note on Cena, *Saggi,* p. 1041.

2. IN SEARCH OF AUTHENTICITY: *UMORISMO*

1. See Pirandello's "Un Critico Fantastico," *Saggi,* p. 373; *Umorismo, Saggi,* p. 138.
2. My word "sense" does not adequately render the emotional coloration apparently intended by Pirandello. In letters to Ugo Ojetti

recently published he emphasized the term *sentimento* in the phrase and contrasted it with *visione, pensiero, avvertimento.* See *Carteggi Inediti,* ed. Sarah Zappulla Muscara, Quaderni dell' Istituto di Studi Pirandelliani 2 (Rome, 1980), pp. 33, 37.

3. Pirandello, *Umorismo, Saggi,* p. 134.
4. Ibid., p. 126.
5. See the early chapters of ibid., passim.
6. Luigi Pirandello, letter of 24 June 1890, "Lettere di Studente: 1889–1890 [to Ernesto Monaci]," *Nuova Antologia* 426 (1 Apr. 1943), 147.
7. Benedetto Croce, "L'Umorismo: del Vario Significato della Parola e del Suo Uso nella Critica Letteraria," *Journal of Comparative Literature,* vol. 1, no. 3 (1903), 220–28.
8. Pirandello, *Art and Science, Saggi,* p. 167.
9. Ibid.
10. See Antonio Piromalli's excellent article, "Pirandello e Croce," in *Atti del Congresso Internazionale di Studi Pirandelliani* (Florence, 1967), pp. 863–75.
11. Luigi Baccolo, "Pirandello e la Storia," *Teatro di Pirandello,* Convegno di Studi, Centro di Studi Alfieriani, ad Asti, 1967 (Asti, 1968), pp. 17–20. The article had appeared earlier in *Tempo Presente* 12 (1966), 61–64.
12. Luigi Pirandello, "Lettere al Figlio Stefano durante la Grande Guerra," *Sipario,* vol. 7, no. 80 (July 1952), 31.
13. Pirandello, *Umorismo, Saggi,* p. 127.
14. For an excellent account of this tendency see Massimo Castri's *Pirandello Ottanta,* ed. Ettore Capriolo (Milan, 1981).
15. The singular exception to this is probably *The Mountain Giants* (*I Giganti della Montagna,* 1932–36).
16. Letter dated 15 December 1893 (Rome). "Dodici Lettere alla Fidanzata," *Omnibus,* vol. 1, no. 1 (18 Oct. 1946), 10.
17. Giovanni Marchesini, *Saggi sulla Naturale Unità del Pensiero* (Florence, 1895) and *Le Finzioni dell'Anima* (Bari, 1905). Franz Rauhut was the first to study Pirandello's debt to Marchesini. See his "Wissenschaftliche Quellen von Gedanken Luigi Pirandellos," *Romanische Forschungen* 53 (1939), 185–205, and *Der Junge Pirandello* (Munich, 1964).
18. Pirandello, *Novelle,* 1:451.
19. Ibid., p. 87.
20. Ibid., p. 95.
21. Pirandello, "Sincerità e Arte," p. 12.
22. See chapter 1, n. 38.
23. Luigi Pirandello, *Tutti i Romanzi,* [ed. Corrado Alvaro], *Opere di*

Luigi Pirandello, vol. 3, I Classici Contemporanei Italiani (Milan, 1957), 217–18.

24. Pirandello, *Romanzi,* p. 265.
25. Ibid., pp. 303–4.
26. Piero Cudini, *"Il fu Mattia Pascal:* Dalle fonti chamissiane e zoliane alla prima struttura narrativa di Luigi Pirandello," *Belfagor* 26 (1971), 702–13.
27. Benedetto Croce, "Luigi Baccolo—*Luigi Pirandello,*" *La Critica* 36 (20 Jan. 1938), 68–70.

3. A MEDITATION ON CONSCIOUSNESS AND SELF-CONSCIOUSNESS

1. Pirandello, *Romanzi,* pp. 383–84.
2. Pirandello, "Dodici Lettere alla Fidanzata," p. 17.
3. Pirandello, *Romanzi,* pp. 1179–85. In the first edition this novel was entitled *Roll 'Em (Si Gira).* See also Pirandello's review of Rosso di San Secondo's *La Fuga,* in *Saggi,* p. 970.
4. "Pirandello on Writing Plays," *Living Age,* 326 (Aug. 1925), 473.
5. Adriano Tilgher reproduces this statement in "Theater of Mirrors" "Il Teatro dello Specchio," first printed in *La Stampa* (18, 19 Aug. 1920), then reprinted in *Il Problema Centrale,* ed. Alessandro D'Amico (Genoa, 1973), p. 109.
6. The fullest account of this early work is to be found in Sandro D'Amico, "Itinerario," p. 83.
7. Pirandello, *Novelle,* 1:1065.
8. Ibid., p. 1069.
9. Ibid., p. 1079.
10. Pirandello, *Romanzi,* pp. 727–28.
11. Pirandello, *Maschere Nude,* 4: 531–32.
12. Ibid., p. 532.
13. Ibid., p. 429.
14. Pirandello, "The Secret Notebook," p. 7.
15. In Diego Manganella's "Conversando con Pirandello," *Epoca,* vol. 6, no. 157 (5 July 1922), 3.
16. Appeared in *L'Impero,* Nov. 11–12, 1924. Quoted by Giudice, *Pirandello,* p. 496.
17. Castri, *Pirandello Ottanta,* p. 16.
18. Pirandello, "Lettere a Stefano," p. 29.
19. Pirandello, "Lettere ai Familiari," p. 311.
20. Luigi Pirandello, "Una Pagina Inedita di Luigi Pirandello: Una

Lettera a Marta Abba, 29 Aprile 1930," *Realismo Lirico* 51 (July 1962), 17.

21. Luigi Pirandello, "Will Talking Films Abolish the Theater?" ("Se il Film Parlante Abolirà il Teatro?" 1929), *Saggi,* p. 996.

22. "Pirandello Quits Europe," *Living Age* 339 (Nov. 1930), 317.

23. Gaspare Giudice, *Pirandello,* p. 33.

24. See Giudice's careful study of Pirandello's political experience, *Pirandello,* pp. 201–30 and passim.

25. Giuseppe Villaroel, "Colloqui con Pirandello," *Il Giornale d'Italia,* vol. 24, no. 110 (8 May 1924), 3.

26. Quoted from Emil Ludwig's "Colloqui con Pirandello" by Gian Franco Venè, *Pirandello Fascista* (Milan, 1971), p. 116.

27. "La Vita Creata," *L'Idea Nazionale,* vol. 13, no. 256 (28 Oct. 1923), 2.

28. See the interview with Villaroel, p. 3.

29. Corrado Alvaro reports the story and the statement in his preface to *Novelle,* 1:22. On returning from an interview with Mussolini, Pirandello said that the Duce had reproved his restraint concerning Marta Abba. "When you love a woman," Pirandello reported him as saying, "you don't talk so much: you throw her on a couch." Pirandello's disaffection with Mussolini as a leader is perhaps most succinctly summed up in Eligio Possenti's report of a conversation on a walk during the height of fascism (*in pieno fascismo*). Pirandello described Mussolini as "a top hat, an empty top hat that by itself cannot stand upright. But into this hat, after Vittorio Veneto, many Italians have put something. The pure have put their noblest national aspirations; the impure their basest interests. And now the hat, filled in this way, stands upright. On the day when, for one reason or another, the pure and the impure take back what they have put inside, the hat will fall amid general disinterest." "Pirandello Fu Profetico nel Definire Mussolini," *Corriere della Sera,* vol. 81, no. 178 (29 July 1956), 3.

30. Guido Lopez, "Epistolario D'Amico, Lopez, Pirandello," *Il Dramma,* vol. 32, no. 241 (Oct. 1956), 45.

31. Pirandello, *Quaderni, Romanzi,* pp. 1206–7.

32. See Pirandello's *Umorismo, Saggi,* p. 81, and *Tonight We Improvise, Maschere Nude,* 4:210.

33. Pirandello, *Maschere Nude,* 4:208–11.

34. Umberto Bosco, *Cammino di Pirandello* (Rome, 1969), pp. 1–5.

35. See Vincenzo Chieppa, *Pirandello e Sartre* (Florence, 1967) and Nicola Chiaromonte, "Pirandello e Dopo," *Tempo Presente,* vol. 12, no. 2 (Feb. 1967), 62–64.

36. Mario Missiroli, "Colloqui con Luigi Pirandello," *L'Illustrazione Italiana,* vol. 61, no. 40 (7 Oct. 1934), 543.

37. Pirandello, *Saggi,* pp. 875–76.
38. Pirandello, "Il Poeta Ludwig Handsteken," *Saggi,* p. 964 (first published in *La Tribuna,* 7 July 1916).
39. Pirandello, *Umorismo, Saggi,* p. 153, and "The Secret Notebook," pp. 16–17.

4. IN THE GRIPS OF ARCANE FORCES

1. Mario Missiroli, "Colloqui," p. 544.
2. Pirandello, *Maschere Nude,* 5:838.
3. Pirandello, *Romanzi,* p. 387.
4. Ibid., p. 1104.
5. See especially Giovanni Macchia, *Pirandello o la Stanza della Tortura* (Milan, 1981), pp. 46–62.
6. Renato Simoni, "Tragedia di Pirandello," *Sipario,* vol. 1, no. 7–8 (1946), 44.
7. Massimo Bontempelli, "Pirandello e il Candore," *Introduzione e Discorsi 1936–1942* (Milan, 1945), pp. 9–28.
8. Pirandello, *Romanzi,* p. 354.
9. Ibid., p. 121.
10. Ibid., pp. 148–49.
11. Pirandello, *Novelle,* 1:470.
12. Pirandello, "Lettere ai Familiari," p. 312.
13. Pirandello, *Maschere Nude,* 4:505, 508.
14. Ibid., p. 508.
15. Pirandello, *Novelle,* 2:815.

5. RELATIVITY AND THE FICTIONS
OF THE SPIRIT

1. See, for example, Pirandello's "Theater and Literature," ("Teatro e Letteratura," 1918), *Saggi,* p. 987, and his "Discourse on Verga Presented in Catania," ("Discorso di Catania [su Verga]," 1920), *Saggi,* p. 419.
2. Pirandello, *Saggi,* pp. 874–75.
3. Joseph Wood Krutch, "Pirandello and the Dissolution of Ego," *"Modernism" in Modern Drama: A Definition and an Estimate* (Ithaca, N.Y., 1953), pp. 77–87.
4. Pirandello, *Saggi,* pp. 149–51.
5. The two basic books on Pirandello during his formative years are Franz Rauhut's *Der Junge Pirandello* and Gösta Andersson's *Arte e Teoria.*

6. Pirandello, *Saggi*, p. 151.
7. Pirandello, "Lettere al Figlio Stefano," pp. 31–32.
8. Pirandello, *Romanzi*, p. 914.
9. Until the recent publication of the correspondence between Pirandello and Martoglio, Pirandello's critics had assumed that he had changed to Italian for its wider audience. Although that issue probably played a part in his decision, the correspondence with Martoglio makes clear that he was also motivated by a dislike for Angelo Musco, his chief Sicilian interpreter. See *Pirandello / Martoglio: Carteggio Inedito*, ed. Sarah Zappulla, Quaderni dell'Istituto di Studi Pirandelliani 3 (Milan, 1980), passim.
10. Douglas Radcliffe-Umstead, *The Mirror of Our Anguish* (Cranbury, N.J., 1978), pp. 262, 273.
11. Pirandello, *Romanzi*, p. 1206.
12. Pirandello, "Lettere al Figlio Stefano," p. 29 (18 Aug. 1916).
13. Ibid., p. 32 (18 Apr. 1917).
14. Richard Gilman, *The Making of Modern Drama* (New York, 1972), pp. 170–71.
15. Pirandello, *Maschere Nude*, 4:365–66.
16. Ibid., p. 368.
17. Pirandello frequently made this argument about madness. See especially the interview with Villaroel, 8 May 1924, p. 3: "The madman constructs without logic. Logic is form, and form stands in opposition to life. Life is formless and illogical. Therefore I believe that madfolk are closer to life. There's nothing fixed or determined in us. We have all possibilities within. Thus it is that suddenly, without thought, we turn thief or madman. All we need to do is to relax this elastic netting called consciousness, and everything slips out. We order our lives with thought. When the brain dominates, life takes on a healthy aspect." A good part of this is reproduced by Giudice, *Pirandello*, p. 354.
18. Pirandello, *Maschere Nude*, 4:349.
19. Ibid., p. 355.
20. Ibid., p. 326.
21. Ibid., pp. 326–27.
22. Pirandello, *Umorismo, Saggi*, p. 153.

6. THE THEATRICAL MATRIX OF EXPERIENCE

1. Pirandello, *Maschere Nude*, 4:176.
2. Giudice, *Pirandello*, p. 531.

3. Pirandello, *Maschere Nude,* 4:196–97.

4. Ibid., p. 198.

5. See especially Arcangelo Leone de Castris, *Storia di Pirandello* (Bari, 1975), pp. 139, 141, 224–25; Piromalli, "Pirandello e Croce," pp. 868, 871–72; Nicola Chiaromonte, "Pirandello and Contemporary Theatre," *Le Théâtre dans le Monde,* vol. 16, no. 3 (1967), 228; Jörn Moestrup, *The Structural Patterns of Pirandello's Work* (Odense, 1972), p. 128; Eugène Ionesco, "Négation de Brecht," *Artes, Lettres et Spectacles* 602 (16 Jan. 1957), 2.

6. Luigi Pirandello, "The Primacy of Italian Theater" ("Primato del Teatro Italiano"), *Scenario* 4 (May 1935), 235–41, passim.

7. Elder Olson, *Tragedy and the Theory of Drama* (Detroit, 1966).

8. Reprinted in Leonardo Sciascia, *Pirandello e il Pirandellismo* (Palermo, 1953), p. 89.

9. See especially Tilgher's "Theater of Mirrors" ("Teatro dello Specchio") in *Il Problema Centrale,* pp. 108–18 and "Il Teatro di Luigi Pirandello" in *Studi sul Teatro Contemporaneo* (Rome, 1923), pp. 135–93.

10. Luigi Pirandello to Silvio D'Amico, 29 Nov. 1927, reprinted by Franz Rauhut in *Der Junge Pirandello,* p. 417.

11. The "essay" referred to is the long chapter cited in n. 9 from Tilgher's *Studi sul Teatro Contemporaneo.* The quotation is from his "Le Estetiche di Luigi Pirandello," *Il Problema Centrale,* p. 388.

12. Tilgher, *Studi sul Teatro Contemporaneo,* p. 138.

13. See Tilgher, "Le Estetiche di Luigi Pirandello," *Il Problema Centrale,* pp. 386–87.

14. See n. 10.

15. Adriano Tilgher, *La Scena e la Vita. Nuovi Studi sul Teatro Contemporaneo* (Rome, 1925), pp. 136, 138.

16. Luigi Pirandello, "Will Talking Films Abolish the Theater?" *Saggi,* p. 997.

17. Giudice, *Pirandello,* p. 325.

18. See Luigi Pirandello, "Lettere di Pirandello a Ruggero Ruggeri," *Il Dramma,* vol. 31, no. 227–28 (Aug.–Sept. 1955), 57–70, passim; "Spoken Action," *Saggi,* p. 983; "The *Francesca da Rimini* of G. A. Cesareo," *Saggi,* p. 941; and "Illustrators, Actors, and Translators," *Saggi,* p. 221.

19. See Giudice, *Pirandello,* p. 471–79; and the reminiscences in Anton Giulio Bragaglia, "Pirandello: Uomo," in *Almanacco Letterario Bompiani, 1938* (Milan, 1938), pp. 87–88; Dario Niccodemi, *Tempo Passato* (Milan, 1929), pp. 83–88; Marta Abba, "Marta Abba: 'Parlo del Maestro,'" *Il Dramma,* vol. 11, no. 202 (15 Jan. 1935), 37–38.

20. Pirandello, *Saggi,* p. 1235.

21. Quoted by Vicentini from Bernardino Varisco's *Conosci Te Stesso* (1912), in *L'Estetica di Pirandello,* p. 55.
22. Pirandello, "Lettere ai Familiari," p. 311.
23. Pirandello, *Maschere Nude,* 5:943.
24. Ibid., pp. 961–62.
25. Ibid., p. 968.
26. To these might be added the minor matters of the moving table in *The Life I Gave You* and the animate statues in *When One Is Somebody.*
27. Pirandello, "Lettere al Figlio Stefano" (23 July 1917), p. 37.
28. Adriano Tilgher, "Ratti e Pirandello," first appeared in *La Stampa* (21, 22 May 1921), reprinted in *Il Problema Centrale* in a note on p. 132.
29. Tilgher, *Il Problema Centrale,* pp. 129–31.
30. The article first appeared in *Comoedia* 7 (1 Jan. 1925), 5–10, then as the preface to *Six Characters, Maschere Nude,* 4:35–46. I quote from the preface, pp. 39–40.
31. Pirandello, *Maschere Nude,* 4:40.
32. Sciascia, *Pirandello,* p. 90.
33. Pirandello, *Maschere Nude,* 4:81.
34. Ibid., p. 54.
35. Ibid., p. 87.
36. Pirandello, "Lettere a Ruggeri," p. 70.
37. Pirandello, *Maschere Nude,* 4:81.
38. Gino Rizzo, "Luigi Pirandello in Search of a Total Theatre," *Italian Quarterly,* vol. 12, no. 45 (1968), 3–26. See also Richard Gilman, *The Making of Modern Drama,* p. 181.
39. Pirandello, *Maschere Nude,* 4:116.
40. Ibid., pp. 99–100.

7. PIRANDELLO: THE ONE AND THE MANY

1. Lopez, "Epistolario D'Amico, Lopez, Pirandello," p. 45.
2. Dated 29 November 1927. Rauhut, *Der Junge Pirandello,* p. 417.
3. Luigi Pirandello, "Abbasso il Pirandellismo," *Il Dramma* 7 (15 Dec. 1931), 27.
4. See Pirandello's letter to Tilgher of 29 August 1921 already quoted, in Sciascia, *Pirandello,* p. 90.
5. Pirandello, "Lettere ai Familiari," p. 312.
6. Pirandello, *Novelle,* 2:750.
7. Pirandello, *Romanzi,* pp. 692–93.
8. Giovanni Calendoli, *Luigi Pirandello* (Catania, 1962), pp. 71–72;

Arminio Janner, *Luigi Pirandello* (Florence, 1948), pp. 259–70; Radcliff-Umstead, *The Mirror of Our Anguish*, p. 20.

9. Pirandello, *Novelle*, 1:447.

10. Ibid., p. 446.

11. See especially Pirandello's comments in the interviews with W. V., *Il Messaggero della Domenica*, vol. 2, no. 8 (23 Feb. 1919), 1.

12. Pirandello, never averse to using a second time a passage he thought effective, was especially given to self-plagiarism in this novel. See *Tutti i Romanzi*, ed. Giovanni Macchia, 2 vols., (Milan, 1973–75); Mario Costanzo's textual notes are excellent in this respect: 2:1068–84, 1104–9. The principal works borrowed from are "City Trees" ("Alberi Cittadini," 1900), *The Late Mattia Pascal* (1904), "Stefano Giogli, One and Two" ("Stefano Giogli, Uno e Due," 1909), "Sing the Epistle" (1911), "To Reconstruct Oneself" ("Ricostruirsi," 1915), "The Trap" (1912), *Six Characters* (1921), "Return" ("Ritorno," 1923), and *Each in His Own Way* (1924).

13. Pirandello, *Romanzi*, pp. 1415–16.

14. Ibid., p. 1416.

15. Ibid.

16. Biasin, *Literary Diseases*, p. 125.

17. The figure of fireflies anticipates in some respects the metaphors of "phosphorescence" and "self-luminousness" discussed by Gilbert Ryle as descriptive of the process of becoming conscious or what I call passing into wakefulness. *The Concept of Mind*, pp. 159–60.

18. Pirandello, *Maschere Nude*, 5:1344.

19. Ibid., p. 1340.

20. Ibid., p. 1344.

21. Pirandello, *Saggi*, p. 880.

22. See, for example, Pirandello's "Discourse on Verga Presented in Catania," *Saggi*, p. 420.

23. I borrow this distinction from Sir Isaiah Berlin's *The Hedgehog and the Fox: Essay on Tolstoy's View of History* (New York, 1977).

24. Domenico Vittorini, *The Drama of Luigi Pirandello*, (Philadelphia), p. vi.

25. See Silvio D'Amico, *Il Teatro dei Fantocci* (Florence, 1920), p. 90, and his *Cronache del Teatro* (Bari, 1963), pp. 82, 105.

26. See Benedetto Croce's "'L'Umorismo' di Luigi Pirandello," *La Critica* 7 (1909), 220–21; his *Conversazioni Critiche: Scritti di Storia Letteraria e Politica*, 5 vols., (Bari, 1939), 5:163; and Italo Siciliano's *Il Teatro di Pirandello: Ovvero dei Fasti dell'Artificio* (Turin, 1929).

27. Georges Neveux, "Il a Tout Fait Naître," *Artes, Lettres et Spectacles* 602 (16 Jan. 1957), 2.

28. Jean Bastaire, attempting a reevaluation in 1958, saw clearly the

limitations of the traditional view; see "Pirandello ou la Dérision Baroque," *Esprit* 26 (June 1958), 977.

29. Luigi Pirandello, "Viaggi," *L'Illustrazione Italiana,* vol. 62, no. 25 (23 June 1935), 1033–34.
30. The leaders in this critical reevaluation were Bastaire (see n. 28); Bernard Dort, "Pirandello et la Drammaturgie Française Contemporaine," in *Atti del Congresso Internazionale di Studi Pirandelliani* (Florence, 1967), pp. 51–73; and Guy Dumur, *Le Théâtre de Pirandello,* (Paris, 1967).
31. See n. 24.
32. See n. 29.

BIBLIOGRAPHY

WORKS BY PIRANDELLO

COLLECTED WORKS, CHRONOLOGICALLY

Novelle per un Anno. [Edited by Corrado Alvaro]. *Opere di Luigi Pirandello,* vols. 1 and 2. I Classici Contemporanei Italiani. Milan, 1956–57.

Tutti i Romanzi. [Edited by Corrado Alvaro]. *Opere di Luigi Pirandello,* vol. 3. I Classici Contemporanei Italiani. Milan, 1957.

Maschere Nude. [Edited by Silvio D'Amico]. *Opere di Luigi Pirandello,* vols. 4 and 5. I Classici Contemporanei Italiani. Milan, 1958.

Saggi, Poesie e Scritti Vari. Edited by Manlio Lo Vecchio-Musti. *Opere di Luigi Pirandello,* vol. 6. I Classici Contemporanei Italiani. Milan, 1960.

Tutti i Romanzi. Edited by Giovanni Macchia with the collaboration of Mario Costanzo. 2 vols. Milan, 1973–75.

OTHER WORKS, CHRONOLOGICALLY

"L'Altalena delle Simpatie." *Folchetto,* vol. 3, no. 279 (9 Oct. 1893), 2.

"Studi Letterari" (review of Francesco Flamini's *Studi di Storia Letteraria Italiana e Straniera*). *Roma Letteraria,* vol. 3, no. 13 (10 July 1895), 305–10.

"Come si Scrive Oggi in Italia." *La Critica,* vol. 2, no. 33 (15 Sept. 1895), 779–84.

"Novelle Siciliane." *Rassegna Settimanale Universale,* vol. 1, no. 15 (12 Apr. 1896), 2–4.

"Sincerità e Arte." *Il Marzocco,* vol. 2, no. 5 (7 Mar. 1897), 11–11v.

"Fede e Bellezza I." *Roma Letteraria,* vol. 6, no. 22 (Nov. 1898), 518–22.
    "Fede e Bellezza II." *Roma Letteraria,* vol. 6, no. 23 (Dec. 1898), 542–46.

"Leopardi Cieco." *Roma Letteraria,* vol. 8, no. 3 (10 Feb. 1900), 51–54.

"Il Marchese di Roccaverdina." *Natura e Arte* 10 (1 July 1901), 184–85.

"Per un Libro di Novelle." *La Fanfulla della Domenica,* vol. 27, no. 3 (15 Jan. 1905), 2v.

"Libri di Versi." *Nuova Antologia* 204 (16 Dec. 1905), 639–47.

"Il Teatro Stabile di Roma." *Il Marzocco,* vol. 11, no. 23 (10 June 1906), 52–52v.

"Novelle e Novellieri." *Nuova Antologia* 207 (16 June 1906), 657–68.

"Uomini, Donne e Burratini." *Le Cronache Letterarie,* vol. 3, no. 98 (3 Mar. 1912), 17–17v.

"Il Fatto Estetico." *Aprutium* 3 (Apr.–May 1914), 179–88.

"La Vita Creata." *L'Idea Nazionale,* vol. 13, no. 256 (28 Oct. 1923), 2.

"Abbasso il Pirandellismo." *Il Dramma* 7 (15 Dec. 1931), 26–27.

"Primato del Teatro Italiano." *Scenario* 4 (May 1935), 235–41.

"Viaggi." *L'Illustrazione Italiana,* vol. 62, no. 25 (23 June 1935), 1033–34.

"Taccuino Segreto di Luigi Pirandello." *Sipario,* vol. 7, no. 80 (Dec. 1952), 2–20.

LETTERS, IN THE ORDER IN WHICH THEY WERE REPRINTED

"Lettere di Studente: 1889–1890 [to Ernesto Monaci]." *Nuova Antologia* 426 (1 Apr. 1943), 144–49.

"Dodici Lettere alla Fidanzata." *Omnibus,* vol. 1, no. 1 (18 Oct. 1946), 10–11; no. 2 (25 Oct. 1946), 16–17.

"Lettere al Figlio Stefano durante la Grande Guerra." *Sipario,* vol. 7, no. 80 (July 1952), 25–37.

[Letters to Tilgher.] In Leonardo Sciascia's *Pirandello e il Pirandellismo,* pp. 89–99. Palermo, 1953.

"Lettere di Pirandello a Ruggero Ruggeri." *Il Dramma,* vol. 31, no. 227–28 (Aug.–Sept. 1955), 57–70.

[Letters Pirandello/D'Annunzio.] Edited by Emilio Mariano. *L'Osservatore Politico Letterario* 4 (Mar. 1958), 39–40.

"Lettere ai Familiari di Luigi Pirandello." Edited by Sandro D'Amico. *Terzo Programma,* 3 (1961), 273–312.

"Una Pagina Inedita di Luigi Pirandello: Una Lettera a Marta Abba, 29 Aprile 1930." *Realismo Lirico* 51 (July 1962), 17.

"Due Lettere di Pirandello a Jenny." Edited by Nino De Bella. *Narrativa,* vol. 9, no. 1 (1964), 155–56.

[Letter to Silvio D'Amico, 29 Nov. 1929.] In Franz Rauhut's *Der Junge Pirandello,* pp. 417–18. Munich, 1964.

"Lettere di Pirandello al Cesareo." Edited by A.M. Dotto. *Nuovi Quaderni del Meridione* 5 (1967), 473–81.

Carteggi Inediti. Edited by Sarah Zappulla Muscara. Quaderni dell' Istituto di Studi Pirandelliani 2. Rome, 1980.

Pirandello / Martoglio: Carteggio Inedito. Edited by Sarah Zappulla. Quaderni dell'Istituto di Studi Pirandelliani 3. Milan, 1980.

INTERVIEWS, CHRONOLOGICALLY

W. V.. "Conversando con Pirandello." *Il Messaggero della Domenica,* vol. 2, no. 8 (23 Feb. 1919), 1.

Manganella, Diego. "Conversando con Pirandello." *Epoca,* vol. 6, no. 157 (5 July 1922), 3.

Villaroel, Giuseppe. "Colloqui con Pirandello." *Il Giornale d'Italia,* vol. 24, no. 110 (8 May 1924), 3.

"Pirandello on Writing Plays." *Living Age* 326 (Aug. 1925), 473.

"Pirandello Interviewed." *Living Age* 331 (1 Oct. 1926), 80–81.

"Pirandello Quits Europe." *Living Age* 339 (Nov. 1930), 317.

"Pirandello in Search of Himself." *Literary Digest* 114 (1 Oct. 1932), 18.

Missiroli, Mario. "Colloquio con Luigi Pirandello." *L'Illustrazione Italiana,* vol. 61, no. 40 (7 Oct. 1934), 543–44.

"Pirandello Parla di Pirandello." *Quadrivio,* vol. 5, no. 3 (15 Nov. 1936), 8.

WORKS ABOUT PIRANDELLO

Abba, Marta. "Marta Abba: 'Parlo del Maestro.'" *Il Dramma,* vol. 11, no. 202 (15 Jan. 1935), 37–38.

———. "Una Fedele Interprete." *Il Tempo* (10 Mar. 1979), 10.

Adank, Mathias. *Luigi Pirandello e i Suoi Rapporti col Mondo Tedesco.* Bern, 1948.

Allavena, Oreste. *Pirandello dalla Narrativa al Dramma.* Savona, 1970.

Alley, John N. "French Periodical Criticism of Pirandello's Plays." *Italica* 25 (1948), 138–49.

Allmayer, Vito Fazio. "Il Problema Pirandello." *Belfagor,* vol. 12, no. 1 (Jan. 1957), 18–34.

Alonge, Roberto. "Pirandello dalla Narrativa al Teatro." *Comunità,* vol. 22, no. 153 (1968), 113–21.

———. "La Tragedia Astratta dell'*Enrico IV.*" In *Teatro di Pirandello* (Convegno di Studi, Centre di Studi Alfieriani, ad Asti, 1967), pp. 29–45. Asti, 1968.

Alvaro, Corrado. "Teatro e Letteratura Teatrale." *Il Dramma* 21 (1 Dec. 1945), 55–56.

———. "Commento al 'Taccuino Segreto di Luigi Pirandello.'" *Sipario,* vol. 7, no. 80 (Dec. 1952), 19–20.

———. Preface to *Novelle per un Anno.* In *Opere di Luigi Pirandello,* vol. 1. I Classici Contemporanei Italiani, pp. 5–41. Milan, 1956.

Andersson, Gösta. *Arte e Teoria: Studi sulla Poetica del Giovane Luigi Pirandello.* Uppsala, 1966.

Antonucci, Giovanni. "La Critica e il Teatro di Pirandello: 1910–1922." *Veltro* 12 (1968), 125–61.

Assunto, Rosario. "Pirandello e le Teorie dell'Arte Significativa di 'Altro.'" *Realtà del Mezzogiorno,* vol. 7, no. 1 (Jan. 1968), 9–17.

Aste, Mario. *Two Novels of Pirandello: An Essay.* Washington, D.C., 1979.

Baccolo, Luigi. "Dopo Pirandello, Sartre." *Sipario,* vol. 5, no. 52 (Aug. 1950), 7.

——. "Pirandello e la Storia." In *Teatro di Pirandello* (Convegno di Studi, Centro di Studi Alfieriani, ad Asti, 1967), pp. 15–21. Asti, 1968.

Baldacci, Luigi. "Il Teatro di Bontempelli e l'Esempio di Pirandello." In *Atti del Congresso Internazionale di Studi Pirandelliani*, pp. 276–83. Florence, 1967.

Barbina, Alfredo. *Bibliografia della Critica Pirandelliana, 1889–1961.* Florence, 1966.

Barilli, Renato. *La Linea Svevo-Pirandello.* Milan, 1972.

Bartolucci, Giuseppe. "La Didascalia Drammaturgica." *Nuova Corrente* 52 (1970), 184–94.

Bastaire, Jean. "Pirandello ou la Dérision Baroque." *Esprit* 26 (June 1958), 976–84.

Battaglia, Salvatore. "Pirandello Narratore." In *Atti del Congresso Internazionale di Studi Pirandelliani*, pp. 25–36. Florence, 1967.

Bentley, Eric. "Note on Pirandello." *Sipario,* vol. 7, no. 80 (Dec. 1952), 66.

——. "Pirandello's Joy and Torment." In his *In Search of Theatre,* pp. 297–314. New York, 1953.

——. "Father's Day: In Search of Six Characters in Search of an Author." *Drama Review,* vol. 13, no. 1 (Fall 1968), 57–72.

Bergin, Thomas. "Luigi Pirandello: Pathfinder and More." *Books Abroad* 41 (1967), 413–14.

Biasin, Gian-Paolo. *Literary Diseases: Theme and Metaphor in the Italian Novel.* Austin, 1975.

Bishop, Thomas. *Pirandello and the French Theatre.* New York, 1960.

Blasich, Gottardo. "Situazione Drammatica e Personaggio Pirandelliano." *Letture,* vol. 23, no. 1 (Jan. 1968), 3–26.

Boni, Marco. "La Formazione Letteraria di Luigi Pirandello." *Convivium, Raccolta Nuova* 3 (1948), 321–50.

Bontempelli, Massimo. "Pirandello o del Candore." In *Introduzione e Discorsi (1936–1942)*, pp. 9–28. Milan, 1945.

Borlenghi, Aldo. *Pirandello o dell'Ambiguità.* Padua, 1968.

Borrello, O. "Pirandello, Croce, e il Problema Estetico." *Rassegna di Scienze Filosofiche* 14 (Jan.–Mar. 1961), 91–111.

Borsellino, Nino. *Immagini di Pirandello.* Cosenza, 1979.

Bosco, Umberto. *Cammino di Pirandello.* Rome, 1969.

——. "Liricità del Ragionare Pirandelliano." In *Quaderni I,* pp. 99–107. Quaderni dell'Istituto di Studi Pirandelliani. Rome, 1973.

Bragaglia, Anton Giulio. "Pirandello: Uomo." In *Almanacco Letterario Bompiani, 1938,* pp. 87–88. Milan, 1938.

Bragaglia, Leonardo. *Gli Interpreti Pirandelliani, 1910–1969.* Rome, 1969.

Bruno, Francesco. "Tilgher e Pirandello." In *Adriano Tilgher: l'Uomo, il Pensiero, i Luoghi, l'Attualità,* edited by Liliana Scalero, pp. 21–26. Padua, 1962.

Brustein, Robert. "Pirandello nella Drammaturgia Contemporanea." *Veltro* 12 (1968), 53–77.

Büdel, Oscar. *Pirandello.* New York, 1965.

Calendoli, Giovanni. *Luigi Pirandello.* Catania, 1962.

———. "Dai Futuristi a Pirandello attraverso il Grottesco." *Sipario* 260 (Dec. 1967), 14–16.

Cambon, Glauco, ed. *Pirandello: A Collection of Critical Essays.* Englewood Cliffs, N.J., 1966.

Caserta, Ernesto G. "Croce, Pirandello e il Problema Estetico." *Italica* 51 (1974), 20–42.

Castri, Massimo. *Pirandello Ottanta.* Edited by Ettore Capriolo. Milan, 1981.

Chaix-Ruy, Jules. *Pirandello: Humour et Poésie.* Paris, 1967.

Chiaromonte, Nicola. *La Situazione Drammatica.* Milan, 1960.

———. "Pirandello e Dopo." *Tempo Presente,* vol. 12, no. 2 (Feb. 1967), 62–64.

———. "Pirandello e l'Umorismo." *Tempo Presente,* vol. 12, no. 5 (May 1967), 11–17.

———. "Pirandello and Contemporary Theatre." *Le Théâtre dans le Monde,* vol. 16, no. 3 (1967), 224–37.

Chieppa, Vincenzo. *Pirandello e Sartre.* Florence, 1967.

Clark, Hoover W. "Existentialism and Pirandello's *Sei Personaggi.*" *Italica* 43 (1966), 276–84.

Corrigan, Beatrice. "Pirandello as a Director." *Theatre Research / Recherches Théâtrales,* vol. 12, no. 1 (1972), 155–63.

Croce, Benedetto. " 'L'Umorismo' di Luigi Pirandello." *La Critica* 7 (1909), 219–23.

———. "Luigi Pirandello." *La Critica* 33 (1935), 20–33.

———. "Il Pirandello e la Critica." *La Critica* 34 (1936), 79–80.

———. "Luigi Baccolo—*Luigi Pirandello.*" *La Critica* 36 (20 Jan. 1938), 68–70.

———. *Conversazioni Critiche: Scritti di Storia Letteraria e Politica.* 5 vols. Bari, 1939.

———. "*Luigi Pirandello e la Letteratura Europea Contemporanea* di A. Janner." *Quaderni della "Critica,"* vol. 4, no. 10 (1948), 80–81.

Cudini, Piero. "*Il Fu Mattia Pascal:* Dalle Fonti Chamissiane e Zoliane alla Prima Struttura Narrativa di Luigi Pirandello." *Belfagor* 26 (1971), 702–13.

Cuminetti, Benvenuto. "Indicazioni su *Quaderni di Serafino Gubbio Operatore.*" *Vita e Pensiero* 50 (Sept. 1967), 854–65.

D'Ambra, Lucio. "Malinconia Autunnale di Pirandello." *Comoedia* 10 (15 Oct. 1928), 9–11.

D'Amico, Sandro. " 'Presentazione' to 'Lettere ai Famigliari,' " *Terzo Programma* 3 (1961), 273–80.

——. "Itinerario di Pirandello al Teatro." *Veltro* 12 (1968), 81–97.

D'Amico, Silvio. *Il Teatro dei Fantocci.* Florence, 1920.

——. "Il Bisogno di Credere." *Sipario,* vol. 1, no. 7–8 (1946), 43.

——. "Il Messaggio di Luigi Pirandello." *Sipario,* vol. 7, no. 80 (1952), 63–64.

——. *Cronache del Teatro.* Bari, 1963.

De Castris, Arcangelo Leone. *Storia di Pirandello.* Bari, 1975.

Della Terza, Dante. "The Italian Novel and the Avant-garde." In *Petrarch to Pirandello: Studies in Italian Literature in Honor of Beatrice Corrigan,* edited by Julius A. Molinaro, pp. 231–49. Toronto, 1973.

Di Collalto, Orlando. "Introduzione a una Interpretazione Scenografica del Teatro Pirandelliano." *Letteratura* 28 (1964), 201–6.

Doglio, Federico. "Appunti per una Lettura dell'*Enrico IV*." *Quaderni I,* Quaderni dell'Istituto di Studi Pirandelliani 1, pp. 46–64. Rome, 1973.

Dombroski, Robert S. "La Concezione dell'Uomo in Pirandello e la Mitologia Fascista: Appunti per uno Studio." *Paragone* 292 (June 1974), 35–56.

Dort, Bernard. "Pirandello et la Dramaturgie Française Contemporaine." In *Atti del Congresso Internazionale di Studi Pirandelliani,* pp. 51–73. Florence, 1967.

Dumur, Guy. *Le Théâtre de Pirandello.* Paris, 1967.

Fabbri, Diego. "A Rip in a Paper Sky." *Le Théâtre dans le Monde,* vol. 16, no. 3 (1967), 218–23.

Fergusson, Francis. *The Idea of a Theater.* Princeton, N.J., 1949.

Ferrante, Luigi. *Teatro Italiano Grottesco.* Rocca San Casciano, 1954.

——. *Pirandello.* Florence, 1958.

——. "Pirandello e la Drammaturgia Italiana." *Quaderni del Piccolo Teatro della Città di Milano* 1 (1961), 13–20.

——. "La Poetica di Pirandello." In *Atti del Congresso Internazionale di Studi Pirandelliani,* pp. 370–78. Florence, 1967.

Frateili, Arnaldo. "Pirandello Uno e Due." *Almanacco Letterario Bompiani, 1938,* pp. 83–86. Milan, 1938.

Freedman, Morris. "Moral Perspectives in Pirandello." *Modern Drama* 6 (1964), 368–77.

Giacalone, Giuseppe. *Pirandello.* Brescia, 1966.

Gigli, Lorenzo. "Sicilianità di Pirandello." *Comoedia* 14 (15 Mar. 1932), 17–18.

Gilman, Richard. *The Making of Modern Drama.* New York, 1972.

——. "Pirandello." *Yale / Theatre* 5 (Spring 1974), 94–117.

Giudice, Gaspare. *Pirandello.* Turin, 1963. An English translation (abridged) has been done by Alistair Hamilton, London, 1975.

Golino, Carlo L. "Pirandello's Least-Known Novel." *Italica* 26 (1949), 263–68.

Gordon, Jan. "*Sei Personaggi in Cerca d'Autore:* Myth, Ritual, and Pirandello's Anti-Symbolist Theater." *Forum Italicum* 6 (1972), 333–55.

Guglielminetti, Marziano. *Struttura e Sintesi del Romanzo Italiano del Primo Novecento.* Milan, 1964.

——. "Il Teatro Mitico di Pirandello." In *Teatro di Pirandello* (Convegno di Studi, Centro di Studi Alfieriani, ad Asti), pp. 47–85. Asti, 1968.

Illiano, Antonio. "Pirandello's *Six Characters in Search of an Author:* A Comedy in the Making." *Italica* 44 (1967), 1–12.

——. "Momenti e Problemi di Critica Pirandelliana: L'Umorismo, Pirandello e Croce, Pirandello e Tilgher." *PMLA* 83 (1968), 135–43.

Ionesco, Eugène. "Négation de Brecht." *Artes, Lettres, et Spectacles* 602 (16 Jan. 1957), 2.

Jacobbi, Ruggero. "Attualità ed Inattualità di Pirandello." *Quaderni del Piccolo Teatro della Città di Milano* 1 (1961), 21–27.

Janner, Arminio. *Luigi Pirandello.* Florence, 1948.

Kennedy, Andrew K. "*Six Characters:* Pirandello's Last Tape." *Modern Drama,* vol. 12, no. 1 (May 1969), 1–9.

Krutch, Joseph Wood. "Pirandello and the Dissolution of Ego." In his *"Modernism" in Modern Drama: A Definition and an Estimate,* pp. 77–87. Ithaca, N.Y., 1953.

Lanza, Giuseppe. "Modernità di Pirandello." *Tempo Presente,* vol. 9, no. 12 (Dec. 1964), 20–30.

Laurentano, Bruno. "Pirandello, l'Incomunicabilità e il Dialogo." *La Cultura,* vol. 2, no. 6 (Nov. 1964), 660–64.

Licastro, Emanuele. "The Anti-Theatre in Pirandello: *The Man with a Flower in His Mouth.*" *Romance Notes,* vol. 15, no. 3 (Spring 1974), 513–15.

——. *Luigi Pirandello: Dalle Novelle alle Commedie.* Verona, 1974.

Livio, Gigi. "Il Periodo Grottesco del Teatro Pirandelliano." *Lettere Italiane,* vol. 23, no. 4 (Oct.–Dec. 1971), 519–47.

Lo Curzio, Gugielmo. *La Poesia di Luigi Pirandello.* Palermo, 1935.

Lopez, Guido. "Epistolario D'Amico, Lopez, Pirandello." *Il Dramma,* vol. 32, no. 241 (Oct. 1956), 37–46.

Lopez, Robert S. "Pirandello Old and New." *Yale Review* 60 (Winter 1971), 228–40.

Loriggio, Franco. "Life and Death: Pirandello's *Man with a Flower in His Mouth.*" *Italian Quarterly,* vol. 12, no. 47–48 (Winter–Spring 1969), 151–60.

Macchia, Giovanni. *Pirandello o la Stanza della Tortura.* Milan, 1981.

MacClintock, Lander. *The Age of Pirandello.* Bloomington, Ind., 1951.

Maira, Salvatore. "Ideologia e Tecnica nella Narrativa di Luigi Pirandello." *Nuovi Argomenti* 29–30 (Sept.–Dec. 1972), 187–224.

Mariano, Emilio. "Pirandello e il Teatro. Con Lettere Inedite." *Nuova Antologia* 97 (Dec. 1962), 487–506.

Matthaei, Renate. *Luigi Pirandello.* New York, 1973.

May, Frederick. "A Neglected Article by Pirandello: Tendencies of the Modern Novel." *Italian Quarterly,* vol. 6, no. 23–24 (Fall–Winter 1962), 30–45.

Moestrup, Jörn. *The Structural Patterns of Pirandello's Work.* Odense, 1972.

Momigliano, Attilio. *Impressioni d'un Lettore Contemporaneo,* pp. 246–60. Milan, 1928.

———. *Storia della Letteratura Italiana dalle Origini ai Nostri Giorni,* pp. 668–75. Messina-Milan, 1936.

Monti, Silvana. *Pirandello.* Palermo, 1974.

Moravia, Alberto. "La Lezione di Pirandello." *Sipario,* vol. 1, no. 7–8 (1946), 40.

———. "Il Dramma di Ersilia Drei senza i Sofismi di Pirandello." *Europeo,* vol. 10, no. 8 (21 Feb. 1954), 37.

Munafò, Gaetano. *Conoscere Pirandello.* Florence, 1968.

Nardelli, Federico. *L'Uomo Segreto.* Milan, 1932.

Neveux, Georges. "Il a Tout Fait Naître." *Artes, Lettres, et Spectacles* 602 (16 Jan. 1957), 2.

Niccodemi, Dario. *Tempo Passato.* Milan, 1929.

Oliver, Roger W. *Dreams of Passion. The Theater of Luigi Pirandello.* New York, 1979.

Paolucci, Anne. "Pirandello: Experience as the Expression of Will." *Forum Italicum,* vol. 7, no. 3 (Sept. 1973), 404–14.

———. *Pirandello's Theater: The Recovery of Modern Stage for Dramatic Art.* Carbondale, Ill., 1974.

Passeri Pignoni, Vera. "Il Pensiero Filosofico di Luigi Pirandello." *Sapienza* 20 (1967), 477–503.

Personè, Luigi. "Pirandello Scrittore Umoristico." *Osservatore Politico Letterario,* vol. 13, no. 8 (Aug. 1967), 10–29.

Pes, Nelia. *L'Idea come Personaggio nell'Arte di Luigi Pirandello.* Pisa, 1947.

Pettinati, Mario. "A Colazione fra Pirandello e G. B. Shaw." *Eloquenza Siciliana,* vol. 9, no. 1 (Jan.–Feb. 1969), 262–66.

Pirandello, Stefano [pseudonym Stefano Landi]. "La Vita Ardente di Pirandello." *Quadrivio,* vol. 5, no. 7 (13 Dec. 1936), 1, 3.

———. "Pirandello è Sempre nel Nostro Cuore." *Il Dramma* 15 (1 Feb. 1939), 20–21.

Piromalli, Antonio. "Pirandello e Croce." In *Atti del Congresso Internazionale di Studi Pirandelliani,* pp. 863–75. Florence, 1967.

Poggioli, Renato. "Pirandello in Retrospect." *Italian Quarterly,* vol. 1, no. 4 (Winter 1958), 19–47.

Possenti, Eligio. "Pirandello Fu Profetico nel Definire Mussolini." *Corriere della Sera,* vol. 81, no. 178 (29 July 1956), 3.

Prosperi, Giorgio. "Un Ritratto di Pirandello." *Quaderni del Piccolo Teatro della Città di Milano* 1 (1961), 9–11.

Radcliff-Umstead, Douglas. *The Mirror of Our Anguish.* Cranbury, N.J., 1978.

Ragusa, Olga. *Luigi Pirandello: An Approach to His Theatre.* Edinburgh, 1980.

Rauhut, Franz. "Wissenschaftliche Quellen von Gedanken Luigi Pirandellos." *Romanische Forschungen* 53 (1939), 185–205.

——. "Il Motivo Psicologico in Pirandello." *Veltro* 12 (1968), 99–121.

Rizzo, Gino. "Luigi Pirandello in Search of a Total Theatre." *Italian Quarterly,* vol. 12, no. 45 (1968), 3–26.

Rosenberg, Marvin. "Pirandello's Mirror." *Modern Drama* 6 (1964), 331–45.

Rossarè, F. T. *L'Essenzialità Problematica e Dialettica del Teatro di Pirandello.* Florence, 1972.

Rosso di San Secondo, P. M. "1908/1918." *Sipario,* vol. 1, no. 7–8 (1946), 40–41.

——. "Vitalità di Pirandello." *Giornale d'Italia,* vol. 51, no. 293 (11 Dec. 1951), 3.

Russo, Luigi. *I Narratori (1850–1950).* Milan, 1951.

Scalero, Liliana, ed. *Adriano Tilgher: l'Uomo, il Pensiero, i Luoghi, l'Attualità.* Padua, 1962.

Scherer, Jacques. "Marivaux and Pirandello." *Modern Drama,* vol. 1, no. 1 (May 1958), 10–14.

Sciascia, Leonardo. *Pirandello e il Pirandellismo.* Palermo, 1953.

——. *Pirandello e la Sicilia.* Rome, 1961.

Siciliano, Enzo. "Pirandello e Dintorni: Il Fascismo." *Nuovi Argomenti* 6 (1967), 48–57.

——. "Marinetti, Pirandello, etc." *Nuovi Argomenti* 10 (1968), 257–59.

——. "Per Alcune Novelle di Pirandello." *Nuovi Argomenti* 11 (1968), 71–78.

Siciliano, Italo. *Il Teatro di Pirandello: Ovvero dei Fasti dell'Artificio.* Turin, 1929.

Simoni, Renato. "Tragedia di Pirandello." *Sipario,* vol. 1, no. 7–8 (1946), 44.

——. "I Giganti della Montagna," *Il Dramma* 23 (1 Nov. 1947), 48–53.

Starkie, Walter. *Luigi Pirandello.* London, 1926.

Strehler, Giorgio. "Réflexions sur la Mise en Scène des *Géants de la Montagne* de Pirandello." *Cahiers de la Compagnie Madeleine Renault–Jean-Louis Barrault* (May–June 1967), 52–60.

Surchi, Sergio. "Kafka e Pirandello." *Il Dramma* 26 (15 Oct. 1950), 52–53.

Terracini, Benvenuto. *Analisi, Stilistica, Teoria, Storia, Problemi.* Milan, 1966, pp. 283–385.

Tilgher, Adriano. *Voci del Tempo.* Rome, 1921.

——. *Studi sul Teatro Contemporaneo.* Rome, 1923.

——. *La Scena e la Vita. Nuovi Studi sul Teatro Contemporaneo.* Rome, 1925.

——. *Il Problema Centrale.* Edited by Alessandro D'Amico. Genoa, 1973.

Torresani, Sergio. "Gramsci e Pirandello." *Vita e Pensiero* 50 (Sept. 1967), 866–77.

Venè, Gian Franco. *Pirandello Fascista.* Milan, 1971.

Vicentini, Claudio. *L'Estetica di Pirandello.* Milan, 1970.

——. "Dalla Filosofia di Pirandello alla Culturologia di Barilli." *Rivista di Estetica,* vol. 17, no. 2 (May–Aug. 1972), 232–36.

Vittorini, Domenico. *The Drama of Luigi Pirandello.* Philadelphia, 1935.

Weiss, Auréliu. *Le Théâtre de Luigi Pirandello dans le Mouvement Dramatique Contemporain.* Paris, 1964.

Young, Stark. "Pirandello Plays." *Theatre Arts Magazine* 8 (Mar. 1924), 209–10.

GENERAL WORKS

Arnold, Matthew. *Culture and Anarchy: The Works of Matthew Arnold.* 15 vols. London, 1903.

Bergson, Henri. *Creative Evolution.* Translated by Arthur Mitchell. New York, 1911.

Berlin, Sir Isaiah. *The Hedgehog and the Fox: Essay on Tolstoy's View of History.* New York, 1977.

Binet, Alfred. *Alterations of Personality.* Translated by H. G. Baldwin. New York, 1896.

Binni, Walter. *La Poetica del Decadentismo Italiano.* Florence, 1936.

Büdel, Oscar. "Contemporary Theatre and Aesthetic Distance." *PMLA,* vol. 76, no. 3 (June 1961), 277–91.

Cesareo, Giovanni Alfredo. "L'Arte Creatice." *Nuova Antologia* 158 (16 Apr. 1912), 569–89.

Croce, Benedetto. "L'Umorismo: del Vario Significato della Parola e del Suo Uso nella Critica Letteraria." *Journal of Comparative Literature,* vol. 1, no. 3 (1903), 220–28.

Dennett, D. C. *Content and Consciousness.* London, 1969.

De Sanctis, Francesco. *Storia della Letteratura Italiana.* Edited by Maria Teresa Lanza. 2 vols. Milan, 1956.

Dionisotti, Carlo. *Geografia e Storia della Letteratura Italiana.* Turin, 1967.

Evreinov, Nikolai. *Theatre in Life.* Translated by Alexander I. Nazaroff. New York, 1927.

Fodor, Jerry A. *The Language of Thought.* New York, 1975.

Gramsci, Antonio. *Opere di Antonio Gramsci.* 9 vols. Turin, 1947–54.

Hazard, Paul. *The European Mind: The Critical Years (1680–1715).* Translated by J. Lewis May. New Haven, 1953.

Kayser, Wolfgang. *The Grotesque in Art and Literature.* Translated by Ulrich Weinstein. Bloomington, Ind., 1963.

Ojetti, Ugo. "Individualismo e Arte." *Il Marzocco,* vol. 2, no. 4 (28 Feb. 1897), 8–8v.

Olson, Elder. *Tragedy and the Theory of Drama.* Detroit, 1966.

Puppo, Mario. "Illuminismo e le Polemiche sulle Lingue." In *La Cultura Illuministica in Italia,* edited by Mario Fubini, pp. 222–32. Turin, 1957.

Ryle, Gilbert. *The Concept of Mind.* New York, 1949.

Salinari, Carlo. *Miti e Coscienza del Decandentismo Italiano.* Milan, 1960.

Shaw, George Bernard. *The Collected Works of Bernard Shaw.* 30 vols. New York, 1930—.

Sypher, Wylie. *Loss of Self in Modern Literature and Art.* New York, 1962.

Tommaseo, Niccolò. *Poesie e Prose.* Edited by P. P. Trompeo and P. Ciureanu. 2 vols. Turin, 1966.

Trilling, Lionel. *Sincerity and Authenticity.* Cambridge, Mass., 1972.

White, Hayden V. *Tropics of Discourse.* Baltimore, 1978.

INDEX

NOTE ON THE AUTHOR

Anthony Caputi was born and raised in Buffalo, N.Y. During World War II he served with the U.S. Army in France and Belgium, after which he resumed his education at the University of Buffalo and Cornell University. He has spent his entire academic career at Cornell teaching dramatic literature and creative writing. His scholarly writings include a book on Renaissance drama, *John Marston, Satirist,* and one on farce, *Buffo, the Genius of Vulgar Comedy,* as well as articles on Shakespeare and modern drama and two drama anthologies. More recently he has published two novels.